P9-APH-132

3 2044 059 928 705

Justice and Reconciliation

Justice and Reconciliation

AFTER THE VIOLENCE

WITHDRAWN

Andrew Rigby

LYNNE
RIENNER
PUBLISHERS

BOULDER
LONDON

BPX 0040 - 3/2

JC 578 .R54 2001
Rigby, Andrew, 1944-
Justice and reconciliation

RECEIVED

APR 2 5 2002

Kennedy School Library

Published in the United States of America in 2001 by
Lynne Rienner Publishers, Inc.
1800 30th Street, Boulder, Colorado 80301
www.rienner.com

and in the United Kingdom by
Lynne Rienner Publishers, Inc.
3 Henrietta Street, Covent Garden, London WC2E 8LU

© 2001 by Lynne Rienner Publishers, Inc. All rights reserved

Library of Congress Cataloging-in-Publication Data
Rigby, Andrew.
    Justice and reconciliation :   after the violence /   Andrew Rigby.
       p.   cm.
    Includes bibliographical references and index.
    ISBN 1-55587-960-8 (alk. paper)
    ISBN 1-55587-986-1 (pbk.: alk. paper)
    1. Restorative justice. 2. Reconciliation. I. Title.
JC578.R54   2001
320'.01'1—dc21

                                  00-045985

British Cataloguing in Publication Data
A Cataloguing in Publication record for this book
is available from the British Library.

Printed and bound in the United States of America

The paper used in this publication meets the requirements
of the American National Standard for Permanence of
Paper for Printed Library Materials Z39.48-1984.

5 4 3 2 1

For Carol

Contents

Preface

The origins of this book go back further than I care to think about. Ever since I came across what some people now call the "global ethic," the golden rule—to treat your neighbor as you would have them treat yourself—I became caught up in the dilemma of how to live up to such a demanding moral code. As a consequence, I became fascinated by those "moral deviants" who had the courage of their convictions—unlike me—and refused to compromise their ethics for the sake of material comfort and short-term advantage. I read about the history of utopian experiments in communal living, about people who saw each and every dimension of their individual and collective life as significant in the struggle to transform the world, and I wondered about the power of personal and collective exemplary action as a means of non-violent social change.

Later on I read Max Weber's essay, "Politics as a Vocation," and recognized his distinction between the two ideal types of ethical systems to be pursued in the world of politics: the ethic of ultimate ends or conviction, characterized by an uncompromising commitment to a set of values and ideals, and the ethic of responsibility, which acknowledges the need to be guided in one's political conduct by an awareness of what is practically possible within the world as it is and the parameters of existing conditions. Weber came to the pessimistic conclusion that neither of these two modes could act as infallible guides to action. The ethic of conviction can lead to the belief that the good end justifies morally dubious means, a path that can lead to the Gulag and the concentration camp; or it can lead to a disdain for all but the purest of means and a consequent failure to resist immediate evils in any effective manner. The pathway directed by the ethic of responsibility has equally great pitfalls. You compromise once, then another time, and you are on the slippery slope of choosing between relative evils, with all vision of what ought to be driven from your mind.

Hence the ongoing problem of trying to figure out how to live in the world-as-it-is, while trying to bear witness to a world-as-it-ought-to-be, without withdrawing to a separatist community or sect.[1] This enduring dilemma struck me acutely during the late 1980s and early 1990s when I was doing research on the Palestinian Uprising, or Intifada. I began to see that so many of the people who were being accused of collaborating with the Israeli occupying force were people caught in difficult circumstances, people who made their choices as best they could according to their morality and their interests. I began to wonder what I would have done in their place. What if my daughter needed medical treatment only available overseas? What if the occupiers agreed to let me take her out, as long as I returned the favor by agreeing to talk with them once a month about this and that?

I became fascinated by the phenomenon of collaboration, identifying with the dilemmas faced by those living under occupation. This led me to study the collaboration that took place during World War II, which reinforced the realization that my early assumptions about the clear distinction between resister and collaborator, victim and perpetrator, were completely naive. I appreciate the feeling behind Ian Buruma's reflections on the Dutch experience of occupation:

> Occupation is always a humiliating business—not just because of the loss of sovereignty and political rights but because it dramatically shows up human weakness. Heroes are very few in such times, and only a fool would put himself or herself among the imaginary heroes. It is easier to understand the ugly little compromises people make to save their own skins, the furtive services rendered to the uniformed masters, the looking away when the Gestapo kicks in the neighbour's door. When I grew up, everything was done to forget the humiliation and to identify with the heroes.[2]

As I started to read further I began to see that under occupation, as in so-called open societies, most people are damaged by the systems and institutional structures that they themselves sustain and reproduce. We, like they, are victims of oppression, and pillars of that oppression also. We all accommodate ourselves to the realities of life. But under occupation or in authoritarian political systems those everyday compromises are cast in sharper relief, as people continue to live within the lie and thereby reproduce the system in the rituals of everyday life.[3]

So, for me, thinking about life under occupation or in repressive regimes, culpability, guilt, and innocence became matters of degree. And when I came across a growing body of literature on what people were calling "transitional justice," especially the invaluable volumes edited by Neil Kritz of the United States Institute of Peace, I began to reflect on the alternative approaches adopted by successor regimes to police the past.[4] What I have tried to do in the following pages is explore by means of illustrative case studies the range of alternative approaches to coping with the legacy of human rights abuses available to societies emerging out of protracted conflict and collective trauma. Informing the treatment that follows is the deep awareness that those of us who have never been placed in extremis should not be quick to judge those who somehow failed to live up to the moral and legal codes that we claim to follow. Not only do we all make compromises, but until we ourselves have faced up to the same fears, pressures, and temptations of those we condemn, then we never know—would we have acted any differently?

As the work on the manuscript progressed I became increasingly fascinated by the different ways in which people cope with loss. During July 2000, two senior police officers in Britain were charged with criminal negligence relating to the death of 96 football fans who suffered fatal injuries at Hillsborough Stadium, Sheffield, on 15 April 1989 at the start of a football match between Liverpool and Nottingham Forest. The case was brought by the Hillsborough Family Support Group. Their quest for the formal acknowledgment of the truth about the causes of the overcrowding in that particular section of the stadium on that day, and their determination to pursue those police officers who they believed bore some responsibility for the overcrowding and hence for the tragic outcome, reminded me of the ongoing struggle by the relatives of the disappeared in Argentina and Chile who refuse to let bygones be bygones. And I have to confess that I wondered to myself why such folk continued to fight for their version of truth and justice. It would not bring their loved ones back.

I have had loved ones taken from me in tragic circumstances. I will not forget them; to do so would dishonor them in some way. But I do not want the pain of those times to come back. It took many years to learn how to live with the memories in such a way that every moment was not dominated by them. The realization that has come to me is that we all have different ways of coping with painful memories, the impoverishment of our lives, and the bitterness occasioned by the loss of our loved ones. And while the focus of this book is on the alternative approaches adopted by different societies to deal with the legacy of division and abuse of human rights left by previous regimes, I do believe that so many of us who have not had to endure life under dictatorships or unusually repressive regimes can still identify with the moral, legal, political, and human dilemmas that are the subject matter of the following chapters.

*   *   *

A considerable range of people have helped me in writing this book. Just to single out a few: Bassem 'Eid in Jerusalem and Roberta Bacic in London gave freely of their time and interest. Laurie Nathan and Sally Schramm of the Centre for Conflict Resolution in South Africa shared their insights. My relatives in San Feliu and Girona, especially Enric Tremps, were happy to share their recollections and opinions. My new colleagues within the School of International Studies and Law at Coventry University have been very supportive. My longtime friends Mahdi Abdul Hadi, Howard Clark, Marwan Darweish, Bob Overy, Michael Randle, and Stuart Rees responded when called upon, while Carol Rank and Evan Rigby agreed to go away on a family holiday without me so that I could complete the manuscript.

Notes

1. This is the same dilemma faced by Raymond Chandler's detective Philip Marlowe, the man who is not himself mean, but who chooses to walk down the mean streets of life. See Chandler, "The Simple Art of Murder."
2. Buruma, *The Wages of Guilt,* p. 6.
3. See Havel, "The Power of the Powerless."
4. See especially Kritz, *Transitional Justice.*

1

Reconciliation and Forgiving the Past

It's a poor sort of memory that only works backwards.
—White Queen, in *Through the Looking Glass* by Lewis Carroll

H OW do people come to terms with a legacy of past atrocities, abuses, and criminal acts? How can the wounds caused by division and conflict be healed? How can a people recover from collective trauma? In exploring such questions one frequently comes across parallels being drawn between the manner in which a society might come to terms with the pain of its past and the Western approach to helping victims deal with post-traumatic stress disorder. You can find the same assumptions about the significance of being able to tell one's story in a secure environment so as to purge the demons and thereby create a new life on sure foundations.

I am not convinced of the appropriateness of opening up the past and talking about it as a means of dealing with the hurt. At a common-sense level it would seem obvious that most people want to forget the pains of the past and get on with their lives. Why should anyone want to relive past traumas by talking about them? Those who do are often people whose core identity is as a victim. In April 2000 one of the main stories in the British press was the failure of a libel case brought by author David Irving against an American professor, seeking vindication for his claim that the Holocaust never happened. Irving was branded by the judge a racist, an anti-Semite, and a pro-Nazi polemicist who distorted the history of the Holocaust to fit his own ideological prejudices. Interestingly, in his commentary on the case, journalist Jonathan Freedland called for an end to this Jewish absorption with the traumatic events of more than half a century ago, arguing that it was time to give "the victims and survivors of the holocaust some peace." Following themes developed by other Jewish writers and historians, Freedland

1

basically argued that it was imperative for the Jewish people to find something else to put at the center of their identity, that the collective fascination with and focus on the Shoah was deeply unhealthy.[1]

Of course one should honor the memory of victims of the past, but one could argue that you can have too much memory. Too great a concern with remembering the past can mean that the divisions and conflicts of old never die, the wounds are never healed. In such circumstances the past continues to dominate the present, and hence to some degree determines the future.

How to move on? How to address the past in a constructive future-oriented manner? This is a crucial issue, not just for individuals, but for societies and communities emerging out of division, bloodshed, and collective nightmare. There is no simple authoritative model for such a collective process of moving on, but there are a number of possible approaches. This book aims to review these alternative models.

Amnesia—Forgive and Forget?

The Spanish dictator Francisco Franco came to power through a military rebellion and subsequent civil war; after his victory in 1939, his regime became infamous for its barbaric treatment of the defeated Republicans and the repression practiced throughout the country. Yet, after his death in 1975 and the transition to democratic rule, there was no purge, but rather an exercise in collective amnesia. Everything was subordinated to the peaceful transition to democratic rule—and this exercise in letting bygones be bygones would appear to have worked; the roots of democracy in Spain have deepened. (See Chapter 3.)

In the Spanish case, this decision to ignore the past, this pact of oblivion, was made by elites to ensure political stability. There were good grounds for believing that any attempt to sully the reputation of Franco and purge the military and security forces would lead to a coup attempt. But this desire to cover up the past can also be the wish of people at the grassroots. This is particularly so if many of them share a past that they would rather forget because of their active involvement in, or complicity with, the evil that was perpetrated in their name. For people who have been involved in phenomenena such as the mass violence that can happen in a civil war, it can certainly seem as if the past is best left behind. To introduce it into the present might lead to further bloodshed, conflict, and pain.

Here the case of Cambodia comes to mind. There is no denying that in large part the emphasis on reconciliation and avoidance of "the spirit of revenge," which has characterized the Cambodian approach to dealing with the pain of the past, is a consequence of agreements between the Cambodian political elite and the surviving leadership of the Khmer Rouge. But it is also important to realize that although in each Cambodian family network there will be people who were killed or died unnecessarily during the terrible years of the Khmer Rouge, in each family there are also likely to be people who participated in the killing or were complicit in allowing people to die from malnutrition and preventable disease before the overthrow of the Pol Pot regime by the Vietnamese in 1979. Is it so surprising in such circumstances that there has been no great demand for an uncovering of the past or any overwhelming cry for justice against the perpetrators of the genocide? Where would it end? Who would remain untouched?

However, just because one generation might want to forget the past does not mean that subsequent generations will remain satisfied with leaving it covered up. In the case of Cambodia, half the population was born after the Vietnamese drove the Khmer Rouge out of Phnom Penh, and there is some evidence that they are beginning to voice their demands to know what actually happened during those years in the 1970s, a period to which some current school textbooks devote less than ten lines.[2]

Trials, Purges, and the Pursuit of Justice

At the opposite pole from amnesia is the active attempt to police the past and prosecute those guilty of perpetrating human rights abuses. Here the example comes to mind of the prosecution of Nazi war criminals and their collaborators, which took place at Nuremberg and elsewhere in Europe after World War II. More recently there has been the prosecution of former East German border guards charged with the killing of fellow citizens trying to escape to the West in the years before the European political map was transformed in 1989.

A number of factors come into play in determining whether or not the path of prosecution and purge is adopted. Thus, in the newly liberated countries of Western Europe after 1945, and in countries like Czechoslovakia and Germany after the transitions of 1989, the new regimes had the will to engage in a purge, and believed they had the means to pursue such a policy. The path of the purge is likely to be followed under the following conditions:

1. When there is the will, such as when there is an overwhelming desire on the part of the vast majority of the citizenry to call to account those who betrayed the common good and welfare of the society.
2. When the new regime feels confident of its power and ability to pursue justice without risking political and social stability.
3. Such conditions usually prevail when the new regime has come to power as a result of a popular comprehensive victory over those who are the potential targets of such a purge.

There is something appealing about the idea and practice of holding people accountable for their misdeeds, making them pay their dues. There is also a certain common-sense appeal to the notion that by prosecuting and punishing those who abused the rights of others, future potential perpetrators might be deterred.

Furthermore, another important dimension of trying people for crimes committed in the past is that it individualizes guilt. As the German theologian Karl Jaspers said of the Nuremberg trials in 1946, "For us Germans this trial has the advantage that it distinguished between the particular crimes of the leaders and that it does not condemn the Germans collectively."[3] In a similar vein Serbs today might applaud the work of the International Criminal Tribunal for Yugoslavia in The Hague for showing the rest of the world that the horrendous abuses perpetrated during the war in Bosnia were not committed by the Serbs as a people, but by individual and identifiable concentration camp guards and paramilitary members who happened to be part of the Serbian community. (See Chapter 8.)

The advocates of trials and of the pursuit of justice also argue that the punishment of the perpetrators through due legal process not only helps prevent the incidence of private acts of revenge and *self-help justice,* but also demonstrates that there are other ways of coping with difference than resorting to violence.[4]

Such is the theory, but the practice invariably leaves some room for doubt. The debate over the Nuremberg trials is ongoing. Was it due process or revenge? The accused were not prosecuted by their peers but by their conquerors. If the German leaders were tried for war crimes, what about those responsible for bombing Dresden, Hiroshima, and Nagasaki? Were they not also war crimes? For many Germans the justice meted out at Nuremberg was victor's justice. As Ian Buruma has pointed out, the big question is, "How to achieve justice without distorting the law, and how to stage a trial by victors over the vanquished without distorting history"?[5]

Certainly the more recent experience of attempts to punish those responsible for the abuse of human rights under the state socialist regimes of Central and Eastern Europe, to purge them and their collaborators from positions of influence and public office, leads to the conclusion that such efforts all too easily degenerate into witch-hunts motivated by narrow political considerations rather than a concern with justice. (See Chapter 5.)

There is a further problem with trials, which we can call the problem of the *lampistes,* the term used to refer to those in occupied Europe who suffered summary justice at the hands of vengeance-seekers in the immediate aftermath of liberation. (See Chapter 2.) The problem is that invariably the small fry suffers the penalties for crimes committed while implementing the policies devised by people with "clean hands" who sit behind desks, far from the scenes where the blood was shed and the abuses perpetrated. For those who pay the price for their actions while seeing others escape punishment, justice can appear not so much blind as arbitrary. The danger is that there is then left a significant section of the population that feels victimized and scapegoated—and the divisions of the past are thereby reproduced into the future. So, while trials and purges can serve to make the victims feel happy that justice has been done, they might not assist the process of healing division.

The prosecution of human rights violators exercises a strong appeal for those who are convinced that there is a clear division between guilty and innocent, perpetrators and victims. But this Manichean paradigm does not reflect the complexity of life under repression. As we shall see, President Vaclav Havel of the Czech Republic was initially reluctant to endorse any kind of purge following the Velvet Revolution of 1989. He was too aware of the manner in which the machinery of the old regime could colonize people, turning them into unwitting accomplices in the repressive apparatuses of the state. In the Guatemalan civil war, particularly during the 1970s and 1980s, many of the soldiers responsible for committing horrendous abuses of people's rights were themselves poor, uneducated conscripts, overwhelmed by the culture of violence that permeated the military and security forces. Moreover, they faced summary and extreme punishment if they refused to carry out orders. Clearly they were guilty of perpetrating terrible acts, but were they not also victims?

Karl Jaspers, reflecting on the Holocaust, distinguishes between four types of guilt: the *criminal* guilt of those who actually committed the crimes; the *political* guilt of those who helped such people get to power; the *moral* guilt of those who stood by, doing nothing as the crimes were being committed; and the *metaphysical* guilt of those who survived while others were killed, thereby failing in their responsibility to do all that they might have done to preserve the standards of civilized humanity. Trials might be valid processes for determining criminal guilt, but they are not best suited to coping with each of the different forms of culpability.[6]

Moreover, trials have their limitations when it comes to unveiling the truth about the past. They are combative encounters where defendant and prosecutor compete to get their version of the truth accepted as authoritative. In this process both sides are engaged in what we might term the manipulation of history, insofar as they each have an interest in concealing some aspects of the past and highlighting others.

It can be argued that trials can serve as morality plays, where good triumphs over evil and the guilty are made to pay the price for their misdeeds. As such, they might function as symbolic history lessons, but they are not the best means for dealing with all the subtleties of the past. For that, another approach seems best suited—that of the truth commission.

Truth—for the Sake of Peace?

Whereas trials and purges are aimed at punishing the perpetrators of crimes against their fellow citizens, the prime concern of the truth commission approach is with the victims. The aim is to identify them, to acknowledge them and the wrongs done to them, and to arrive at appropriate compensation. The intention is that through such a process the victims and their families might be helped to come to terms with their anger and bitterness. The pattern was set by the National Commission on the Disappeared, which was set up by Argentina's president Raúl Alfonsín in 1983. In its report the Commission tried to unveil the secrecy surrounding the torture, killing, and disappearance of the thousands of victims of the military regime. Chile followed the example of

Argentina, and in 1991 the report of the Chilean National Commission on Truth and Reconciliation was published. Chile's president, Patricio Aylwin, marked the occasion by appearing on television to apologize on behalf of the nation to the families of the victims of Pinochet's regime. (See Chapter 4.) More recently there has been the South African Truth and Reconciliation Commission. (See Chapter 6.)

When one considers the situation that faced the civilian regimes that succeeded the military juntas in South America, and the unstable law and order situation that confronted the new postapartheid regime in South Africa, it would seem that the truth commission is the approach adopted by regimes that lack either the will or the means to prosecute the perpetrators of political crimes, and where the policy of forgive and forget is not viable because of the depth of division and level of bitterness in society. Such a situation is generally associated with the following conditions:

1. When the number of those complicit in past evils is such that their prosecution would destroy any possible basis for future reconciliation and the development of a common sense of nationality and citizenship.
2. Where a significant proportion of those who would be targets of any purge are from one particular ethnic group or community within the wider society, with the result that a purge might lay the basis for future social and political division in the form of ethnic or communal conflict. An important factor in such a situation would be the desire on the part of the new regime to avoid provoking any secessionist tendencies on the part of any community or ethnic group.
3. Where the new regime is not confident that it possesses the power or the ability to carry out a purge, because of the relative resources controlled either by those who would be the chief targets of any purge or by their patrons within and outside the country.

Such conditions are likely to prevail when, rather than enjoying an outright victory over the old regime, the new regime has come to power through some negotiated process involving either the likely targets of any purge and/or their patrons.

Samuel Huntington distinguished between three types of transition with different consequences for processes of democratization: transformation, when elites take the initiative to bring about change; replacement, when the initiative is solely from the opposition; and transplacement, when democratization comes about through joint action by government and opposition.[7] Like all ideal types or models, Huntington's threefold distinction is only useful to the extent that it throws light on the phenomena under consideration. But in thinking about the kinds of factors that predispose new regimes to adopt a particular approach to the legacy of past abuses, the typology does seem to have some utility. Thus, we might depict the transition in Spain as one of transformation, an elite-negotiated process that resulted in a strategy of letting bygones be bygones. The transitions in Eastern and Central Europe during 1989, like the liberation of continental Europe in 1945, were more clearly forms of replacement, the defeat and overthrow of the established regime through pressure from below and from outside, which resulted in a greater emphasis on the pursuit of justice against those responsible for human rights abuses. Finally, the transitions in Argentina and Chile, and in South Africa, can be classified as forms of transplacement, the result of pressure from below forcing the regime to negotiate the terms of transition, and which resulted in the acceptance of the pursuit of truth over justice as the means of dealing with the legacy of abuse, bitterness, and suffering.

The advocates of the truth commission approach argue that truth commissions are central to the promotion of reconciliation in divided societies, healing wounds that trials and purges can deepen. In the literature one often comes across the quote from a bereaved Uruguayan woman who confessed, "I am ready to forgive, but I need to know whom to forgive and for what."[8] Certainly we know that for the family and friends of victims there can be no closure, no moving on and leaving the past behind, without knowing what happened to their loved ones. Too many, of course, never do discover the final destiny of those who were "disappeared," even after the best efforts of a truth commission. In Argentina the secret burial grounds of those tortured and killed by the security forces more than a quarter of a century ago are still being uncovered.[9]

In defense of the truth commission approach, it is often claimed that without the kind of amnesty that the Argentinean and Chilean military and security personnel enjoyed, then the truth would have remained hidden. After all, why should people acknowledge their role in shameful actions if, as a consequence, they would face prosecution and penalty? But of course the truth that is revealed by truth commissions can only be a partial truth. In fact the very process of uncovering a part of the truth and granting it the status of official, public, and authoritative record can serve to cover up other aspects of the truth. Thus, as we shall see in the cases of the Latin American truth commissions, their remit prevented them from naming and identifying the actual individuals responsible for the abuses. From the perspective of the survivors, this meant that the perpetrators continued to enjoy impunity. Not only did they escape any kind of judicial trial, but they were not even required to acknowledge their shameful deeds. It is a painful paradox that truth commissions can in fact cover up exactly those aspects of the past they might be expected to uncover. For this reason some observers have criticized the Latin American type of truth commission as a relatively cost-free way to meet popular demands for an accounting, creating the impression that the past has been dealt with, so that people will be prepared to move on and face the future together.[10]

At the heart of such criticisms is the argument that justice is forgotten in the proclaimed quest for truth, and that the alleged reconciliation is false. To put it at its crudest, the criminals provide a version of the truth in return for amnesty, and the victims are then left to do the reconciling. The survivors are expected to accept their loss and relinquish the quest for justice. But maybe this is the price that has to be paid for democracy and the restoration of human rights. The Latin American regimes that inherited power from the military juntas opted for truth commissions and eschewed trials because they believed they had to make a choice to forfeit justice for the sake of peace and democratic pluralism, settling for truth and peace rather than justice and bloodshed.

Because of such criticisms, the South Africans introduced the element of *conditional* amnesty into their model. Under the South African scheme, any perpetrators of human rights abuses who sought amnesty were required to make a full disclosure of all their relevant acts and have their case considered by an Amnesty Committee. They did not have to express regret or remorse, but if they were to be free from the fear of prosecution, then they needed to admit to their crimes and, moreover, convince the Amnesty Committee that these had been political in nature and were not committed out of personal malice or for private gain.

Even though the successful applicants may escape formal punishment, there is still a kind of justice involved in such cases, insofar as it is not a cost-free exercise for the perpetrator. There is a public shaming in having to reveal and have entered into the public record all the evil that a person has done to his or her fellow citizens. Moreover, those at the heart of the South African Truth and Reconciliation Commission articulated a broader restorative concept of justice that went beyond the narrow retributive demand that the culprits should pay for their crimes. Archbishop Tutu, in particular, has written and spoken much about the notion of *ubuntu*, the understanding that we are all part of one community and that by creating a space within which the perpetrators of abuses might rejoin this community, they can be helped to regain something of their lost humanity and thereby enrich us all through the restoration of social harmony and wholeness.

Compensation and Reparations

For those who have suffered loss and pain, bereavement and trauma, to be denied justice and required to accept an inadequate and incomplete version of the truth must be a bitter pill to swallow. It can be sweetened to some degree by offers of compensation and reparations. Thus, the report of the Chilean truth and reconciliation commission included recommendations for reparations to be made to the surviving victims of the repression. The proposals included both symbolic measures for restoring the good name of victims, such as the erection of monuments to honor their memory, and material measures such as financial compensation and educational and welfare benefits for the relatives of the victims. Drawing on the Chilean experience, the South Africans provided for a Reparations and Rehabilitation Committee within their truth and reconciliation process. Its task was to recommend appropriate measures "aimed at the granting of reparation to, and the rehabilitation and the restoration of the human and civil dignity of the victims of violations of human rights." Its report went beyond setting the level of financial grants to be made to victims of abuse and advocated far-reaching changes in the provision of the means to satisfy the basic needs of the deprived and excluded sectors of South African society. In so doing, the members of the committee raised profound issues regarding the relationship between reparations and justice.

New regimes can try to compensate the primary and secondary victims of gross human rights violations with cash payments, educational bursaries, access to health care, the construction of memorials, and other forms of material and symbolic reparations. But how do you address the issue of reparations for the vast majority of people who were not affected directly by the torturers and murderers, the people whose children were not disappeared or killed, but who were denied the opportunity to fulfill their potential as human beings because of the quiet violence of socioeconomic inequalities and the banal everyday reality of repression? How do you acknowledge their suffering; how do you compensate them for the violence they endured? Can peace and reconciliation in the deepest sense be achieved without addressing such matters?

In the 1980s, as a lecturer in Peace Studies, I used to give students essay questions such as, "There can be no peace without justice. Discuss." The "good student" argued that peace was something more than the absence of interpersonal violence (negative peace); it entailed a condition under which people might fulfill their potential as human beings in productive and cooperative relationships with others. That is, true peace involved the absence of structural violence—the dominant institutional arrangements and practices within society that resulted in so much avoidable suffering, injury, and death. In other words, positive peace required some degree of socioeconomic justice and political equality.[11] Nowadays I fear I have become more sensitive to the tensions between peace and justice and I would be more likely to turn the essay question around to read: "There can be no peace with justice. Discuss."

Over the years I have studied various conflicts around the world, and I have had a particular interest in the Israeli-Palestinian conflict. I still remember the moment 20 years ago when I was in Beach Camp in Gaza City, meeting Palestinian refugees for the first time and realizing that they were victims of history. They might still hold the keys to their old homes "across the Green Line,"[12] but they could never return to claim their patrimony outside of a bloody war that could threaten lives not only in the Middle East but much farther afield, given Israel's nuclear capabilities. In other words, if the dispossessed Palestinians were ever sufficiently determined to seek restitution and justice, whatever the price, then it would be at the cost of peace in the region and beyond. Therefore, for the sake of peace, the rest of us must hope that the Palestinians, and other dispossessed groups around the globe, never do put the thirst for justice above all else. To do so would mean that so many conflicts around the world would be locked into an endless cycle of violence and vengeance.

But if the victims of history are to be denied full restitution of what they have lost, then it is the responsibility of the rest of us to do what we can to ensure that they do receive appropriate compensation and reparations, material and symbolic, so that they can transcend and leave behind their status as victims locked into a past of injustice and suffering.

Toward Reconciliation

Of course, for the bereaved and dispossessed everywhere, that which they have lost can never be restored to them. Even if they were to regain their property, it would not be the same as it was. But individuals, like collectivities, for the sake of peace, must somehow become capable of accepting loss and moving on. This ability to let go of the pain of the past is at the heart of what many understand to be forgiveness. Hatred and the quest for revenge can consume people, turning them into a mirror image of those whom they hate. In order not to remain trapped in the confines of past injuries and injustices, individuals must learn to forsake the search for vengeance. Without this there can be no new beginning, no transformation of relationships. As Hannah Arendt phrased it in her book, *The Human Condition,* "forgiving serves to undo the deeds of the past, whose 'sins' hang like Damocles' sword over every new generation."[13]

Forgiveness is a personal process. It refers to the past and it does not require the involvement or even the knowledge of those who committed the perceived wrong, although many would argue that some expression of repentance is a prerequisite. But in fact many people remain unaware that they have committed any wrong for which they should seek forgiveness.

Reconciliation, in contrast, refers to the future and requires the active participation of those who were divided by enmity. At the core of any reconciliation process is the preparedness of people to anticipate a shared future. For this to occur they are required not to forget but to forgive the past, and thus be in a position to move forward together.

But how can people begin to forgive the past and orient toward a shared future if that past remains shrouded in secrecy and if their present circumstances daily remind them of the violations they have suffered? As I have tried to illustrate with my reference to the Palestinians and in my review of the different models available to successor regimes when dealing with a legacy of human rights violations, there is an ongoing tension between the need for truth, the quest for justice, and the desire for peace.

The most perceptive exploration of these tensions that I have come across has been in the writings of John Paul Lederach. Lederach is a Mennonite with wide experience in peace-building work in deeply divided societies. His insight came from a reading of Psalm 85, verse 10, where the psalmist, referring to the return of people to their land and the opportunity for peace, says:

> Truth and Mercy have met together.
> Justice and Peace have kissed.

For Lederach, reconciliation is the process and the place where these four meet. In his words:

> *Truth* is the longing for acknowledgement of wrong and the validation of painful loss and experience, but it is coupled with *Mercy,* which articulates the need for acceptance, letting go, and a new beginning. *Justice* represents the search for individual and group rights, for social restructuring, and for restitution, but is linked with *Peace,* which underscores the need for interdependence, well-being and security.[14]

Following Lederach we can agree that for reconciliation to take place and wholeness and harmony to be approached, then some degree of truth, mercy (or forgiveness), justice, and peace must be woven into the process. This is the ideal against which the case studies that follow should be judged. They all fall short in one component or another. But there is an additional dimension that must be borne in mind—time.

Just as it takes time for wounds to heal and for people to work through their anger and bitterness so that they are in a position to offer the gift of forgiveness, so it takes time to achieve truth, justice, and peace. These struggles do not end with the sentencing of a war criminal, the publication of a truth commission report, or the attempt of successor regimes to sweep the past under the carpet. A recent newspaper article reported that human rights lawyers in Chile, aided by the government, had convinced the supreme court to take legal action against General Augusto Pinochet, despite the amnesty that he and his associates granted themselves to cover their human rights abuses between 1973 and 1978.[15] This advance in the pursuit of justice came just seven weeks after Pinochet had been released from house arrest in Britain. Here we have a heartening example of the way in which governmental and non-governmental groups and organizations within a country and around the world can work together to create the conditions necessary for genuine reconciliation.

Notes

1. Jonathan Freedland, "Let's Close the Book," *The Guardian*, 12 April 2000.

2. John Gittings, "Silence Marks Cambodia's Bloody Anniversary," *The Guardian*, 18 April 2000.

3. Quoted in Ignatieff, *The Warrior's Honor*, p. 178.

4. See Rosenberg, "Overcoming the Legacies of Dictatorship."

5. Buruma, *The Wages of Guilt*, p. 144.

6. Jaspers's friend Hannah Arendt wrote to him that the scale of the Nazi crimes revealed the limits of the law, for no punishment could match the enormity of what had been done. Cited in Minow, *Between Vengeance and Forgiveness*, p. 47.

7. Huntington, *The Third Wave*.

8. Quoted in Cohen, "State Crimes of Previous Regimes," p. 41.

9. See, for example, Michael McCaughan, "Argentina Unearths 90 Torture Victims," *The Guardian*, 18 April 2000.

10. See, for example, Popkin and Roht-Arriaza, "Truth as Justice," p. 83.

11. For a seminal discussion of some of these concepts and ideas, see Galtung, "Violence, Peace, and Peace Research."

12. The term current among Palestinians until after the Oslo Accords to refer to the pre-1967 territorial borders of Israel.

13. Arendt, *The Human Condition*, p. 213. More prosaically, President Bill Clinton, speaking at the funeral of the assassinated Israeli premier Yitzak Rabin, advised, "Those who cannot let go of the hatred of their enemies risk sowing the seeds of hatred within their own communities" (news coverage, 6 November 1995).

14. Lederach, *Building Peace*, p. 29.

15. Jonathan Franklin, "Chile Faces Moment of Truth," *The Guardian*, 22 Aprill 2000.

2

European Purges
After World War II

On 1 September 1939, German troops invaded Poland. Two days later France and Britain declared war on Germany, and World War II had started. By the spring of the following year the Germans had achieved their military breakthrough in Europe. In April 1940 the invasions of Denmark and Norway were launched. The following month Belgium and Holland were occupied, and by mid-June French troops had surrendered and a new government under Marshal Philippe Pétain sued for an armistice. Within a few months, much of continental Europe had fallen under Nazi occupation.

The occupation of a country by a foreign power confronts the indigenous population and its political leadership with severe dilemmas. Beyond the strategic issues of how to bring about an end to occupation, there are the more immediate questions of how to relate to the occupier. What is the proper relationship between vanquished and victor? For the political leadership there is the immediate choice to be made of whether to go into exile or seek to establish ways of living with the enemy.

Pétain was responsible for the term "collaboration" entering the political vocabulary, when he declared that the German victory left France with a choice between the "traditional peace of oppression" and "an entirely novel peace of collaboration."[1] Pétain claimed to speak for France, and many French people considered him to be their legitimate national leader. He believed that the national interest would be best served through cooperation with the victors. It was a policy of national collaboration, orchestrated by the administration established at Vichy to

15

govern the part of central and southern France that was not occupied directly by the Germans in 1940.

Denmark followed a similar policy of national collaboration, with the elected government deciding to stay in office after the German invasion, to act as a shield to protect the civilian population from the worst excesses of occupation. In both the French and Danish cases, the decision to collaborate was taken by the national authority within the borders of the conquered territory and justified in terms of the defense of national interests. Such policies of national collaboration involved various forms of institutional collaboration, whereby different administrative apparatuses and organizational networks cooperated, as a matter of policy, with the conqueror.

Unlike France and Denmark, the governments of Belgium, Holland, and Norway went into exile. But in each case they instructed civil servants to remain at their posts to maintain the services upon which the civilian population continued to rely.

For the civilians of each newly occupied country there were more general dilemmas to be confronted. The routine practices of everyday life appeared through a new prism; the established assumptions could no longer be taken for granted. Old recipes for action and interpretation had to be revised and new strategies for living had to be developed. Under occupation, what was once unquestioned becomes problematic. Thus, while obedience to the law might once have been a duty, how should one respond to the regulations imposed by the occupier? For a newly occupied people the world must be reinterpreted and reconstructed.

This chapter examines how people in continental Europe responded to the challenge of occupation, and explores the attempts that were made after the war to purge and punish those who were deemed to have collaborated with the occupiers and profited from their relationship. As we shall see, the pursuit of justice against those who were accused of betraying their country and their fellow citizens was severely flawed in several respects, providing us with some insight into the problems of "cleansing" a society following occupation—a theme to which we shall return in subsequent chapters.

Adjusting to Occupation

The process of building up a new mode of life based on the novel circumstances of occupation is particularly problematic if there is a lack of unambiguous directives from an authoritative source. This is the case when there is no clear legitimate authority, such as a government-in-exile, that can lay claim to de jure authority to set against the de facto power of the occupier, or where there are competing national factions contesting the right to instruct and advise the civilian population. When there are no clear guidelines emanating from a legitimate national authority, people have to make their own decisions as to where to draw the line in terms of their relationship with the occupying power. The result is that many can drift inadvertently into relationships with the occupier that are subsequently deemed to constitute collaboration.

In his study of Belgium during World War II, Martin Conway explored aspects of this phenomenon, emphasizing the way in which, under occupation, the private realm was invaded by political concerns and everyday actions took on a new significance:

> The unemployed worker who volunteered for work in Germany, the woman who crossed the street to avoid (or to meet) German soldiers, or the family which offered food to a fugitive who called at their door were all making choices which—though they rarely lacked a certain human ambivalence—possessed a significance which extended beyond the personal sphere.[2]

If, under occupation, the "personal is political" in a far more obvious manner than during normal times, it has to be acknowledged that the life strategy of most of those living under occupation in Europe during World War II was dominated by the impulse to survive rather than to be heroic martyrs. Although the parameters of reality might have changed, the bulk of people continued to reveal all the normal contradictory human traits of courage and cowardice, defiance and submission, resistance and collaboration.

In other words, in adapting to the new conditions of occupation, the majority of people did not become full-time members of resistance groups, nor did they become abject collaborators. Rather, they concentrated on survival. This meant that as people arrived at their own balance between adaptation to and rejection of the constraints imposed by the occupying power, the boundaries between collaboration and resistance became blurred. Thus, according to historian David Thomson, the majority of people in occupied Europe belonged to neither of the two extremes of active resisters or craven collaborators, "but included infinite shades of semi-collaboration, acquiescence, surrender to necessity, neutralism, and mild piecemeal resistance."[3]

Collaboration with the Enemy

In contrast with the majority of folk who, if they collaborated with the occupier, did so unwittingly or unwillingly, there were in each country in occupied Europe, with the exception of Poland, organized groups and movements that collaborated willingly with the Germans because they shared at least some of the tenets of National Socialism.[4] In Norway there was Vidkun Qisling and his National Unity Party; in Holland there was Anton Mussert's National Socialist Party; in Belgium there were several sympathetic organizations, including Leon Degrelle's Rexist Movement; in France there were a number of fascist groupings; and in Denmark there were no less than 22 political organizations sympathetic to Nazism.[5]

Although the membership of such collaborationist organizations never constituted more than a small minority of the population in each country, some idea of the general extent of collaboration with the German occupiers can be gauged from the number of people charged at the end of the war, although one does need to bear in mind that the numbers of people brought to trial reflected the energy and determination with which the purging process was pursued as much as the actual level of collaboration. In Holland somewhere between 250,000 and 450,000, out of a population of 9.2 million, were investigated, and 150,000 were charged with collaboration.[6] In Belgium, with a population of around 8 million, over 300,000 were investigated, and about 100,000 arrested, with 77,000 found guilty and punished.[7] In Denmark, with a population of some 4 million, approximately 22,000 were arrested within two days of liberation, of which 15,000 were brought to trial and 14,000 found guilty.[8] In Norway, with a population similar in size to that of Denmark, a total of more than 90,000 were investigated, and approximately 63,000 were found guilty.[9] In contrast, in France, with a population more than twice the size of that of Holland and Belgium combined, only 125,000 were brought to trial—a figure that reflects the relative lack of vigor with which the purge was pursued in that country.

The significance of these figures lies in the evidence they provide to show that collaboration in occupied Western Europe during World War II was not a rare or unusual occurrence. It was commonplace. But to understand why this was so, we need to understand something of the fluidity of the phenomenon and explore the different forms it took.

Varieties of Collaboration

World War II was unlike any previous war insofar as it touched every aspect of life; it was total war. The division between military and civilian, combatant and noncombatant, broke down. Especially in the countries of Axis-occupied Europe, everyone was a participant in the war in some form or another. It was virtually impossible to be a neutral bystander. Hence, one approach to distinguishing between different manifestations of collaboration is according to the area of life within which the collaboration took place. Thus, one might refer to the *political* collaboration of people like Qisling and Mussert and their followers, or the *military* collaboration of the 50,000 Dutch who fought alongside the Germans. There were also the *horizontal* collaborators, those women who had affairs with Germans during the war—a particular form of *social* collaboration. The most common form of collaboration, however, was *economic*.

Throughout occupied Europe thousands of ordinary workers volunteered to work in German industry before the introduction of forced labor. Indeed, according to Werner Rings, "By the end of August 1941, a grand total of over two million European workers, male and female, had voluntarily gone to the Third Reich to work for Hitler's war machine."[10] Furthermore, insofar as the economy of each of the occupied countries was geared to assisting the German war aims, the only kind of employment or economic activity available to most people involved some form of service to the enemy. As Rings has provocatively expressed it, during the early years of World War II, "the whole of occupied Europe worked primarily for Hitler's war machine."[11] This is a view supported by John Sweets's study of the French city of Clermont-Ferrand under occupation. By 1943 France had become the most important supplier of raw materials, foodstuffs, and manufactured goods to the German economy and, according to Sweets, "most employed persons were working, directly or indirectly, for German ends."[12]

The problem with categorizing collaboration according to the area of life within which it took place is that it tells us nothing about the orientation of the collaborators. There are a number of criteria that seem to be more pertinent to any efforts to calculate the degree of culpability to be attached to different types of collaboration than the area of life within which it has occurred. One obvious factor is the degree of damage, harm, or violence inflicted upon compatriots or the national interest by the actions of the collaborator. However, this factor relates to the consequences of collaboration rather than the predisposition of the collaborator, and as such can be taken into account only on a case-by-case basis. But there are two other factors that relate to the type of motivation behind the collaboration that can be used for purposes of categorization. One concerns the spirit with which the collaborator provided services to the occupier. Did people collaborate willingly or reluctantly, with enthusiasm or as a necessary evil? The other factor concerns the extent to which services were offered by the collaborator out of some sense of communal loyalty, however misguided, or out of unbridled self-interest. On the basis of these two criteria, a fourfold typology can be used to present an overview of the range of collaborative activity prevalent in occupied Europe during World War II.[13] It is presented in Table 2.1.

Table 2.1   Range of Collaborative Activity in Occupied Europe During World War II

Motivation	Cooperation offered willingly	Cooperation offered reluctantly
Individual/self-interest	*The traitor:* unconditional collaboration for private gain	*The accommodationist:* collaboration in order to survive
Community interest	*The patriotic traitor:* collaborationism in service of the occupier's cause	*The conditional collaborator:* to serve the wider community

The Traitor and the Patriotic Traitor: The Treason of the Unconditional Collaborator and the Collaborationist

From the perspective of a particular community or society under occupation, there was little difference in moral turpitude between those who offered their services to the enemy for reasons of self-interest, and those who did so on behalf of what they considered to be the best interests of their society. Both types were generally stigmatized as traitors. Moreover, in practice, those who served the cause of the occupier enthusiastically were likely to be motivated by a mixture of both self-interest and idealism, making it difficult to distinguish between the two.

However, in trying to evaluate the degree of moral wrong entailed in different forms of collaboration, it would seem worthwhile to try to distinguish between those opportunists who offered their services for private gain and had no justification for their action other than personal greed, vanity, or desire, and those who cooperated with the occupier because they identified with the enemy's cause, principled collaborators who believed that through their actions they could help bring about positive changes in their own society. The term *collaborationist* has been applied by some writers to such people.[14] Unlike the unscrupulous collaborators who betrayed their neighbors and fellow community members for the sake of silver, at least the principled collaborationist could claim a devotion to a cause beyond his or her narrow self-interest.

As was remarked above, every country in occupied Europe during World War II, with the exception of Poland, produced its indigenous collaborationist movement. Despite their differences, the leadership of these movements identified with the German cause and, through collaboration, hoped to acquire the political power necessary to transform their own societies so that they might take their rightful place in the German-dominated New Europe. Although the collaborationist movements that they led undoubtedly attracted corrupt and brutal individuals who sought to enrich themselves through cooperation with the enemy and the exploitation of their compatriots, it is equally clear that a considerable proportion of the membership of such movements were "patriotic traitors," to use David Littlejohn's apt description, who were convinced of the need for a radical transformation of their own society. People like Vidkun Quisling believed that the fate of their country was linked to that of Germany, and that through serving the German cause they were serving the interests of their own nation. Quisling went to his death sure that history would judge him a martyr.

The Accommodationist

The archetypal accommodationist was the impoverished worker who needed a job, even if that job ultimately benefited the enemy. In this category, we should also include industrialists who produced and sold goods to the enemy to keep factories running and farmers who sold produce to feed the Germans. They all cooperated with the occupier, and as such can be deemed to have been collaborators. However, their collaboration frequently stemmed from the belief that they had no alternative but to deal with the enemy. They had no other realistic option if they were to avoid destitution. They did not collaborate for a "cause" but so that they and their families might live.

Such accommodationism would seem to have been the most common form of collaboration, and it brought about some contradictory situations. Thus, the typical accommodationists might well have been collaborators during working hours and resisters in their "free time." By day they helped the occupier, at night they assisted the partisans. One example concerns the head of the Michelin company in France, who was acknowledged to have been one of the leading figures in the French resistance. Despite this, by the time the company's main plant in Clermont-Ferrand was destroyed in a bombing raid in March 1944, 80 percent of production was exported to Germany.[15] John Sweets has expressed the dilemma of people like Monsieur Michelin very clearly:

> In reality, what practical alternative did a French factory owner have to keeping his business going by taking up German contracts? Refusal to co-operate might mean confiscation of the factory's material stocks and equipment for shipment to Germany; by 1943 it definitely would have threatened the workers with transfer to Germany under the forced labour draft. . . . choices were not simple and without consequence in occupied France.[16]

It is impossible to judge the culpability of the accommodationist. As in everyday life, a common excuse made by the cowardly and the weak was that they had no option; to seek to do otherwise would have been impossible and unrealistic. In such a manner they tried to evade responsibility for their actions. They were, after all, human beings faced with difficult moral choices under the anomic conditions of occupation. As Werner Warmbrunn has remarked with regard to the Dutch experience in World War II:

> No nation is composed predominantly of heroes, and for many citizens the necessity of making this choice never presented itself. It is sufficient to say, therefore, that individual Dutchmen who had to face such often heartbreaking alternatives, whether to work in Germany or to go into hiding, whether to offer shelter to Jews, or whether to join a resistance group, arrived at their decisions probably with the same mixture of heroism, cowardice, and common sense that other persons

would display under similar circumstances. . . . Because each instance
of 'accommodation' has to be judged on its own merits, it is impossible to make a generalised judgement with respect to this category of
collaboration.[17]

For many businessmen who argued that they had no alternative but
to trade with the Germans, the temptation to boost profit margins
proved irresistible. They ended up as profiteers, making money out
of other people's hardship through activities such as taking over the
businesses of dispossessed Jews. Down such a slippery slope the
respectable accommodationist would join company alongside black
marketeers and workers who voluntarily gave up their prewar jobs to
earn more money making munitions for the Germans—the collaboration of such people went beyond accommodation.

The Conditional Collaborator

Conditional collaborators consented to cooperate with the enemy in
some way or another, albeit reluctantly, because they believed that by
their actions they could serve the interests of the wider public or of special groups within the general population.[18] Ideal conditional collaborators believed that the benefits derived by the enemy from their services
were outweighed by the advantages that accrued to their compatriots.
Another way of putting it would be that they collaborated to assist their
fellow nationals, and in some cases collaborated so that they might be
more effective resisters.

As such, this category embraces individuals that Rings depicted as
tactical collaborators, who worked for the enemy during the day to
obtain documents or whatever else was necessary to enable the partisans to carry out their activities. There were also the civil servants who
stayed at their posts under occupation, albeit reluctantly, not to serve
the new regime, but to continue to provide needed services to the general public. In pursuing a strategy of conditional collaboration, such people might also have been trying to fulfill a shielding function, seeking
to protect their compatriots from the worst aspects of foreign domination.

Whatever the specific motivation, in each case the collaboration
was entered into reluctantly and for the sake of the wider community
rather than for personal gain. But all too frequently, conditional collabo-

rators could find themselves on a slippery slope as the moral ambiguities of their position came into ever-sharper focus. Should law officers have stayed at their posts to prevent the complete subordination of legal process to the will of the occupier? Should they have continued trying to maintain the "rule of law," if they ended up providing a spurious legitimacy to the rules and regulations imposed by the occupiers? Should the Dutch judiciary have remained in office after their Jewish colleagues had been dismissed? Should university administrators and faculty have struggled to keep their universities open and functioning in occupied Europe after the Jews and other "undesirables" had been excluded? Was the Danish government protecting its citizens from the worst excesses of German rule when it handed over communists and veterans from the Republican side of the Spanish Civil War for deportation to concentration camps, from which the majority never returned?[19] Could the Danish government claim any moral superiority over that of the Vichy regime, which, in the interests of good relations with the Germans, rounded up for deportation all non-French Jews in August 1943?

There is a terrible poignancy to some of the examples of conditional collaboration during World War II, none more so than the case of the Jewish Councils who acted as liaison committees to carry out dealings with the Nazis. It is clear that people participated in the Councils reluctantly. But a key rationale was the belief that they had a duty to protect their fellow Jews from as much persecution as possible, however minuscule. Thus, a German rabbi who survived the Holocaust expressed the view:

> When the question arose whether Jewish orderlies should select Jews for deportation, I took the view that it would be better for them to do it because they would at least treat them more gently and be more likely to assist them and make their lot easier than the Gestapo. Effective resistance to the task was beyond our power.[20]

In the process, of course, they helped the Nazis implement their genocidal project.

On the basis of the experience of World War II, it would seem that any sustained cooperation with an evil so obscene as National Socialism, however necessary such cooperation might have seemed, ultimately corroded and contaminated the noble intentions of the conditional collaborators.

The Purging of Collaborators

Self-Help Justice

The typology presented in the previous section was constructed to high-light the different degrees of culpability associated with the various forms of collaboration. Unconditional collaborators who were prepared to betray, torture, and murder their compatriots for personal reward and gratification clearly occupied a different moral world from conditional collaborators who, rightly or wrongly, cooperated with the enemy in the sincere belief that they were performing a service for their fellow citizens, assisting in some way the struggle against complete subjugation to the occupying power.

Certainly, it would appear that resistance groups during World War II operated with such distinctions in mind. Thus, while there is no agreement on the exact figure, most contemporary historians would agree that in France around 10,000 alleged collaborators were assassinated or summarily executed during the war, the bulk of them in the last few weeks before liberation. Most of these executions were directed against members of the *milice,* a collaborationist paramilitary force that concentrated on antiresistance activity. So hated were they that their families were deemed legitimate assassination targets by certain resistance groups. Often such executions were preceded by secret "trials," with the accused being informed of the judgment of the "court" by means of public warnings daubed on walls or printed in underground leaflets. Indeed, so quickly did the number of executions accelerate during the last months of the war in France that the leaders of the resistance tried to control it, fearful that it was opening the door to personal vendettas and simple banditry. As it was, the pattern of "crossroads justice" continued in France for a number of months after liberation, with at least 4,500 summary executions taking place.[21] According to official government estimates, a quarter of these summary executions were preceded by some form of de facto trial convened by local liberation committees. As for the remainder, although some of the killing was politically motivated or carried out for private gain, the majority resulted from spontaneous and uncontrollable rage fueled by frustration with the slow pace of official justice.[22]

The level of self-help justice (or lynch law) was unusually high in France. But throughout the rest of occupied Europe, unconditional collaborators and collaborationists were deemed to be legitimate targets for the resistance. There were at least 170 summary executions in Denmark, with four collaborators shot dead in a single day in Copenhagen in May 1943. In Holland there were 300 executions in 1944 alone—a particularly large figure for a country where there had been no political murder since 1672.[23] Interestingly, an attack on three Dutch collaborationists in April 1943 provoked considerable discussion in the underground press. The victims were Dutch fascists, but they were not directly responsible for the deaths of any of their compatriots. Therefore, it was argued by a significant section of opinion, these attacks were nothing more than irresponsible political murders.[24]

Retroactive Legislation

The level of antipathy toward the unconditional collaborators, traitors, and "patriotic traitors" alike was revealed in the aftermath of liberation. Denmark, Holland, and Norway passed retroactive legislation introducing the death penalty to deal with extreme cases of collaboration and such crimes against humanity as the torture of prisoners. In Norway 30 death sentences were passed, of which 25 were carried out.[25] In Denmark there were 112 death sentences, and 46 people were executed.[26] In Holland 138 death sentences were imposed, but only 36 of them were carried out.[27] Belgium had the highest proportion of death sentences, with 4,170 people condemned, of which 230 were eventually executed.[28] There were more official executions in France than anywhere else, with 6,763 death sentences delivered by the courts (3,910 were handed out in absentia), of which 767 were carried out.[29]

In each country there was concern that the process of purging collaborators should be carried out by the legitimate state authorities to avoid the worst excesses of lynch law and political murder, and to facilitate the reestablishment of legitimate state authority. The question of how thorough and how severe the purging should be became a focal point of political discussion. One noteworthy debate took place between Albert Camus and François Mauriac in France. In the interests of national reconciliation, Mauriac urged forgiveness. For his part, Camus, while rejecting hatred as repugnant, felt that forgiveness was an insult to his dead comrades, and the failure to "clean the house" would sabotage the chance of building a new social order in postwar France.[30]

Special Tribunals

Special courts and tribunals were established to deal with collaborators. Among the problems faced were the floods of denunciations that occurred in each country, with quite a number coming from criminal elements masquerading as resisters to cover their tracks. The processing of accusations was handicapped by the felt need to purge the police of collaborators before it could act as an investigatory and law enforcement agency. For example, 13.7 percent of the Dutch police force was dismissed in the aftermath to liberation.[31] Alongside the dilemma of determining sentences that were appropriate to the type of collaboration, there were also problems of inconsistency in sentencing between different courts and regions.

France

The *épuration,* or purging process, was most demanding and difficult in France, where the level and extent of collaboration presented particular problems. A purge commission was established for each government department to consider any charges made against civil servants. Most of those accused claimed they had been conditional collaborators: staying in post either to meet the needs of the wider community or to play the "double game," collaborating with the enemy to help the resistance more effectively. To cope with this defense it was agreed that any civil servants who confined collaboration to the normal performance of duty were not culpable, unless they showed excessive zeal for activities that were antinational in their consequences, or failed to evade their official obligations when such avoidance would have served the nation.

The general aim was to exclude from public office all those who had worked directly or indirectly for the establishment in France of a political order modeled on that of Germany. However, there would not have been enough room in the prisons for all the people guilty of such a crime, in addition to those who had collaborated with the Germans in other ways. Therefore, the French introduced an ordinance dealing with the national indignity incurred by anyone who had voluntarily aided Germany and her allies and thereby harmed the French nation. Over 100,000 French citizens were charged with bringing dishonor on the nation. They were unworthy citizens, *inciviques,* and were deprived of their rights of citizenship for five years or more. During this period they were excluded from voting, holding any elected office, or occupying any position in the civil service or in any of the public utilities in which the state played a significant role. Other discretionary penalties included the confiscation of property and the loss of state pension rights.

In relative terms France had the lowest rate of arrests and imprisonment in Western Europe, with a total of 38,000 imprisoned, a ratio of around 94 out of every 100,000 in the population.[32] The figure for Denmark was 374 out of every 100,000 (a total of 14,000 prison sentences), while the 40,000 sentenced in Holland accounted for a ratio of 419 for every 100,000 citizens. An approximate total of 50,000 Belgians were imprisoned, 596 out of every 100,000. At the top of the league came Norway with a total of around 21,000 imprisoned, equivalent to 633 for every 100,000 Norwegians.[33]

Although other countries were more vigorous than France in pursuing collaborators, in each country this initial approach gave way over time to a more lenient stance vis-à-vis the convicted collaborators as the rage for vengeance of the immediate postoccupation period gave way to more considered concerns about reconciliation and rehabilitation. Thus, in the case of France, of the 38,000 imprisoned for collaboration, more than two-thirds had been released by the end of 1948. Also during that year over one-third of the sentences of national degradation were suspended by presidential decree. By the time of the first important Amnesty Law of 1951, only about 4,000 remained in prison.[34] Two years later, in the context of Cold War–inspired attacks on leftists, a further amnesty bill was passed, which led to the release of all those except those guilty of the most serious crimes. This amnesty was extended to those who had fought as conscripts in the German army.

It has been estimated that half of the French losses during World War II were civilians who were killed by their fellow citizens.[35] For understandable reasons, perhaps, the French state sought to cover up this shameful level of complicity and culpability. However, this failure to examine in any official or public fashion the reason why so many French citizens collaborated with the occupying regime and identified with its project did not mean that the issue disappeared. From time to time the past has returned to plague France with the belated indictment and trial of collaborators, particularly those more or less directly involved in the deportation of the Jews of France to the death camps, such as Klaus Barbie (1983) and more recently Maurice Papon (1998).

Norway

The most far-reaching prosecution of suspected collaborators was adopted by Norway. During its exile in London the Norwegian government had passed a number of ordinances dealing with collaboration. Although it reintroduced the death penalty, which had been abolished in 1876, it acted on the recommendations of a special committee established at the instigation of the resistance movement to lay down a series of lesser penalties for forms of treachery that did not merit the ultimate sanction. Collaborators were also charged under sections of the penal code dealing with such activities as illegal attempts to overthrow the government and providing illicit help to the enemy. Others were prosecuted under articles of the military penal code that related to the behavior of civilians in time of war and in the theater of war. For this purpose Norway was considered to be a theater of war from the invasion of 1940 to liberation in 1945.

Over 90,000 were investigated. Twenty-five unconditional collaborators and collaborationists were executed, the majority of them responsible for inflicting gross suffering on their fellow citizens. A system of local tribunals was established to deal with the less serious charges, and by April 1947 6,000 to 8,000 had been sentenced to terms of imprisonment of three years or more. Fifteen thousand had been sentenced to shorter terms, while some 33,000 to 34,000 had been fined and/or deprived of their civil rights. In addition, a number of collaborators had restrictions placed on their movements and were excluded from certain areas to avoid social disturbance and situations where their lives might be endangered. A total of 6,000 Norwegians were exempted from punishment because their offense was deemed to be minimal.[36] In subsequent years a series of amnesties was granted, culminating in July 1948 when all collaborators who had served more than half of their sentence were released.

The Norwegians found it particularly problematic dealing with economic collaborators: where was the dividing line between reasonable accommodationism and outright profiteering? Was the man who gave up his job on the farm for a better paid one in a German-run factory guilty of collaboration, or was he merely acting as a normal *homo economicus,* seeking the best return for his labor? In the end the distinction was deemed to revolve around the issue of whether or not a person had provided direct assistance to the German war effort, like involvement in munitions manufacture or the construction of defenses. People who had derived material benefit from collaboration during the occupation had their property confiscated. In addition the charge of national indignity allowed for various economic sanctions, including prohibitions on the ownership of certain kinds of property and pursuing certain professions. However, the full sanctions were rarely applied once it was realized that if they were, then people would be prevented from earning any kind of livelihood.

Denmark

A similar pattern of vigorous prosecution of collaborators, followed by relative leniency, was followed in Denmark. Within two days of the capitulation of Germany, special arrest committees, which had been prepared in advance and were equipped with file cards and transport, emerged to take into custody some 22,000 alleged collaborators. By April 1948 approximately 15,000 had been charged, with 23 executed and the remainder of those deemed to be "unworthy of common confidence"[37] sentenced to various combinations of terms of imprisonment, fines, confiscation of property, and deprivation of civil rights.

Holland

In Holland approximately 130,000 to 150,000 were investigated, and by October 1945 there were 96,044 suspected collaborators in custody. Like the Norwegians and Danish, the Dutch had introduced retroactive legislation so that the death penalty might be passed on those guilty of the worst crimes of treason. Among those sentenced to death were Dutch military officers who served in the German armed forces. According to Dutch law, a person forfeited his citizenship on entering foreign military service without permission of the crown. It has been estimated that at least 25,000 Dutch men fought alongside the Germans during the war. The surviving Dutchmen were among the 60,000 who were stripped of their citizenship and had their property confiscated after the war.[38]

As in the other countries, those guilty of less serious forms of collaboration faced a range of lesser penalties, including the deprivation of civil rights. Even having a "Nazi state of mind" or a "disloyal attitude," displayed by being sympathetic to Nazism or being friendly with Germans, was deemed to be an offense entailing national indignity. Special courts, including a series of occupational purge boards, had to be established to deal with the numbers accused of collaboration. By January 1947 there were over 50 such courts or boards in existence, each with its own standards of patriotic conduct by which to judge the behavior of those who appeared before them. They covered all the branches of industry and commerce, the different public services and government employees, university students, the press, and artists. Most boards consisted of a judge, assisted by two or more lay jurors from the appropriate occupational group who possessed exemplary resistance records.

Many of the men and women who were released from internment or avoided imprisonment altogether had some kind of supervision order placed on them by the Dutch authorities.[39] Many were forced to live as social outcasts, ostracized and treated as pariahs, and their children were discriminated against in local schools. Most ex-collaborators dealt with this problem by moving to new locales where they were not known. To assist them in the difficult process of rehabilitation and reentry into society a voluntary association was established—the Foundation for the Supervision and Care of Collaborators. Although it received funding from the Dutch government, the Foundation was staffed by more than 17,000 volunteers. Its founder explained the thinking behind the venture:

> Our aim is always to prevent the creation of a pariah class in our nation. "Resocialisation" does not only consist of overcoming material difficulties or finding a suitable job [for the pupil]. Resocialisation must be in the first place a mental reorientation along the lines of the ideals and life of our society. The religious, moral, cultural and political traditions of our nation must gradually penetrate the minds of Quislings. Without such a voluntary submission to the values of our society they will remain strangers and even enemies in our midst. . . . This mental purge must come . . . through ordinary, day-to-day life, work, and social intercourse.[40]

Belgium

Alone among the occupied countries of Western Europe during World War II, Belgium had experienced occupation during World War I. As a consequence legislation was passed during the interwar years specifying the punishment for various forms of collaboration. The sanctions for economic collaboration were particularly severe, laying down the death sentence for all those who aided the enemy by providing soldiers, laborers, money, food, arms, or ammunition. Given the virtual impossibility of avoiding such involvement with the enemy during the occupation, this was far too draconian to be implemented.

Therefore, in May 1945 retroactive legislation was introduced that attempted to distinguish between different degrees of economic collaboration and culpability, but the Belgians had no more success than any other country in dealing with the tricky question of distinguishing between profiteering and accommodationism. As one Belgian legal expert observed at the time,

> It is easy to punish the guilty one when the offence is to have worn a certain uniform, to have denounced to the enemy one's fellow countryman, or to have written in a newspaper in support of the occupation; but it is infinitely more difficult to decide in what measure an industrialist who worked under the control of the occupant provided him with "guilty goods."[41]

Under the Belgian penal law, offenses relating to the external safety of the state in wartime were the concern of the military courts. The Belgian government-in-exile decided to stay with this procedure, but in cases of collaboration the three military officers who sat in judgment were joined by two civil magistrates. As in other countries, the heaviest penalties were imposed on those responsible for denouncing and betraying their fellow citizens to the enemy, those who had fought alongside the German forces, and the representatives of the media who had produced propaganda for the enemy. Similarly, the *inciviques,* whose conduct during the occupation had fallen short of what it should have been, suffered the suspension of their civil and political rights.

The "Cleansing" of Germany

In July 1943 the allies and exiled governments had formed the United Nations War Crimes Commission, having emphasized their determination to punish those responsible for inhuman acts. The International Military Tribunal that resulted from this commitment tried 24 major war criminals, including Albert Speer, at Nuremberg. In subsequent months the Western occupying powers prosecuted just over 5,000 high-ranking officials, military officers, ministers, and industrialists—of whom nearly 800 were executed.[42] The implementation of the purge was then handed over to German courts but, despite widespread convictions, by 1951 half of those convicted had been released. In 1950 clemency boards had been established and they recommended releasing nearly everyone who came before them.

In addition to prosecuting those implicated in the Nazi crimes, the Allies tried to cleanse German life to eradicate any threat of a resurgence of National Socialism. Thus, under a law of 1946 the entire adult population of the Western-occupied area was subject to screening, with the possibility of being grouped into one of five categories according to the degree of guilt. Those charged with offenses appeared before local lay boards for punishment, but there was considerable dissatisfaction with the process all around. Local people were reluctant to staff the local tribunals and be implicated in the imposition of victors' justice. Moreover, the tribunal decisions were subject to appeal, and the system was particularly vulnerable to corruption. Most of the individuals sanctioned received minor fines, and only when these had been paid were they issued a certificate of rehabilitation to guard against any further stigma.

One further problem with this attempt at a thoroughgoing purge was that in a society where few people were untarnished, to effect a full purge would have decimated the number of skilled and experienced people available to rebuild the economy and reconstruct the state structure.

In addition, and perhaps most significantly, the impulse to purge was severely undermined as the fear of a resurgence of fascism was superseded by concern with the burgeoning communist menace from the Soviet Union. Thus, with the escalation of the Cold War and the United States' felt need for German cooperation in the struggle against the perceived Soviet-led threat, the pressure to root out the remnants of the old Nazi regime dissipated. As early as 1947 the United States was urging ending the screening boards, and by late 1947 through 1948 a series of amnesties was awarded. Meanwhile, in East Germany there were thorough purges of the judiciary, the civil service, and the industrial sector, with about 200,000 people losing their jobs. War crimes trials were held until 1947 by the Soviets, and then by the purged German courts. Overall, 30,000 were tried in the German Democratic Republic and 500 were executed.[43]

Conclusion

Despite the differences in the treatment of collaborators between each country, some common features are discernible.

Restoring the Power of the State

In each country the government sought to control the actions of vigilantes in pursuit of self-help justice and impose the power of the state over the purification process. This was most difficult in the immediate aftermath to liberation, when the anger and fury against collaborators was at its greatest. Therefore, collaborators who came before the courts in the early days after liberation tended to receive the most severe sentences. In general, the severity of the sentencing eased with the passage of time. This led to many inconsistencies in the levels of sentencing, but reflected the cooling of popular anger.

Retroactive Legislation

Norway, Denmark, and Holland each passed retroactive legislation to introduce the death penalty for the worst cases of treason, despite the concern of jurists and others that this involved a drastic departure from the principle of *nulla poena sine lege* (no punishment without law, or due legal process). In Belgium and France the death penalty had not been abolished; like the other countries, they found it necessary to modify their legal code to deal with the phenomenon of mass collaboration. Basically, the prewar legislation that dealt with matters of treason was too rigid and severe for the punishment of people who were not so much treacherous as weak, greedy, and opportunistic. Therefore, in each country a new set of offenses was introduced, relating to bringing dishonor upon the nation, and punishable by a sliding scale of sentences involving imprisonment, fines, confiscation of property, and the deprivation of civil rights.

Shortcutting the Judicial Process

Because of the absolute numbers of collaborators that confronted the judiciary in the newly liberated countries, and because of the nature of the offense, it was felt necessary to modify the existing judicial machinery. There were three noteworthy dimensions to these changes. First of all there was the introduction of local courts and tribunals to deal with the less serious cases. A second feature was the introduction of lay jurors into the judicial system in countries that did not normally employ them. This reflected the general feeling that there should be some popular participation in the administration of justice to collaborators, particularly in deliberations about the sentence to be imposed.[44] The third modification, adopted in Belgium, Holland, and Norway, was the widespread use of negotiated settlements, which took place either in or out of court. In such cases the accused would be offered a fairly standardized penalty for the kind of offense with which he or she was charged. If this was accepted, the matter was dealt with administratively and the need for a trial was obviated. By shortcutting normal procedures in this manner, judicial systems were able to deal with the huge backlog of cases that faced them. This process could also lead to popular indignation if it was suspected that collaborators were getting off too lightly.[45]

The Problem of the Lampistes

One of the criticisms made of the purge process as it was carried out in each country was that too often the big fish escaped serious punishment, while their subordinates suffered the full force of public anger and state justice. Of course, it must have been all but impossible to feel any sympathy for collaborators who had blood on their hands, such as the police who had arrested resistance activists and those who participated in their interrogation and torture. They were obvious targets for vigilantes in search of vengeance, and hence the term *lampistes*—such people were the most likely to be strung up from the nearest lamppost.

But what of the bureaucrats and the decisionmakers camouflaged behind their desks upon whose instructions such people acted? Too often, by the time the trail of collaboration had been traced back to such people, public anger had subsided. Invariably there were influential figures to speak on their behalf, and the courts had grown more tolerant of the defense ploy of those who claimed to be conditional collaborators playing the double game, working for the enemy to help the resistance. The result was that they tended to escape with relatively light sentences.

Rehabilitation and Amnesties

As popular resentment against collaborators waned with the passage of time, concern grew about the need for reconciliation and the eventual rehabilitation of collaborators. This was reflected in the series of amnesties that were decreed during the late 1940s. The result was that by 1950 there were few collaborators still serving prison sentences in the states of formerly occupied Western Europe.

Laying the Foundations
for a New Democratic Order

One final point needs to be made before concluding this chapter. Norway, Denmark, Holland, Belgium, and France prided themselves on their democratic state systems. Thus, the new postliberation political authorities felt they stood in sharp contrast to the totalitarian system imposed on their countries by the Germans during the war. Consequently, in their active pursuit of collaborators they were not just responding to public anger and the desire to punish those who, to some degree or other, had betrayed their fellow citizens. They also felt they were laying the foundations for a new democratic postwar order. The purging was a purification process; part of it was about revenge and retribution, but primarily it was about cleansing society. The whole process was seen as integral to the construction of a new order, one that was the complete antithesis of the fascist totalitarianism of National Socialism.

There were problems with this project, of course. The introduction of retroactive legislation under which people were punished, and indeed executed, was contrary to basic canons of natural justice. Moreover, as we have seen, the pursuit and punishment of collaborators and those guilty of gross human rights abuses were severely compromised by the changing international environment and, in particular, the escalation of the Cold War, which meant that yesterday's enemy and traitor could become a valued ally in the struggle against the dark forces—whether such forces were those of communist dictatorship or warmongering capitalism.

Moreover, the experience of France since the end of World War II would seem to indicate that too early an attempt to effect a closure on the shame of the past can mean an incomplete and inadequate cleansing. However, in the next chapter we shall examine the case of Spain where, after the death of Franco in 1975, the transition to democracy was effected without any official attempt to uncover, and hence cleanse, the history of human rights violations carried out during the years of dictatorship.

Notes

1. Rings, *Life with the Enemy*, p. 110.
2. Conway, *Collaboration in Belgium*, p. 2.
3. Thomson, *Europe Since Napoleon*, p. 812.
4. The main reason there was no collaborationist movement in Poland was that the Germans were not interested in collaborating with any section of the Polish population—it takes two sides to collaborate.
5. Littlejohn, *The Patriotic Traitors*, p. 59.
6. Mason, *The Purge of Dutch Quislings*, p. 138.
7. Littlejohn, p. 182.
8. Givskov, "The Danish Purge Laws," pp. 447–460.
9. Johs Andenoes, "La répression de la collaboration avec l'ennemi en Norvège," *Revue de Droit Penal et de Criminologie*, vol. 27, part 7, April 1947, p. 606.
10. Rings, p. 80.
11. Rings, p. 82.
12. Sweets, *Choices in Vichy France*, p. 198.
13. The following typology is based on that presented by Werner Warmbrunn; see Warmbrunn, *The Dutch Under German Occupation, 1940–1945*, pp. 272–275. See also the typology presented in Rings.
14. See, for instance, Semelin, *Unarmed Against Hitler*.
15. Sweets, p. 12.
16. Sweets, p. 14.
17. Warmbrunn, p. 273.
18. This is the type of orientation labeled "reasonable collaboration" by Warmbrunn. Rings, in his typology, attempted to distinguish between neutral, conditional, and tactical collaborators. Despite the value of Rings's work, there are a number of inconsistencies in his typology; for the sake of clarity I have grouped them all together, following the example of Warmbrunn.
19. See Kari, *De Danske spaniensfrivillige*, pp. 187–194.
20. Quoted in Rings, pp. 140–141.
21. Novick, *The Resistance Versus Vichy*, p. 71.
22. Novick, p. 72.
23. Warmbrunn, pp. 206–208.
24. Zondergeld, "Non-violent Resistance in the Netherlands During World War II," p. 175.
25. Littlejohn, p. 48.
26. Littlejohn, p. 82.
27. Mason, p. 64.
28. Littlejohn, p. 182.
29. Novick, p. 186.
30. See Novick, pp. 166–167.
31. Mason, p. 92.
32. Of all the cases brought before the French military and civilian courts, approximately 45 percent were dismissed or acquitted, 25 percent were convicted of national dishonor, and 24 percent were imprisoned. Around 7,000

were sentenced to death and 1,500 were actually executed. See Roht-Arriaza, *Impunity and Human Rights in International Law and Practice,* p. 76.

33. Novick, p. 187.

34. Novick, pp. 187–188.

35. Roht-Arriaza, p. 77.

36. These figures are taken from Andenoes.

37. See Givskov, pp. 447–460.

38. This figure included 20,000 wives who lost their citizenship automatically along with their husbands. See Mason, p. 66.

39. The male-female ratio of collaborators was 3:1. See Mason, p. 40.

40. Quoted in Mason, p. 156.

41. Vermeylen, "The Punishment of Collaborators," p. 75.

42. About 10,000 are thought to have been prosecuted by the USSR in its zone. Figures from Roht-Arriaza, p. 74.

43. See Buruma, *The Wages of Guilt,* pp. 155–156.

44. In support of such an innovation, the Dutch Minister of Justice observed that while "the administration of penal justice . . . presupposes a very carefully defined punishable deed . . . there are ten thousand and more forms of unpatriotic behaviour" that ordinary laypeople could judge as well as jurists. Quoted in Novick, p. 213.

45. For a discussion, see Novick, pp. 209–214.

3

Spain:
Amnesty and Amnesia

There is a school of thought that believes the best way to deal with trauma is for the individual to talk about the pain from the past, to acknowledge it, and, if this process takes place in a supportive environment, learn to live with the memories. This therapeutic model is then applied to the collective or national level—unless a community or nation faces up to the trauma of its past, then the ghosts will return to haunt them, distorting their future development. Hence, so the reasoning goes, for the sake of future generations, we in the here-and-now must uncover the sins of our collective past. If we fail in this, we are likely to repeat the same mistakes that led to the trauma of yesterday.

Not everyone shares this belief in being open to the past and the therapeutic value of uncovering our shame, guilt, and pain so that we might become healthy once again. Some of us would rather not talk about it, thank you. Much better to forget the pain of the past, brush it under the carpet as the phrase goes, and get on with life. This is exactly what happened on a national level in Spain after Franco's death in 1975. Franco's regime, established after his victory in the Spanish Civil War in 1939, had been notorious for its barbaric treatment of the defeated Republicans and for the suppression of civil liberties and the abuse of human rights. And yet, after his death, there were no purges, no reprisals. There was an unwritten, if not unspoken, agreement that the Francoist past should be forgotten, at least in public. There was a generally accepted exercise in collective amnesia. Everything was subordinated to the need to ensure the peaceful transition toward parliamentary democracy.

39

This approach was in marked contrast to the stance adopted by Franco himself after 1939, when he was concerned to keep alive a particular collective memory. He determined that the bloody conflict should not be forgotten, but should be remembered for what it was: a war of victory over those who would have destroyed Mother Spain.

This chapter will examine these two contrasting approaches to dealing with the legacy of the past.

The Legacy of the Civil War: The Culture of Revenge

The legitimacy of Franco's regime rested on the victory in the Civil War. He would remind his people that "we did not win the regime we have today hypocritically with some votes. We won it at the point of the bayonet and with the blood of our best people."[1] Every year on 1 April there would be public celebrations in honor of the Nationalist victory and to commemorate all those who gave their lives in the crusade to save Spain from the evil forces of international socialism and secularism.

The number of lives lost in that one-thousand day, 32-month-long war has been a matter of debate and dispute. It would appear, however, that of a population of 25 million in 1936, up to 1 million were lost by mid-1939 either through violent death or exile. Between 100,000 and 150,000 people were killed in battle, and some 350,000 to 400,000 political refugees had fled across the Pyrenees into France by March 1939. Following the fall of France to Germany in 1940, many of the Spanish exiles were imprisoned, and an estimated 10,000 died subsequently in Nazi concentration camps. Some of the better-known activists were arrested and returned to Spain to face execution. In truth, far more Spaniards were slaughtered through executions and reprisal killings than on the battlefield. This terror was not the preserve of just one side. The Republicans were responsible for about 20,000 such deaths, mainly committed during the first three months of the war. Almost 7,000 priests and members of religious orders were murdered during this period, with the anarchist newspaper *Solidaridad Obrera* calling for "the church to be torn out by the roots . . . we must seize all their possessions . . . the bishops and cardinals must be shot."[2] Later in the war, of course, terror was practiced more methodically by the communists on their enemies within the Republican camp.

It was this kind of official terror that characterized the killings carried out within the Nationalist zones during and after the war. The American historian Gabriel Jackson has estimated that between 1936 and the end of the mass executions in 1944, the Nationalists liquidated some 150,000 to 200,000 of their compatriots. Others have challenged this figure, insisting that the maximum number of people killed in this manner was 40,000.[3] Whatever the exact figure, the magnitude of the slaughter was far in excess of anything that might have been justified by military logic in the interests of victory. It can only be understood as an integral part of the war aim of Franco—which was to purge Spain of the degenerate forces that threatened the fatherland. As Richards has remarked, "The primary objective was not simply to defeat but to exterminate the enemy," eliminating as many as possible and terrorizing those who survived.[4] The imperative was to engage in as far-reaching a cleansing operation as possible. Terror and mass killings were central to the rebel mission: the regeneration of the *patria*.

One of the cities that suffered in this manner was Seville. The initial occupation of the city by the Nationalists took only a week. Wave after wave of executions of workers and other suspect elements then followed. It was a period of mass shootings in the streets and cemeteries, without recourse to even the thinnest veneer of due legal process. This is not to say that it was indiscriminate. The militias and the Nationalist army were assisted by lists of targets drawn up by informants, usually associated with the local landowning elite.

One woman later recalled those fear-filled days in the summer of 1936:

> We were five days without going out at all . . . There were executions against the wall, right opposite where we lived. But I never saw them. There were those who got up in the morning and went to see who had been shot. They left them there for two or three hours so that the people could see them . . . The lorries loaded with people destined for the cemetery also passed down my street . . . But we didn't want to see those either. When the shots sounded at night we covered up our ears.[5]

So many disappeared in this manner, with relatives afraid to identify the bodies of loved ones for fear of sharing their fate. It was enough to be found with a membership card of a socialist trade union to be put against a wall and shot. In such a climate of fear, brutalities went unrecorded, and deaths were not registered. Squads of men were organized into Purification Brigades, which scoured the environs of Seville, cleaning up suspect elements. No one knows how many were killed. Estimates range from 2,400 to 20,000. Even at the end of the war, in mid-1939, when it must have become very difficult to find any surviving agents of "anti-Spain," it was reported that 80 executions a day were still taking place in Seville, with the bodies interred in a common grave covering some 14 square kilometers on the outskirts of the city.[6] Under the Law of Political Responsibilities promulgated on 9 February 1939, Franco decreed it an offense not only to have fought on the Republican side during the war, but also to have failed to join the rebellion. Such vindictiveness against the defeated was highlighted even further by the blanket amnesty that the same ordinance extended to cover any acts perpetrated by the Nationalists in furtherance of their cause.[7]

If extermination, expulsion, and exclusion were necessary to cut away the diseased cells and organs that threatened the fatherland, then clearly there was no reason to halt the process once the formal hostilities of war had ended. You did not make peace with the devil; there could be no compromise with the forces of darkness. The result was that in the wake of their victory, Franco's forces behaved like an all-conquering foreign army. Military victory was only one stage in the struggle. The agents of anti-Spain needed to be rooted out and all those who had been contaminated by them purged. As part of this cleansing process it was determined that people must not be allowed to forget the reasons for which the crusade had been waged. Therefore, Franco did all that he could to reproduce the painful memories of the Civil War, to keep the wounds alive, and to reaffirm the fundamental division between victors and vanquished. At the heart of this project was the institutionalization of a particular interpretation of the Civil War, the creation of an official memory that was then imposed and reproduced as *the* collective memory of the Civil War period. In the words of Paul Preston, "History under the Francoist dictatorship was a direct instrument of the state, written by policemen, soldiers and priests, invigilated by the powerful censorship machinery. It was the continuation of the war by other means, an effort to justify the military uprising, the war, and the subsequent repression."[8]

This official history, this orientation toward the past, came to dominate Spain over the 40 years of Franco's regime. The result was that the majority of Spaniards were robbed of any vision or collective hope for the future, their world being circumscribed by the dead weight of the past that was reproduced in all walks of public life. Thus, 1939 became the Year of Victory. The bulk of national holidays in Franco's Spain, other than saint's days, were victory festivals: the day the war ended, 1 April, was commemorated as Victory Day; 18 July was the Day of the Uprising; 1 October the Day of the Caudillo; and 29 October was the Day of the Fallen. Of course, the only fallen who were honored were the *Caídos por Dios y por España,* those who died for God and for Spain. Nearly 20 years after the war, in 1968, it was suggested that ex-combatants of the Republicans should obtain pensions like the former soldiers of the Nationalists. Franco was outraged: "You cannot combine a glorious army with the scum of the Spanish population."[9]

So, rather than reconciliation, the end of the war brought with it a systematic regime of repression and the institutionalization of revenge against the defeated enemy within. Tens of thousands of veterans, deemed to be political enemies, guilty of war crimes and "with blood on their hands," were brought before special tribunals and sentenced to death or to periods of 20 or 30 years in prison. Firing squads could still be heard regularly in Barcelona until 1942, and it was only with the approaching defeat of the Axis powers in 1944 that mass executions came to a halt.[10]

Forced labor was one of the most common forms of punishment for those who escaped the execution squads. Many of these political prisoners were put to work constructing public monuments to commemorate the Nationalist victory. In Madrid the site of the battle for the city was marked by a huge arch of victory. The most extravagant of the efforts to embody the memory of the Nationalist victory in permanent form was Franco's massive Valley of the Fallen *(Valle de los Caídos),* the gigantic mausoleum that took 20,000 men 20 years to carve out of the mountains some 40 miles from Madrid. A huge basilica topped with a cross 150 meters high, it was the most extreme symbol of Franco's cause and a memorial to those who died in his crusade.

Catherine Moriarty has written of the significance of war memorials as foci of grief in the absence of the dead, as public sites to which personal memories can be attached in such a manner that private grieving becomes enmeshed in the collective experience and memory.[11] The bereaved of the Republican side were denied this solace, just as their own personal and collective history was denied by such public monuments and memorials as the Valley of the Fallen. Indeed, even to express mourning in public for the victims of the firing squads was to risk punishment during the immediate postwar period, and it was not until the 1980s that monuments were erected to honor the memory of *los caídos por la libertad,* those who fell for freedom.

The pursuit of vengeance was driven not just by the need to complete the Nationalist victory and purify Spain. It also served to bind together the disparate forces that had come together in the 18 July rebellion. Their complicity in the brutal repression meant that they were all tied together by *el pacto de la sangre,* the covenant of blood. None of them could expect any mercy should the political situation change and their enemies achieve political power. As a consequence, the diehards were drawn from the ranks of those who feared the revenge of their victims and who had profited under the dictator's regime; they remained intransigent in their opposition to any opening up of the Francoist system until its end.

The Legacy of the Civil War:
The Culture of Evasion

In the immediate postwar years of the 1940s concerns about threats to the impunity enjoyed by the Nationalists were nonexistent. The victors laid claim to their patrimony, while the majority of the population lived in quiet desperation, focused primarily on personal survival. These were the Years of Hunger, when wages were slashed while food prices rocketed. Infant mortality rates rose as gaps in living standards widened. Trade unions were banned and strikers risked long prison sentences. Militarily defeated, weary of the horrors and privations of war, the Republicans who escaped execution and imprisonment were materially cowed and reduced to the status of second-class citizens, robbed of dignity and identity. How to get enough to eat, rather than how to resist the regime, was the enduring preoccupation of much of the population. As Michael Richards has explained, "The appalling conditions under which most of the lower classes were forced to live under Franco determined a necessary obsession with mere survival in the immediate post-war period. The victory of Franco was re-created in the day-to-day degradation of the defeated. It was chiefly this enforced retreat into the private domestic sphere in order to survive which made resistance all but impossible."[12]

Describing life in Barcelona during this period of the early 1940s, Manuel Vázquez Montalban emphasized the primary concern with survival and the attempts to evade confronting the horrors that were still being perpetrated throughout the vanquished city: "The city survived and pretended not to hear the firing squads shooting, not to notice the queues outside the Model Prison, or the systematic destruction of its own identity."[13]

This privatized response to material hardship and the fear of persecution was further reflected in the popular culture of the day, with the revue star Conchita Piquer singing: "I don't want to know / Don't tell me neighbour / I prefer to go on dreaming / To knowing the truth."[14] The regime controlled the media, and during the 1940s and 1950s encouraged this culture of evasion. It was a time when the kind of inner migration that we all engage in from time to time, seeking to evade the harsher realities of the world by escaping into an "other world" of fiction and fantasy, became particularly widespread. Although essentially a privatized response, it came to constitute a cultural movement, a collective movement of evasion. Thus, it was during this period that football became a mass spectator sport in Spain and soap operas on the radio became particularly popular. In the words of two historians of this period, "Football, bullfighting, kiosk literature, radio shows, the cinema, were all part of the culture of evasion, casting its 'artificial silence' around the real problems of a pauperised country. Those struggling to make do on second-hand clothes and scanty rations could escape into a world of illusion."[15]

Franco's Regime

This narrowing of the focus of people's concerns to the private realm suited Franco's project. An authoritarian, conservative military officer, Franco believed in the need for a supreme ruler (himself) to restore a society shattered by war. His regime was sustained by three main pillars (or families): the Nationalist army, the Falange, and the Church. What held them together for forty years, apart from self-interest, was a common ideological framework encompassing a belief in the necessity of the 1936 uprising, an abhorrence of the left, admiration for military virtues, a commitment to Catholicism, the exhaltation of Franco, and a shared vision of Spain restored to the full imperial splendor of its Golden Age. The secret of Franco's personal hold on power, which he maintained unchallenged until his death in 1975, was his manipulation of these different families and of the representatives of the different clans within them, to ensure that none had a monopoly of power.

During the immediate post–Civil War years there was no possibility of developing an open oppositional movement. The most basic rights of citizenship were circumscribed, with severe limits on rights of association and free expression, including the right to vote. There was no independent judiciary. Military courts dealt with what were considered to be serious political crimes involving the threat of violence, while the Tribunals of Public Order (established in 1963) dealt with lesser political offenses such as belonging to an illegal party or trade union. There were also various forms of administrative intimidation and persecution. Those who failed to show adequate respect for the regime and its institutions would find themselves denied a driving license or passport, and discover that avenues of career advancement had been cut off.

The only threats to Franco's peace during the 1940s came from sporadic guerrilla actions, which the Communist Party called off in the 1950s as it began to pursue a strategy of national reconciliation, building bridges with liberal opposition groups within Spain. The bulk of the leaders of the prewar opposition to Franco were in exile, as divided among themselves as ever. The majority of them placed their faith for the future in the liberation of fascist Spain by means of a push from the outside. After all, how could the liberal democracies that had just defeated Hitler allow Franco's regime to survive? The developing Cold War between the NATO and Warsaw Pact powers put an end to such hopes, when the United States broke Spain's international isolation and in September 1953 signed a treaty allowing the U.S. military access to base facilities within Spain in return for economic aid.

By the 1950s Spain was facing severe economic problems, and throughout that decade pressure grew for a change in economic policy. This was the context within which a new breed of technocrats became more influential within the Francoist regime. Associated with a secretive Catholic lay organization known as Opus Dei, from 1957 onward these men urged the integration of Spain into the rest of Europe and the international economy. They pursued the standard World Bank package—wage freezes, devaluation, opening up the domestic market to foreign investment—and after a few years of recession the fruits began to show. The 1960s was a period of rapid economic growth in Spain. The relaxation of visa controls laid the foundation for the mass Spanish tourist industry, while the economic growth enjoyed by the rest of Europe meant a steady demand for Spanish migrant labor to the north of the Pyrenees, and the remittances of Spaniards working in the factories and on the farms of northern and western Europe became a significant element in Spain's invisible export trade.

Those who had pressed upon Franco the imperative of economic modernization had argued strongly that social peace could only be maintained through economic advance. Unforeseen by them, the economic buoyancy of the 1960s started to reveal some of the social and political fissures that lay beneath the imposed order of Franco's Spain. Throughout the decade there was an increase in industrial disputes, as under conditions of full employment and rising demand for labor the working class began to recover some of the self-confidence necessary to start defending its interests.

At no time did the growth in working class militancy threaten the regime, but despite all the instruments of repression under its control, the state found it increasingly difficult to prevent such disputes from disturbing the surface calm of Franco's authoritarian peace. This stability also came under threat from an increasingly vocal student opposition, whose numbers had grown as universities expanded to meet the demands of industry for an educated workforce. These young people had not participated in the Civil War, but they were open to all the social and political influences that emanated from the radical questioning of the status quo that was part and parcel of the transnational cultural youth movement during the latter half of the 1960s. As a consequence, student protest became endemic—focusing on demands for the democratization of student unions and academic freedom. Beyond such internal issues there were wider concerns relating to opposition to the Vietnam War, solidarity with striking workers and the victims of government repression, and the demand for the democratization of Spanish society.

The regime's hegemony was further weakened by developments within the Catholic Church. Throughout the Catholic world the 1960s was a period of questioning and reevaluating the role of the church and its ministers in relation to society and the state. Furthermore, young Spanish priests were not immune to the radicalization of youth that took place in Spain and elsewhere throughout the 1960s, just at the time when the old priests and bishops who had been through the Civil War and blessed Franco's crusade were beginning to retire and lose their influence. This predisposition to question the established perspectives within the Spanish church was encouraged by the changes taking place in the Vatican, as exemplified by the debates during the Second Vatican Council. Particularly significant was Pope John XXIII's 1963 encyclical *Pacem in terris,* which acknowledged the dignity of the individual in the context of the universal human family within which all are equal, and urged all to pursue the common good by means that safeguarded and promoted the rights of the human person. In this context priests within the church began to identify with working-class and regional protesters against the Franco regime and began to deny the regime's claim to legitimacy and moral authority. This trend culminated in 1971 when the Assembly of Bishops and Priests issued an apology to the Spanish people, seeking a pardon for its partisanship in the Civil War. The Church of the Crusade had turned into the Church of Reconciliation.

A further foundation of Franco's regime, the suppression of separatism, began to wither as the years passed. One of Franco's first acts after coming to power had been to revoke the statutes of autonomy granted to Catalonia and the Basque region by the Second Republic before the Civil War. Any undue manifestation of regionalist sentiment was anathema to him. He viewed it as a fundamental threat to his mission of restoring Spain to its former glory as a great and united power. Despite this, or perhaps because of the attempt to suppress such movements, separatist feeling in both Catalonia and the Basque country was increasing by the end of the 1960s. In Catalonia the movement was primarily a cultural one, but in the Basque country it took a more violent form.

Within the dominant political class the main division lay between those who believed in the need for reform to ensure the survival of the regime *(aperturistas),* and the intransigent members of the bunker *(immobilistas),* who believed that any easing of the authoritarian rod would mark the beginning of the end of the Francoist system and the privileged position that they occupied within it. Influential among the *aperturistas* were significant sections of the urban middle class and business groups, who sought Spanish entry into the European Economic Community (EEC) but who knew that Spain would only be admitted once she had displayed a commitment to democratic political processes. But the forces of reaction were rising throughout the 1960s, while the old dictator fought against his increasing frailty, struggling to circumscribe his delegated successor, Juan Carlos, and ensure that Francoism would live on after Franco.

Franco finally died in his bed on 20 November 1975, and two days later Juan Carlos was crowned king. By the time of his death, Franco and Francoism had become an anachronism. The political system was completely out of harmony with the society that had emerged during nearly 40 years of dictatorship. It was clear to everyone other than the most reactionary members of the bunker that change was necessary, and

within three years of Franco's death the goal of the opposition—
"democracy without adjectives"—had been achieved. Next, we will
explore some of the key features of this process.

The Transition to Democracy:
The Institutional Framework

By the early 1970s, and with the old dictator's death imminent, the
opposition parties had grouped themselves into a broad coalition
embracing socialists, communists, and regional parties, and were calling for *a ruptura democrática*—a clean break with the old system, a
complete political amnesty, legalization of all political parties, free
trade unions, regional autonomy, an independent judiciary, and a neutral
army. On Franco's death they were out on the streets, chanting "No to
an imposed King! No to the Francoist King!" and "Spain tomorrow will
be Republican" *(España mañana, Será republicana).*[16] Juan Carlos was
aware of the fate that befell the Greek royal family when they revealed
their insensitivity to public demands for reform, and so he knew that his
survival depended on his sensitivity to the popular mood. But he also
knew that in attempting to do this he had to proceed cautiously if he
was to maintain the loyalty of the army and security forces, and counter
the threat of rightist coups.

One obvious step that he could have taken to convince the opposition that he was serious in his self-proclaimed mission to be "the king
of each and every Spaniard" would have been to free the political prisoners incarcerated under Franco's brutal regime. But such a move
would have provoked outrage among the rightists within the army and
security forces, and risked plunging Spain into a renewed civil war. So,
what marked the years of transition was the slow and careful expansion
of political liberties, alongside an equally cautious program of political
amnesty.[17]

The disappointment of those who hoped for immediate and dramatic changes increased as the premier appointed by Franco, Carlos Arias
Navarro, revealed himself to be the most cautious and conservative of
reformers. In May 1976 he presented a bill before the parliament
(Cortes) making it legal to hold meetings and demonstrations; a month
later he presented a bill to legalize political parties except for the
Communists and those to the left of them. But it was clear to all that he
was not comfortable in his role and lacked the determination necessary

to face up to the intransigence of the diehards in the Cortes. The King made his unease known, and Arias resigned on 1 July 1976.

His successor was Adolpho Suárez, a former general secretary of the *Moviemento Nacional,* the national political movement of Franco's regime. The choice was greeted with dismay by all democratically inclined Spaniards. What they did not know was that Suárez had convinced Juan Carlos of his commitment to democratization and of his capacity to carry it out, given his total familiarity with the workings of the Francoist system.

Aware of the lack of public confidence in his capacities, Suárez moved quickly. Shortly after his appointment he appeared on television to promise a referendum on political reform, elections within a year, and a further release of political prisoners. True to his word, in November 1976 he brought before the Cortes a political reform bill that would introduce universal suffrage and a two-chamber parliament. The vote was covered live on television, ensuring that as members were called upon to cast their vote they were fully aware that they did so before the eyes of the public. They had also been advised by Suárez and his colleagues that those who voted for reform could rest assured that no action would be taken against anyone suspected of corruption and the abuse of power. The bill was passed 425 to 59, with 13 abstentions. A month later the reforms were overwhelmingly endorsed in a referendum in which more than three-quarters of the electorate turned out and over 94 percent voted in favor, with less than 3 percent opposed. Further reforms followed. In February 1977 the Socialist Party was legalized. The right to strike was recognized in March, and trade unions were legalized in April 1977, the same month that the National Movement was disbanded and the Communist Party was legalized in time for the elections planned for 15 June.

The main threat to the successful outcome of the elections, apart from the enduring possibility of a rightist coup, was that posed by the Basque political parties and movements who announced their intention to boycott the elections in response to the Suárez government's failure to grant full amnesty to all political prisoners. Following the partial pardon of Coronation Day, which affected less than 10 percent of the 750 Basque prisoners,[18] there had been a few moves to heal the wounds of political division inherited from the past, but all of them left the Basques feeling shortchanged. Despite their differences, the Basque political parties remained solid in their demand for the release of all political prisoners, while the members of the bunker were equally firm that the Spanish state should never submit to separatist demands. Eventually, on 15 October 1977, Suárez conceded a total amnesty covering all politically motivated crimes committed before 15 June 1977, the date of the general election.[19]

His big fear was the reaction of the right, particularly those in the security forces, to the release of terrorists deemed guilty of politically motivated crimes of violence. He was increasingly aware of the urgent need for change among the forces of law and order if he was to maintain at least the minimal trust of those demanding political reform. But efforts to replace some of the reactionary commanders within the police and the civil guard provoked antigovernment demonstrations by some of the most diehard squads. A similar policy with regard to the army fueled the fears of rightists and led certain members of the bunker to contemplate a military coup and the imposition of a "government of national unity." As a result the opposition moderated its demands. Realizing the gravity of the threat posed by the diehard squads, they gave up hope of a radical break with the old order and settled for *refor-ma pactada,* a negotiated transition from dictatorship to democracy that acknowledged the legality of the institutional framework bequeathed by Franco.[20]

The elections of 15 June 1977 were the first democratic elections to be held in Spain in over 40 years. The right-center party led by Suárez, the Union de Centro Democratico (UCD), emerged with the largest number of seats, but without an overall majority. The UCD's victory was followed closely by the social democratic Partido Socialista Obrero Espanol (PSOE) under the leadership of Felipe González. The small percentage of votes obtained by the communists on the left and the Francoists on the right seemed a clear indication that the mood among most of the electorate was for moderation, a desire to avoid upset on the path toward democracy.

As leader of the main party but without an overall majority, Suárez approached the leaders of the other three parties in the new Constituent Assembly and proposed a comprehensive agreement on the legislative program to be pursued during the life of the parliament. This agreement, known as the Moncloa Pact, after the premier's official residence, was arrived at during October 1977.

In October 1978 the new Spanish constitution was approved by both chambers of the Cortes, and in December it was approved in a referendum. Home rule was granted to the Basques and Catalans, and Spain joined the ranks of liberal democracies. The 1978 constitution symbolized the spirit of accommodation that marked the transition period. It represented a compromise between right and left, republican and monarchist, church and anticlericalism, the center and the peripheral nationalist groups. Even so, it aroused the fears of the reactionaries within the military and security forces.

Although the army was by no means a monolithic bloc, in general it was the main bastion of ultrarightist political reaction, and throughout the transition period there was a series of plots to counter the process of political reform. A projected coup, Operation Galaxia, was planned for 17 November 1978 to prevent the referendum on the constitution. It was discovered, but the low-key response of the government revealed the deep-seated fear of provoking the military. Discontent among the military had been heightened by the legalization of the Communist Party, and the terrorists acts of Basque paramilitary and extremist left-wing groups succeeded in provoking impatience with the democratic experiment among significant sections of the armed forces. Their mood was not improved by a draft military amnesty bill presented to the Cortes in June 1980 that aimed to rehabilitate officers who had fought on the Republican side during the civil war. By early 1981 Madrid was afire with rumors of an imminent military coup. The attempt was launched on 23 February when a group of civil guards burst into the Cortes and held all present hostage. They were hoping that they would be joined by other units. Juan Carlos went on television to make it clear to all that as head of state and commander in chief of Spain's military forces, he was totally committed to the political reform process, and the rebels would have to shoot him before he would abdicate. After 18 hours occupying the Cortes, the plotters surrendered and the coup was defeated. On 27 February over 3 million people throughout Spain demonstrated in favor of democracy.

The coup attempt, which came to be known as 23 F, marked a significant stage in Spain's democratic transition process. The defeat of the plotters and the crown's display of total commitment to the reform project finally convinced the majority of skeptical Spaniards that democracy was a fact; it was real. The time of appeasement of the ultrarightists in the military was over. It was no longer a crime to be a socialist, a communist, an anarchist. You could vote for whom you wanted. This new spirit was reflected in the results of the October 1982 elections when Felipe Gonzáles's PSOE obtained nearly half of the national vote while the UCD was annihilated. In light of such a vote, no military plotters could henceforth claim with any conviction that they were acting in the best interests of the Spanish people. Indeed, when one general publicly defended the 23 February coup attempt, he was dismissed within an hour.[21]

Despite these significant institutional changes, people realized that a deeper cultural transformation was required. People looked toward the emergence of a new political culture emphasizing the unity of the Spanish nation and the virtues of democracy. This required a reevaluation of the past that had divided the people into "Two Spains." As Pérez-Díaz has observed, the process of democratic institution building was "paralleled by a collective cultural effort, partly conscious and partly unconscious, to forget some fragments of Spain's history while keeping alive or reinterpreting others."[22] The next section is devoted to an examination of this cultural effort.

Creating a New Political Culture: Coping with the Legacy of the Past

Writing in 1990 about the problems faced by Spaniards in dealing with the legacy of the Francoist era, Paul Preston observed, "For the Spaniards, denied liberation in 1945, the question of coming to terms with the past has been rendered difficult by the fact that 'the past' continued for nearly forty years after the war's conclusion and indeed beyond."[23] We have seen how this past was reproduced in all kinds of ways to maintain the divisions of the civil war. It lived on after the dictator's death in a somewhat subterranean manner. Because the wounds within Spanish society were so deep, and no effort had been made to heal them, the divisions were still there 40 years after the start of the civil war as Spain embarked on its transition to democracy. As a consequence there was a consensus across the political spectrum that there was no space for revenge or the settling of old scores for fear of a renewed bloody conflict.

In this manner the past continued to exert its influence during the post-Franco transition period, as evidenced by the very fact that it was never talked about or referred to in the public domain. In the privacy of their own homes the families of the victims of Franco's purges might harbor their resentments against the torturers and killers, but no effort was made to acknowledge the privatized pain in the form of some official collective memory. It was feared that to have done so would have jeopardized the transition to democracy, and the vast majority of Spaniards had no desire to participate in old ideological battles. As a consequence, and in the pragmatic spirit of compromise and accommodation that characterized the whole transition process in Spain, a "pact of oblivion" was established among all those parties and groupings committed to the transition They engaged in a collective exercise in public amnesia.

Whereas for Franco the past as constituted by the civil war represented his main source of legitimacy and a key element in maintaining unity throughout his regime, the only source of legitimacy for the emergent democratic state was the future. There, in the future, the social and economic benefits of a liberal democracy were waiting to be enjoyed. A democratic Spanish state would no longer be a pariah on the international scene. Entry into the EEC would be a formality. The state would once again be a state for all Spaniards, not just for those who had been victors of the civil war. As Suárez phrased it: "The question is not to ask people where they are coming from, but where they are going to."[24]

The Pact of Oblivion

All those parties and groupings that sought to see Spain transformed into a political democracy agreed on a pact to forget the most painful elements of the past and engage in a form of selective amnesia necessary to construct a new history, one that would provide a sound foundation for the new democratic culture that they sought to build. It is possible to identify a number of dimensions to this understanding and approach to the problems posed by the legacy of the past.

Minimal reference to Franco.   A basic element was the avoidance of any reference to the Franco era. Politicians did not denounce the evils of the old dictator's regime; they focused on proclaiming the virtues of democracy, while the most powerful of Franco's public memorials, the Cross and mausoleum of the Valley of the Fallen, fell into disuse as a setting for official occasions. In similar manner, the old festival days commemorating the nationalist victory are no longer observed or else new symbolic meanings have been attached to them. Thus, Franco's celebration of the Day of Victory has been transformed into Armed Forces Day, when honor and respect are paid to all military personnel, past and present, nationalist and republican.

No purge.   A second aspect of the pact was that no attempt should be made to redress old injustices, let alone seek retribution against those responsible for the killing and the torturing perpetrated during Franco's time. The democratization process was too sensitive and vulnerable for the opening up of old wounds. As one communist member of the Cortes put it, "How can we be capable of reconciliation after years of killing each other if we don't have the capacity to forget our past forever?"[25] As a result, no effort was made to remove the torturers from their posts in the police and prison services. To this day the police files from Franco's era that could be used to purge those implicated in the abuses of the regime have remained sealed.[26] The journalists who had acted as apologists and propagandists for the old regime were allowed to continue with their careers, as were functionaries who continued to occupy the same key positions in the judiciary, the military, and the different national bureaucracies as they had under Franco. When the National Movement was disbanded in 1977, many of its agencies were absorbed by government ministries, along with the employees of party-related organizations who became civil servants. John Hooper made an incisive observation upon this aspect of the transition to democracy in Spain:

> The spirit of transition is sometimes described as being that of "forgive and forget." That is not entirely correct. Since no one in Spain was ever judged, no one was ever deemed guilty. And since no one was ever deemed guilty, forgiveness never entered into it. It was just a matter of forgetting.[27]

But in truth it was not "just a matter of forgetting." A new past had to be created that fit the political imperatives of the transition period.

The Creation of a New History

Reinterpreting the civil war.   With regard to the civil war, the key reference point for the transition to democracy, new historical interpretations had already begun to emerge during the years before Franco's death that challenged the old Manichean readings of the conflict as a straightforward fight between good and evil. In this more nuanced version of Spain's traumatic recent past, history was portrayed as tragedy, with the associated theme of the participants as hapless victims of forces beyond their control leading them toward an inevitable and dreadful outcome. The war had to be located within the wider context of the unfolding global conflict between fascism, communism, and capitalism. Cast in this light, the civil war took on the hue of a Greek tragedy, with the combatants little more than pawns in the larger game of world politics that brought calamity and grief to the Spanish people. This kind of interpretation had profound consequences in terms of evaluating culpability for the sins of the past for, as Pérez-Díaz has pointed out, if the civil war is portrayed as a tragedy,

> The share of the guilt and responsibility must be more or less evenly distributed among the combatants, since both sides were to blame, and the total amount of guilt and responsibility must also be reduced, since neither side was entirely guilty so much as each was responding to threats from the other. Moreover, both sides became pawns in the larger game of world politics which overwhelmed them.[28]

Furthermore, Pérez-Díaz has argued, if the theme of Spanish history as tragedy is applied to developments after the civil war, then it becomes apparent that "the guilt the parties had to bear has been further expiated through suffering: the losers under the repression they endured for well over a generation, and the winners, to a lesser extent, by seeing their heirs renounce their monopoly on political power and lose control of the state a generation later."[29]

Creating new public symbols. As part of this process of incorporating new versions of the past into daily life and creating fresh myths to underpin the imperative for peaceful political coexistence between erstwhile foes, new symbols were attached to public spaces and occasions. The extent to which this has happened has varied considerably, given the devolution of power to the regions. In the autonomous provinces of Catalonia and the Basque country, there has been a wholesale eradication of all signs and symbols of the Francoist era, as the politicians seek to reproduce a past within which historic nationalities have always existed in their own right, with their own space, language, and culture. In other parts of the country, where the people have been more comfortable with the idea of being both Spanish and, for example, Aragonese, and where the authorities have been less eager to remove the public memorials relating to the Francoist past, new ones have been introduced to complement the old, with streets named after Francoist generals from the civil war still found alongside those named after republicans. But even in that heartland of Francoism, Burgos, the signs and symbols of Franco's rule are disappearing with the passage of time.

Contrasts and Continuities

The striking contrast between the collective amnesia and "amnesty for all by all" that characterized the post-Franco approach to the traumas of the recent past and the vindictive purges of the post–Civil War period can be explained in terms of the particular conjunction of forces at different moments in history. Franco was the leader of a victorious crusade against an insidious force that threatened to destroy Spain. There were two Spains, the victors and the vanquished; and the defeated had no resources with which to resist the obsessive vindictiveness of Franco and his forces.

In contrast, during the transition period of the mid-1970s, the Francoist establishment was not defeated. Except for the diehards of the bunker, Francoists had come to realize that once the old dictator was out of the way, it would be time for change. As a consequence, there was no sudden break with the past. The transition was achieved through negotiation and the gradual handing over of power rather than through victory in a revolutionary conflict. It was a classical case of the type of transition that Huntington has termed "transformation." The Francoists did not abdicate so much as arrange the transfer of fragments of their erstwhile power, and one of the understandings underpinning this process was that there would be no reprisals against anyone involved in the old regime. Looming behind the negotiators, of course, was the specter of reactionary elements in the military, all too eager to be let loose to restore pride and unity to Spain by saving it from the threat of democracy and division.

But these obvious contrasts should not mask certain continuities between the two processes. In both cases particular strands of the past were suppressed while new ones were discovered and reproduced for public consumption. In both cases this exercise in selective amnesia and remembrance was driven by fear. This, at least, is the view of my brother-in-law, a Catalan from Gerona:

> As for Spain during the early years of Franco's regime, compared with the early years of this post-Franco era, I see plenty of similarities. I think that the current "pact of oblivion" is perfectly obvious. But something similar happened during at least the first fifteen years of Franco's regime. I was born in 1938, during the civil war, and went to school during the '40s and early '50s. I knew from my family—all of them republicans (mostly anarchists) who had fought against Franco, and therefore LOSERS—that from the fall of the monarchy in 1931

until Franco's final victory in 1939, Spain had been a republic with
autonomous regions and a very progressive legislation. Coming from
a family of printers I grew up in a house full of books, many of which
had been banned (by writers such as Machado or Lorca). But the way
we were taught history in school was curious; it was as if the period
1931–39 had not existed. All physical signs from that period were
eliminated immediately by the occupying troops, all books they could
lay their hands on destroyed, all songs and other expressions forbid-
den . . . Then it happened "by decree," now by a sort of "common
consensus," and yet, the deep down reason seems to be the same:
FEAR.[30]

There is a common root to the fear that has fed the impulse to selective
amnesia during both periods: the experience of the civil war. We have
seen how Franco and his forces behaved like an occupying army, intent
on purging all who they suspected of republican sympathies. Hence, in
the immediate aftermath of the civil war fear of the consequences of
revealing one's past was quite understandable. However, with time that
fear diminished, only to be replaced by a new one—that the old conflicts might be resurrected with the death of the dictator. By the 1970s
no one wanted to return to the ideological politics of the 1930s and the
bloody conflict of that time.

This desire to forget the past and let bygones be bygones can also
be traced back to the divisions of the Franco years not just in terms of
their intensity at the time, and the resultant fear of renewed bloody conflict if old wounds were opened, but also the manner in which most
Spanish people coped with the consequences of defeat in the civil war.
Commentators have referred to the spirit of tolerance among Spaniards
that eased the transition from dictatorship to democracy, insofar as there
was no significant movement demanding retribution against those
responsible for human rights abuses during the Franco era. This tolerance had its origins in the survival habits developed during the Franco
years, when most people focused on survival and could only vent their
grief and anger within the private sphere of the family. Furthermore, as
we have seen, the regime promoted what has been termed a culture of
evasion, facilitating the escape from the harsh realities of the world to a
fantasy realm, with the consequent depoliticization of the public realm.
This privatized response, the focusing on the self and the family to the
exclusion of broader social and political issues, was reinforced during
the 1960s when Spain shared the economic growth experienced
throughout the rest of Western Europe. Spaniards, like their contemporaries, began to enjoy a more affluent lifestyle and the consumer goods

that became available. This narrowing of the focus of concern was in itself a perfectly understandable response to the constraints of living under a dictatorship where the normal democratic rights of free speech and assembly were denied. The result was an impoverishment of civil society, as evidenced by the paucity of voluntary associations such as trade unions, mutual aid societies, interest groups, and political parties. As John Hooper has observed, "Franco's rule made Spaniards more reliant on themselves and on the state. But not on each other."[31] So here we have another continuity between the two processes: the ability of political elites to pursue their own strategy for dealing with the legacy of the past without due concern about grassroots opposition, given that during both periods there was a scarcity of well-organized pressure groups that might have queried and opposed their reforms.

This leads us to another continuity between the two periods—the manner in which the Spanish people were cast in the role of observers rather than participants in the processes of transformation. This, of course, was the status to be expected under an authoritarian regime that seized power through military victory. But the political apathy of the Spanish people manifested during the transition process of the 1970s, which was to some extent a reflection of the survival habits of the Franco era, was also encouraged by the invisible politics of that period, the way in which the transition process was conducted by political leaders bargaining and compromising among themselves, without reference to grassroots opinion.

Conclusion

In 1976 there were still 40,000 Spanish political exiles living in France.[32] With the consolidation of democracy in Spain more of them began to return home. As part of the overall peacebuilding project and the attempt to foster reconciliation between the Two Spains of the recent past, the Spanish government began to pay pensions to disabled Republican veterans and widows, although not on the same scale as those paid to Nationalist veterans. In addition, those who served time as political prisoners under Franco became eligible for state pensions— one year's entitlement for every year spent in prison. But the number of these *sobrevivientas* (survivors) is declining with each passing year, and with them fade the memories of the horrors of the civil war and the excesses of Franco's regime. Since the history taught in schools usually ends with the civil war, many young Spaniards have only the vaguest of notions about Franco. According to an editorial in the newspaper *El Mundo* commenting on the centenary of Franco's birth, Spaniards look at the Franco era "as if from an enormous distance . . . his memory has been blotted out of the collective present. It now serves as a point of reference for almost no one."[33] This was evidenced by the way in which Spaniards rallied to the support of the head of the International Olympics Committee, Juan Antonio Samaranch, when his Francoist past was exposed by British journalists before the 1992 Barcelona Olympics. That same year a poll of young Spaniards revealed that less than half of them considered Francoism to have been a "mistake."[34]

In September 1999, on the sixtieth anniversary of the end of the civil war, the Spanish parliament passed a resolution condemning the 1936 military uprising that had ushered in the decades of Francoist dictatorship. The resolution was supported by all the political parties with the exception of the conservatives, whose general secretary accused the others of trying to divide Spain, arguing that they should not talk about Two Spains but focus on the future and "the Spain of the 21st century."[35] But what is particularly interesting about this episode is the lack of concern on the part of the Spanish public. The resolution was reported in the press but elicited no public debate. It would seem that most Spaniards are happy enough to continue letting bygones be bygones, a fact I was reminded of during a recent visit to family members in Gerona. Talking with my sister-in-law Bea, it transpired that her grandfather had been summarily executed by the Nationalists in Galicia and their family estate confiscated. This was recounted without any apparent anger or resentment. When I commented on this Bea shrugged her shoulders: "Well, it is all in the past now, isn't it?"

Notes

1. Carr and Fusi, *Spain: Dictatorship to Democracy,* p. 17.

2. Pérez-Diáz, *The Return of Civil Society,* p. 129.

3. Figures cited in Richards, "Civil War, Violence and the Construction of Francoism," p. 209. The lowest estimate of deaths by execution in the Nationalist zones during the war years from July 1936 to April 1939 has been 20,000, a figure put forward by a member of the regime's Ministry of Information in the 1960s. One of Franco's generals calculated that there were 57,662 executions during the war, and a further 23,000 between 1939 and 1961. See Richards, p. 210.

4. Richards, p. 215.
5. Quoted in Richards, p. 201.
6. Richards, p. 224.
7. Hooper, *The New Spaniards,* p. 74.
8. Preston, "The Politics of Revenge," in Preston, *The Politics of Revenge,* pp. 30–47.
9. Carr and Fusi, p. 19.
10. This did not mean an end to the killing. Apparently, about 350 death sentences were examined at each meeting of the Council of Ministers during the early months of 1945, with about 40 of the sentences being confirmed and the victims executed immediately. Franco was the most "hawkish" in his insistence that the purge should continue. Richards, p. 236.
11. Moriarty, "Private Grief and Public Remembrance," pp. 125–142.
12. Richards, p. 200.
13. Quoted in Richards, p. 201.
14. Quoted in Carr and Fusi, pp. 94–95.
15. Carr and Fusi, p. 122.
16. Hooper, p. 32.
17. This project was made all the more difficult by the provocative acts of terrorism committed by the most extreme of the Basque separatists in ETA.
18. Preston, p. 82.
19. Page, "The Role of Penal Policy," p. 239.
20. Preston, *The Triumph of Democracy in Spain,* p. 120.
21. Hooper, p. 52.
22. Pérez-Diáz, p. 22.
23. Preston, *The Politics of Revenge,* p. 33.
24. Quoted in Kritz, *Transitional Justice,* p. 299. The parallels with British Prime Minister Tony Blair's pronouncements on the occasion of the 1998 Good Friday Peace Accords in Northern Ireland are obvious.
25. Quoted in Kritz, p. 299.
26. Kritz, p. 298.
27. Hooper, p. 78.
28. Pérez-Díaz, p. 24.
29. Pérez-Díaz, p. 24.
30. Email correspondence, 17 July 1998.
31. Hooper, p. 76.
32. Macdonald, *Homage to the Spanish Exiles,* p. 334.
33. Quoted by Hooper, p. 73.
34. Hooper, p. 78.
35. *El Pais,* 16 September 1999.

4

Truth and Justice as Far as Possible: The Latin American Experience

In the previous chapter we saw how, in Spain at the time of Franco's death, there was a consensus among political, economic, and military elites that bygones should be bygones, that no attempt should be made to seek redress against those responsible for human rights violations during the dictator's rule. The prime concern was that the transition to a pluralist democratic system within the European Common Market (as it was then called) should proceed without hindrance or threat. We also saw how this process was facilitated by the underdeveloped nature of civil society in Spain at that time, insofar as there was a dearth of autonomous associations and voluntary groups that might have articulated and channeled protest from below against the policy of amnesty and amnesia.

At the time of Franco's death a number of Spain's (and Portugal's) former colonies in South America were suffering under repressive regimes in which the military played a dominant and shameful role. As these regimes began to give way to civilian ones, they looked to the Spanish model as the path of transition to be emulated. The degree to which they succeeded in following the example of Spain, however, varied according to the circumstances of the transition to civilian government. The focus of this chapter is upon two case studies drawn from South America that illustrate how the manner in which a successor regime attempts to deal with a legacy of human rights abuses is significantly affected by the conditions under which the transition from dictatorship to democracy takes place.

By way of introduction, three points need to be emphasized:

1. As a general rule it would appear that in situations where key sectors of the former regime retain significant coercive power and the preparedness to exercise it, then the pursuit of those guilty of human rights abuses is likely to be lukewarm, given the fear that too vigorous a pursuance of the culpable might provoke another coup.

2. In circumstances where the new regime has neither the political will nor the resources to challenge the impunity enjoyed by the torturers, executioners, and kidnappers, then the onus falls on civil society groups and networks to take up the struggle. Invariably, where they find the pursuit of retributive justice to be an unreal and impractical goal, then they have to settle for what some might consider to be the lesser target of uncovering the truth about the years of repression and abuse, while seeking adequate reparations for those who have suffered.

3. In the struggle for truth and the public acknowledgment of the narratives of the victims, a crucial support role can fall to international human rights and kindred networks, a role usually filled by the same networks that provided support throughout the years of struggle against dictatorship.

Brazil and Uruguay

These points can be illustrated briefly by the cases of Brazil and Uruguay. In April 1964 there was a military coup in Brazil. The new regime became increasingly repressive, but by the late 1970s a process of political liberalization had been inaugurated and the incidence of torture, kidnapping, and wrongful imprisonment declined drastically. This relaxation of repression and the opening up of a more democratic political life continued over several years before the eventual handover to civilian government in the spring of 1985. As part of this lengthy transition process, a general amnesty had been declared in 1979 for all those accused of political crimes and for state security agents who risked being charged with human rights violations. This amnesty was accepted by the new civilian government, which thereby colluded in the attempt to bury the past as the necessary price to be paid to get the military to stay in their barracks.

However, unknown to the military and to the state authorities in general, human rights activists associated with the office of the Roman

Catholic archbishop of São Paulo had been compiling their own record of human rights abuses that occurred from 1964 to 1979, based on the official records of the police and security services. After the amnesty law was passed volunteers had exercised their legal right to check out the relevant public records dealing with the apprehension, interrogation, and punishment of all those who fell into the clutches of the security services. The files were then photocopied before being returned. Over a million pages were copied and eventually compiled into a twelve-volume report of nearly 7,000 pages. An edited version of this, entitled *Brasil: Nunca Mas,* was published and appeared in Brazilian book shops in July 1985. The funding for this massive enterprise came primarily from the Geneva-based World Council of Churches. In this way a transnational network underpinned the actions of a group of courageous and committed people, and the story of the years of military repression in Brazil was brought out into the public domain. According to Lawrence Weschler, the groundswell of public concern and revulsion that were aroused by the revelations of the report prompted the Brazilian president to sign the United Nations Convention Against Torture on 23 September 1985.[1]

In Uruguay it was a similar tale. During 11 years of military rule thousands of citizens of this small country were tortured and imprisoned for lengthy periods of time under inhuman conditions. In this time some 150 people disappeared and more than 100 were killed by security forces. As in Brazil, by the mid-1980s the military had decided they wanted to hand over power to a civilian government, but on their own terms. These conditions were agreed to during the negotiations that preceded the inauguration of a civilian president on 1 March 1985. A week later he signed a bill that constituted an amnesty for all remaining political prisoners, but excluded the perpetrators of human rights abuses. The following month, in April 1985, the parliament established an investigative committee but its mandate was restricted to studying the disappearances that had occurred during the 11 years of military rule, and excluded the instances of torture and illegal imprisonment. After seven months the committee reported on 164 disappearances involving security forces, and sent the evidence to the Supreme Court. Before judicial proceedings could commence, however, the parliament approved an act on 22 December 1986 that granted exemption from punishment to all military and security personnel responsible for human rights violations committed before the handover of power. Outraged, human rights groups launched a campaign against this impunity law under the slogan *"Ni Olvido, ni Venganza, Justicia!"* ("Neither forgetting nor vengeance, Justice!"), but in April 1989 narrowly lost a national referendum, which resulted in the retention of the law.

Just a few weeks before the referendum, however, the human rights group Servicio Paz y Justicia (SERPAJ) issued a report patterned on the Brazilian publication documenting the abuses of human rights during the years of military rule, which was the result of three years of work interviewing former political prisoners.[2]

As a general rule it would appear that the weakness of successor states in seeking redress is directly proportional to the strength of the core elements of the prior regime. So, in the cases of Brazil and Uruguay, it was left to civil society groups and networks to attempt to uncover and make public the truth about the years of repression in the face of the failure of the state authorities. However, not all military handovers of state power in South America in recent years have been so completely on the military's own terms. In the case studies that follow, an attempt has been made to illustrate in some depth the different circumstances that resulted in different outcomes with regard to the pursuit of justice and truth by successor regimes.

Thus, in the case of Argentina the junta was humiliated and lost legitimacy through military defeat by the British in the Falklands/Malvinas War, which came on top of economic collapse and widespread impoverishment. As a consequence the civilian government of Raúl Alfonsín was able to identify and prosecute a limited number of human rights violators in light of the revelations of the truth commission that was established.

In Chile, by contrast, the handover to a civilian regime was not brought about by the collapse of the military as such, but rather took place in full accordance with the constitution following Pinochet's defeat in the 1988 plebiscite. Even so, the experience in Argentina was a warning to Pinochet. In October 1989, two months before the first free elections since the 1973 coup, he warned: "No one touches anyone. The day they touch one of my men, the rule of law ends. This I say once and will not say again."[3] His democratic successor, Patricio Aylwin, took the warning to heart and chose not to risk it. As a consequence the impunity of the perpetrators of human rights abuses under Pinochet was very largely preserved. However, as a result of the involvement of external actors Pinochet was not to have it all his own way.

Argentina

In 1976 the armed forces in Argentina deposed President Isabel Peron and took power for themselves. Unlike in Chile, where General Pinochet held power throughout the period of military rule, in Argentina the heads of the different armed services shared office among themselves. Thus, in 1980 the first junta gave way to a second, which was replaced in 1981 by a third, led by General Galtieri, which continued in power until 1983.

The coup was welcomed initially by many for bringing to an end a period of economic instability, raging inflation, and political violence. But the military soon unleashed what became known as the dirty war against all subversives—those who opposed their own virulent anti-communism. Between 10,000 and 30,000 people are thought to have been killed or "disappeared" during the seven-year period of military rule.[4] The illegal and clandestine methods employed were designed to eliminate all opposition and to intimidate all those who might be moved to protest. There were no trials; people were apprehended, tortured, and disappeared. Many were drugged and thrown out of the cargo holds of airplanes over the ocean. Others were buried in secret locations and unmarked graves. Secure in their reign of fear, the torturers and the killers acted with impunity.

Mothers of the Disappeared

It was the women who first broke the silence. In April 1977 a small group of mothers who met at police stations and government offices in search of the their kidnapped children decided that they should meet each week in the main square in the center of Buenos Aires, outside the headquarters of the Ministry of the Interior. As one of them explained, "We began to realise we had to move outside our own families and struggle for all the people who had disappeared, that the explanation for the disappearance of our own children could only be found in the explanation for all the disappearances."[5] Their numbers grew and they became known as *Las Madres de Plaza de Mayo* (the Mothers of Plaza de Mayo). They wore white headscarves as symbols, initially made from the diapers that had belonged to their offspring who had disappeared *(los desaparacedos)*. As one of them recalled, "We made proper white scarves and we embroidered on the names of our children.

Afterwards we put on them '*Aparición con Vida*' (literally, 'Reappearance with Life') because we were no longer searching for just one child but for all the disappeared."[6] "We lost them alive and we want them back alive" was their demand.

The weekly silent protest of these women spread from the capital to most of the major cities and became an international symbol of the struggle against human rights abuses and state terror in Argentina. In an attempt to undermine their stance, the military introduced the *Ley de Olvido* (Law of Forgetting): after someone had been missing for a given length of time they could be declared legally dead and the family would become eligible for a state pension. Elsa de Becerra, one of the stalwarts of the Mothers, explained their opposition to this measure: "They wanted to stop the word 'disappeared' being used. This was their way of burying the issue. Perhaps they thought they could buy our silence. Almost no one accepted it, least of all the Mothers. The Mothers will never sign our children's death certificates."[7]

Over time, international condemnation of human rights abuses grew, as did opposition within the country. The eventual collapse of the military regime came quite quickly. Defeat in the Malvinas/Falklands War with Britain in 1982 coincided with drastic economic conditions as commodity prices fell. The self-belief of the military was eroded by opposition from within, their failure to deal with the recurrent economic crises, and the military defeat. The way was cleared for elections. While the political parties selected candidates and put together platforms, the mothers and the grandmothers of the disappeared formulated their own demands. Four days before the elections in 1983 they issued an "Appeal to the New Government," which called for the immediate release of the detained once constitutional government was restored, to avoid the mass slaughter of survivors; the establishment of a parliamentary commission to investigate the disappearances and other abuses perpetrated by the military; and legislation to ensure that the military would be tried in civilian courts with a jury rather than by their fellow officers and accomplices in the military courts.[8]

The National Commission on Disappeared People

In the elections the Radical Party under Raúl Alfonsín defeated the Peronists, and within days of taking power he announced his intention to appoint a presidential commission to investigate the disappearances and to prosecute nine of the leading military figures from the early years of the junta. The brief of the National Commission on Disappeared People (known by its acronym CONADEP, *Comisión National Sobre la Desaparición de Personas*) was to clarify the events relating to the disappearances, to investigate the fate of the *desaparecidos*, and to present a report to the president. It was to have access to all government facilities and the security forces were ordered to cooperate with its researchers. But its terms of reference disappointed human rights activists, who presumed that Alfonsín had made a deal with the military. CONADEP had no power to subpoena witnesses or to seize relevant documentation. Moreover, lacking the authority to require the military to testify, it had no prosecutory powers but was supposed to pass over to the courts whatever evidence of criminal activity it uncovered. Furthermore, the Commission was appointed by and was answerable to the president, not the Congress.[9]

Despite such misgivings, the Commission was composed of ten individuals from different walks of life, who all enjoyed a significant degree of national and international prestige, and were well known for their stand on human rights. At the first meeting on 18 December 1983 the Commission chose author Ernesto Sábato as chairperson. Whatever their reservations, most human rights groups cooperated enthusiastically with its work. The documentation these groups had amassed over the years was handed over to the Commission and many activists were hired as staff and consultants by CONADEP, while others participated in provincial investigatory commissions. Researchers took statements from relatives of the disappeared and those who had survived the camps, inspected detention centers, and visited secret cemeteries and sections of public graveyards where unidentified bodies had been buried. Consulates and embassies abroad were asked to invite exiles to provide testimony as to their experiences, while other exiles returned to Argentina to testify to the Commission.

After a year CONADEP produced its report. It consisted of 50,000 pages of documentation and a summary that was later published under the title *Nunca Más* (Never Again), which documented nearly 9,000 cases of people who had disappeared, and became a national best-seller. Its impact was heightened when a two-hour synopsis of its findings was broadcast on national television on 4 July 1984. This was powerful enough to provoke unrest in the military, with the result that President Alfonsín felt it necessary to dismiss the Chief of Staff of the army.

But for many of the relatives and friends of the victims, who were what can be termed the secondary victims of the military junta, the report was a whitewash. They knew who the victims were; what they wanted was the names of those who had tortured, raped, and killed them. One of the *Madres* made no secret of her disappointment and frustration.

> CONADEP served to waste a year. This Commission did nothing more than reproduce all the information the human rights organisations already had. It collected together all this evidence on the kidnappings and disappearances, put in into a file and presented it to Alfonsín. . . . The only good thing we can say about CONADEP is that the book and the documentary *Nunca Más* informed the public of what had happened. It made those people who hadn't known, or hadn't wanted to know, face the truth about the military governments.[10]

Alfonsín's big fear was that if the new democratically elected government was too vigorous in the pursuance and prosecution of the military personnel responsible for the savagery of the dirty war, then the breach between the military and civil society would be deepened. His concern was to secure social peace, heal the wounds, and try to close this painful chapter of Argentina's recent history. Furthermore, the armed forces were still capable of upsetting the transition to democratic governance if they felt unduly threatened. They had obstructed the workings of CONADEP in various ways, and members of the Commission were targeted by right-wing paramilitary groups linked to the security services. So, the new government felt constrained to operate within the parameters set by the military, and at times portrayed the human rights groups, with their persistent demands for retributive justice, as a threat to the national project of reconciliation and reconstruction.[11]

The Struggle Against Impunity

Before the handover of power the military had done its utmost to protect itself. The clandestine nature of the dirty war was driven by the desire to maintain secrecy and to ensure impunity. As it became clearer that military rule was about to end, they were haunted by the prospect of being held accountable for their human rights abuses. To minimize the risk of prosecution they destroyed most of the documentation relating to their repression. In addition, in April 1983, the regime issued the *Final Document on the War Against Subversion and Terrorism* in which it was conceded that violations of human rights had occurred, but it was made clear that middle and lower-ranking officers who might have erred had been acting in "due obedience" *(obedienca debida)* to their superior officers—they had been following orders. Finally, just before the handover in October 1983, the military junta had enacted the Law of National Pacification, awarding all members of the armed forces full amnesty for any crimes committed during the struggle against subversion and terrorism.[12]

Although the newly elected government quickly repealed the self-awarded amnesty on 27 December 1983, the decision to prosecute only nine members of the junta and to acknowledge the validity of the concept of due obedience was widely seen as a concession to the military, as was the issuing of arrest orders for seven former members of leftist guerrilla groups.[13] But the military did not have it all their own way. Thus, although the military code required military personnel who had committed an offense while on duty to be tried in military courts, Alfonsín amended the law so that any decision made by the military courts could be appealed in the civilian courts, and unwarranted delay in the pursuit of justice evidenced by the military courts could result in the cases being transferred to civilian jurisdiction. It was a gamble. In allowing the accused to be judged by their own tribunals in the first instance, the government was bowing to the realities of military power and the threat that the military still posed to the democratic process. It was also argued that in allowing a section of the military to judge the most culpable of its officers, the institution would be going some way toward purging itself of the taint of the dirty war. The presumption was that a handful of officers would be sacrificed to help rebuild the prestige of the armed forces, the bulk of whose members, it was assumed, had played no active part in the kidnapping, torturing, and murder.[14] In fact, CONADEP's report made it clear that the abuses were the result of a culture of repression that permeated the whole of the military structure and involved the participation of military personnel at all levels. The perpetrators of the violations were not a "bad handful of officers." The abuses had been implemented through the normal command structures throughout the country.

As it turned out, the Supreme Council of the Armed Forces did prevaricate in its deliberations over the trial of the nine junta members arrested when Alfonsín took office. After nine months the Federal Court acted on what it deemed to be an unwarranted delay, and a second trial, by civilians, was set for April 1985. As the date approached a wave of bombings occurred in Argentina's major cities, and military commanders warned of growing unrest in the ranks. Alfonsín made a televised appeal for people to support him in "defending democracy," and 250,000 people gathered in the Plaza de Mayo to denounce the threats from the military. Even so, he felt obliged to declare a state of emergency in October 1985 following the discovery of yet another coup plot by right-wingers associated with the military.

Five of the nine accused were eventually convicted and sentenced to prison terms ranging from under five years to life. They were stripped of their rank, banned from holding public office in perpetuity, and deprived of all state pension rights and decorations. These sentences were confirmed by the Supreme Court in late December 1986 following an appeal by the defendants.

The courts then turned their attention to other military personnel who had been involved in the torturing and killing. This caused considerable anger and anxiety among the armed forces, leading to repeated threats against the Alfonsín government. Intimidated, the government enacted what later became known as the "Full Stop" *(punto finale)* Law in December 1986, which established a two-month deadline for filing criminal complaints against military personnel by victims or their families. Alfonsín denied that the measure was a result of military pressure, arguing that it was time for Argentina to break free from its bitter past and for the military to be integrated into the project of reconstructing a democratic society.[15]

In fact, the new law backfired on the government, because it resulted in a flurry of new cases filed, and by the deadline of 22 February 1987 more than 300 summonses had been issued by federal courts around the country.[16] By March 1987, 51 security personnel had been arrested for alleged human rights violations, and the anger and tension within the army boiled over once again in a series of rebellions during the Easter period of 1987. Shaken and greatly concerned after negotiations with the rebels, Alfonsín introduced to Congress the Due Obedience *(obedencia debida)* Law in June 1987. This established that the violations of human rights perpetrated by all but the most senior officers were committed under orders from their superiors. Perpetrators were only following orders and as a result they were exonerated. Human rights organizations and activists were outraged.

Alfonsín's successor as president, Carlos Menem, continued with this process of reconciliation through amnesty by granting pardons in 1989 to 39 military officers convicted of human rights violations and to more than 200 others, including leftist guerrillas, those who had mutinied against Alfonsín, and those charged in connection with the Falklands/Malvinas war. A year later, in December 1990, he pardoned the convicted leaders of the junta.[17] In 1992 a law was passed that provided financial compensation for those who had been jailed under the military regimes or been forced into exile during the junta period, and for the families of those who had died in custody.

Reflecting back on the experience in 1993, Alfonsín acknowledged that the aim was not retribution but the prevention of any recurrence: "to guarantee that never again would an Argentinean be taken from his home at night to be tortured or assassinated by agents of the state."[18] He went on to argue that in terms of creating a new democratic culture in Argentina, "the revelation of truth through impartial judicial proceedings and the resulting public condemnation serve just as well as the imposition of punishment to impress upon the public mind the kinds of behaviour that society is unwilling to accept."[19]

Neither Forget nor Forgive

Not everyone agreed with his assessment. Whereas many people in Argentina have been happy to forget the past and get on with their new lives under civilian rule, human rights groups and organizations of those directly affected by the shameful deeds of the military and security services during the years of the dirty war have sought to broaden their struggle against amnesia. "Neither forget nor forgive" (*Ni olvidoni ni perdón*) has been the cry, and the pressure has continued for naming the perpetrators, as well as the determination that these perpetrators should not be allowed to enjoy the present as if the past never was. In this struggle against impunity, civil society groups in Argentina have received significant support from external sources in the international community.

Thus, in 1996 a naval officer and former death squad member, Alfredo Astiz, was forced to retire after years of diplomatic pressure from France, where he had been sentenced in absentia to life imprisonment for the murder of two French nuns in 1977. The Swedish authorities had also been demanding his trial for the murder of a teenager that same year. Human rights activists subsequently demanded that he be put on trial in January 1998 after he had defended in print the atrocities committed by the military and threatened that journalists who were hounding him would "come to a bad end."[20] The Spanish authorities also began investigations into the cases of Spanish citizens who had disappeared during the dirty war, and a Swiss magistrate issued an international arrest warrant for Jorge Rafael Videla, a former army commander and leader of the first junta, in connection with the disappearance of a Swiss-Chilean student who went missing in Buenos Aires in 1977.

In fact Videla, who had served only five years of his life sentence before being pardoned by President Carlos Menem, had been under house arrest in Argentina since June 1998, charged with the systematic kidnapping of children. The arrest arose out of an investigation by a federal judge acting on a case brought by relatives of disappeared children. It was known that babies had been abducted during security raids on families, or taken from their imprisoned mothers immediately after birth, and then given or sold to new families, often those of soldiers who did not have children of their own. At least 172 children were "adopted" and acquired new identities in this manner according to the Truth Commission, which predicted in its 1984 report that "the disappeared children constituted and will constitute for a long time one of the most profound open wounds in our society."[21]

The kidnapping of children was one crime that was excluded from the general amnesties issued by Alfonsín's government, and tracing these children has become one of the central methods of reclaiming the past by the relatives of the disappeared. The *Abuelas de Plaza de Mayo* established a genetic data bank, using blood samples from the parents of the disappeared, to establish the true identity of children. By the beginning of 1999 they had succeeded in uncovering the fate of 58 children, of whom 31 had been united with their true families. On their website and through the media they continue to urge, "All youngsters with doubts about their true identity, come to us. We will be waiting for you with love in order to help you."[22]

In contrast with the continuing timidity of the state, it would seem that civil society groups, as they became more confident about the resilience of democracy in Argentina, became more determined that the question of the culpability of the military and the memory of those who disappeared more than 20 years ago should not be allowed to die away. Thus, alongside the mothers and the grandmothers of the disappeared, a new generation of victims' relatives emerged to join in the struggle. During 1996, these sons and daughters of the disappeared formed a network known as *Hijos* (Sons), which is the Spanish acronym for Children for Identity and Justice and Against Forgetting and Silence. One member explained their determination: "We are not interested in being victims, we are taking up where our parents left off."[23] The type of action for which they became best known is the *escrache* (from the English verb "to scratch"). Their aim is to reveal the whereabouts of the former torturers and death squad members, and then to shame them. Once the homes of former torturers have been identified, demonstrations are held, with leaflets distributed to local residents reading "Warning—killer in the neighborhood." Mock road signs are held aloft demanding the trial and punishment of the targets and warning passers-by of the dangers ahead, while jail bars are symbolically placed in front of the homes of the dirty war veterans.[24]

Another increasingly widespread method of reconstructing and reclaiming the past in the struggle against forgetting has been through the use of the Internet. Argentinean human rights groups have launched websites dedicated to the memory of the disappeared, including a very powerful "Wall of Memory."[25] Visitors to the website click on a name, and a photograph appears, the face of one of those predominantly young people who were tortured and killed by the agents of their own state over two decades ago. It is a powerful and emotional experience to see those faces, to see the individuals behind the bald statistics of so many thousands who disappeared, to recognize the reality of pain and loss embodied in the digital images coming up on the monitor. The website also contains a Gallery of Argentinean Torturers and Killers, with photographs of those responsible for the abuses during those years. As always, when I see such photographs, I am left bemused. They look human, and yet they perpetrated such barbaric deeds upon their fellow human beings. How could they? How do they sleep at night? Do they remain cocooned in their conviction that what they did was necessary to defend the fatherland?[26]

Meantime, the relatives of their victims face more immediate dilemmas: whether or not to accept the compensation that the state has offered to those who lost family members. This issue of reparation can be a very sensitive one in situations where victims and their families have been denied any possibility of justice, in the sense of the punishment of the perpetrators. For some it is unthinkable to accept money for the death of their loved ones. For others the financial awards are a minimal reparation for and acknowledgment of the damage that has been done. For all, though, there must be the realization that full retributive justice is neither achievable nor, possibly, desirable—insofar as it might only serve to perpetuate the divisions in society and risk reviving the cycle of terror. A more realistic and perhaps more positive aim should be to work toward a broader, albeit softer, form of justice—the restora-

tive justice that seeks to heal the divisions within a damaged community. At the core of such a process must be the public acknowledgment
and preservation of the record of those terrible years—modes of symbolic reparation, if you like, that honor the memory of the victims and
survivors. The dilemma is how to preserve the memory without letting
it poison the future. This is not some abstract issue, it is a real problem
for all who seek to uncover and reclaim the lives and the deaths of their
loved ones. As the daughter of one of the victims of the junta, Manes
Roque, observed to journalist Michael McCaughan: "I suffered this
trauma and I have to learn to survive it, to convert this search into a permanent struggle for memory without letting it destroy me."[27]

Chile

On 11 September 1973 the democratically elected Popular Unity government of President Salvador Allende was overthrown in a military
coup, during which Allende lost his life. A four-man military junta, rep-
resenting each of the services plus the police, assumed control, with
General Augusto Pinochet at its head. Over the next few days Pinochet
tried to reassure Chile's 11 million people that there had not been a
coup d'etat so much as a military movement aimed at "salvaging the
country," and he called on people to join together in the "brotherly task"
of rebuilding the nation.

For 150 years before Pinochet's seizure of power, Chile had boast-
ed a tradition of democratic rule. All this was trampled underfoot during
the years of dictatorship that lasted until Pinochet was forced to step
down following the presidential elections of 1989.[28] Although Chile had
experienced a period of growing ideological division and social conflict
during the 1960s, which had intensified under Allende, the country was
to become even more divided during the subsequent decade and a half
of military rule, and for significant sections of the population Pinochet's
rule brought fear and repression.

On the day following the coup, 12 September 1973, a State of Siege
or "internal war" was declared, and within a week military rule was
extended to cover virtually all civilian activities. Congress was dissolved, political parties were banned, trade unions were closed down,
rigid censorship was imposed, and mass raids were launched to arrest
anyone with a "belligerent attitude." Within a short time more than

45,000 people were held for questioning in army barracks, military training camps and hospitals, in ships anchored off the coast, and in sports arenas, including the infamous National Stadium in Santiago where more than 7,000 were held and brutally interrogated. Several thousand fled into exile,[29] and by the end of the year somewhere between 1,500 and 2,000 civilians had been killed—tortured to death, executed by firing squads, shot while "trying to escape," or killed in confrontations with security forces or vigilantes.[30] Hundreds of these people were buried in unmarked graves. Between 1973 and 1978 close to 1,000 people were seized and were never seen again, most of them kidnapped from their homes at night by agents of the feared Directorate of National Intelligence (DINA).[31]

The Changing Pattern of Repression

It is common to identify four main periods of the Pinochet regime according to the means adopted to deal with perceived opposition.[32]

11 September 1973–June 1974. This was the period of mass arrests and the systematic use of torture and summary executions. Where trials were held, they were conducted by War Tribunals, special military courts that the regime justified by reference to the state of "internal war."

June 1974–August 1977. During this period the DINA, with its symbol of a clenched, armored fist, waged its secret war against the "red threat." It became, in effect, a Chilean Gestapo. Under the command of Manuel Contreras Sepúlveda, it deployed up to 4,000 agents and a vast network of informants. Answerable only to Pinochet, this shadowy force became a virtual state within a state, and its targeting of suspected leftists was largely responsible for the culture of fear that permeated much of Chilean society during this period.

August 1977–1983. On 21 September 1976 agents of the DINA assassinated Orlando Letelier and his American assistant Ronnie Moffit in Washington, D.C. Letelier had been Allende's foreign minister, and the United States was outraged that Chilean secret agents should export their "war" to their capital. To many Chilean officials this action confirmed that Contreras and his organization were growing out of control.

Eventually, in August 1977, Pinochet removed him, disbanded the DINA, and replaced it with a more circumscribed agency known as the National Information Center (CNI).

During this period there was some relaxation of repression, the State of Siege was lifted, and the War Tribunals were suspended— although military courts continued to deal with all crimes related to "political subversion." By 1982, however, economic recession had led to the first stirrings of large-scale protest against the regime. The result was a renewed wave of repression.

1983–1990. Street protests continued into 1983, and on 11 May of that year organized labor made its first significant move since the coup when it organized a one-day national strike. Dissident student groups were also growing larger and bolder. The regime responded in the only way it knew—repression, which became more intense following a failed assassination attempt on Pinochet in September 1986.

By the mid-1980s, however, the regime's record on human rights had come under intensified criticism from around the world. Most significantly Ronald Reagan's advisers had begun to fear that Pinochet's dictatorship might result in another Nicaragua in South America, and pressure for change grew. Non-Marxist political parties were legalized in March 1987, and confident in his position, Pinochet held a plebiscite on 5 October 1988 to confirm his continued presidency. A "yes" vote would have resulted in another eight years of military rule. To his amazement and disgust he was defeated, with 54.7 percent voting "no."

Despite his humiliation, under the 1980 constitution that he had imposed, Pinochet would remain in power for a further 17 months, until presidential and congressional elections had been held. This constitution was a guarantee of future privilege for the armed forces. Pinochet, like his role model, Franco, intended to leave Chile "tied, and tied up well."

More than anything else, Chile's security forces dreaded the humiliation of being called to account for their actions, as had happened to some of their contemporaries in Argentina. Pinochet tried to reassure them that he would do all he could to protect those who had been loyal to him during the years of repression. He would stay as army commander as long as possible, at least until 1998. He appointed nine judges to life terms on the 16-member Supreme Court. He passed a law protecting civil servants from dismissal to prevent any kind of purge. And, as was noted earlier, he did not mince his words in warning politicians and human rights organizations against pursuing those responsible for human rights violations. Such was the atmosphere when the Christian Democrat Patricio Aylwin was installed as Chile's new president in March 1990.

Mechanisms of Impunity

One of the key reasons that security personnel were able to act with impunity throughout the years of Pinochet's dictatorship was that the judiciary failed in their responsibility to defend human rights and the principle of equality before the law. Unlike in Argentina, where 80 percent of the judiciary were replaced by the military junta in 1976, there had been no purge in Chile. Indeed, probably a majority of the legal profession in the country welcomed the coup.[33]

For the members of the judiciary the junta became the new source of legislative and executive authority, and their task was to operate according to laws and decrees that emanated from this source. This meant that they were complicit in the perversion of the judicial system. They collaborated in the workings of the War Tribunals under which some 6,000 of their compatriots were sentenced without due process. With a few exceptions judges turned a blind eye to human rights abuses perpetrated by the security forces, rejecting out-of-hand accusations of torture and kidnapping in favor of official explanations.[34]

The reluctance of the courts to challenge the abuses of the regime stemmed in part from their ideological sympathies, but also from their rote application of the letter rather than the spirit of the law. Thus, once the legitimacy of the junta had been accepted by the legal profession, they saw it as their duty to implement and apply any decree or law passed by the junta. Given that in the early years after the coup the regime only required four signatures to create or change a law, this meant that the junta was able to cloak its repression in a facade of legality created by the stream of decrees that the judiciary, by and large, accepted.

When the junta wanted to promulgate a particularly controversial law, it adopted the simple expedient of secrecy. The junta sidestepped the constitutional requirement that all laws be published by including them in limited editions of the *Official Daily Record* that were distributed to a selected network of high-level officials. Among the decrees passed in this way was one that granted broad police powers to the DINA.

The key source of impunity was the 1978 Amnesty Law (Decree Law 2191). The junta proclaimed on 19 April 1978 that as the state of internal war had come to an end and peace and order had been established, an amnesty was to be granted to all "authors, accomplices, or concealers" of politically connected crimes since the coup. The aim, so it was claimed, was to "leave hatreds behind" and promote national reconciliation. Although several hundred political prisoners were released, most of them were sent directly into exile. The real beneficiaries were military and security agents who were absolved from responsibility for the disappearances, torture, and extrajudicial killings committed over the four and a half years since the coup. In case after case of alleged human rights abuse, evidence was erased from the record and the matter officially closed. In the process, thousands of Chileans were denied the opportunity of discovering what had happened to their loved ones.

National Commission
on Truth and Reconciliation

Before the 1989 elections, the Christian Democrat-Socialist Coalition for Democracy *(Concertación para la Democracia),* under the leadership of Patricio Aylwin,[35] had pledged that they would try to repeal or annul the Amnesty Law in their attempts to uncover the truth and determine culpability with regard to crimes against human rights. Aylwin was aware of the strength of public feeling in Chile that they should seek a stronger response than that of Uruguay. However, faced with the determined opposition of Pinochet, and the constraints imposed on the incoming government, it became clear that changing the laws of the previous regime would not be easy.

Among these limitations was that although the coalition held a majority in the lower chamber of Congress, they did not control the Senate. So, to pass any new legislation or repeal existing laws, the new government needed the support of one of the right-wing political parties. This meant that they would be unable to obtain the necessary majority to repeal the 1978 Amnesty Law.

Truth, justice, and social peace: these were the three objectives of the new government. Anticipating the threat to social peace that would result from too vigorous a quest for justice, the new government settled for the pursuit of the truth, in the hope that the process of reconciliation might be furthered through a show of repentance by the perpetrators of the violations, and the offer of forgiveness by their victims. Aylwin's inauguration took place on 12 March 1990, not in the presidential palace or the parliament building but in the National Stadium, where so many of Pinochet's victims had been imprisoned, tortured, and executed. In his speech Aylwin called for a full disclosure of the truth about human rights violations, and as he spoke, the names of the disappeared and the dead were projected in lights as a backdrop. As for justice, his approach was summed up by the phrase *justicia en la medida de lo posible* (justice as far as possible). He would try to get as much justice as he could in the circumstances.

In approaching this dilemma of how to balance the tensions between truth, justice, and the maintenance of social peace, Aylwin was influenced by the Argentinean experience. He was committed to uncovering the history of the Pinochet years and the gross violations of human rights that had taken place, but he had no desire to provoke the military by pursuing some form of retributive justice. Thus, within a few weeks of taking office he started discussions about the kind of truth commission to be established. Eventually he decided to appoint one by presidential decree, and on 24 April 1990, less than two months after the new government had taken office, the formation of the Commission for Truth and Reconciliation was announced. To avoid charges of partisanship the eight commissioners were drawn from across the political spectrum, with three members who had been associated with Pinochet and two who had been exiles under the military regime. The chair, Raúl Rettig Guissen, was a distinguished lawyer who had served as an ambassador under Allende. The Commission came to be known as the Rettig Commission.

A number of human rights groups were unhappy with the Commission's purpose and title, arguing that it should be called the Commission for Truth and Justice and be charged with the appropriate mandate. The mandate was not to be, as the Commission's founding decree affirmed, that "only upon a foundation of truth will it be possible to meet the basic demands of justice and create the necessary conditions for achieving true national reconciliation."[36] Its mandate was fourfold: (1) to detail how the whole system of repression had worked; (2) to account for every disappeared and extrajudicially killed person; (3) to propose measures of reparation and compensation for the families of the victims; and (4) to explore ways to ensure that such horrors should never again occur in Chile.

The scope of the Commission was drastically circumscribed before it started its work by the decision to focus on only the worst cases of abuse, those that resulted in the death or disappearance of the victim. Cases of torture, assault, and illegal imprisonment that did not result in death were outside its scope. The rationale for narrowing the focus was that it would have been unrealistic for the Commission to consider every violation of human rights, and furthermore, Pinochet's regime had never disputed that people had been imprisoned. What the military had always denied was that people had been wrongfully killed and disappeared.

That the Commission was appointed by presidential decree was another limitation on its work. Consequently, it lacked subpoena powers to compel witnesses to testify. Only a congressional mandate could grant such powers, and Aylwin had decided against this path for fear that his proposal would be rejected. In addition, in its reporting the Commission determined that no mention should be made of the names of the perpetrators of the crimes, much to the chagrin of many human rights activists and victim support groups. The argument put forward was that if the alleged perpetrators were identified, the Commission would be prejudicing the possibility of subsequent criminal prosecution of individuals so named, being the equivalent of publicly indicting people without due process.[37]

The decision not to identify the individual perpetrators of abuses would seem to have deprived the Commission's project of what many would consider to be a core element in the pursuit of justice—the notion of retribution, of someone paying for the pain they have caused. Instead its focus was on that other restorative approach to justice—the effort to put things right, to make things whole again. From this perspective the gathering of facts about human rights violations and the fate of the victims was not guided by a determination to punish the perpetrators but rather by the desire to restore the dignity of those who had suffered from the human rights violations of the old regime. By creating the space where people could tell their stories, on the basis of which the Commission could produce an authoritative history of the period, the aim was to translate *knowledge* of the truth into an officially sanctioned *acknowledgment* of that history, and in so doing honor the sacrifice of those who paid such a high price in the struggle against dictatorship. In a similar manner, reparations for the victims were seen as a means of promoting the healing of wounds borne by those whose lives were shattered by the years of repression; it was a step toward the restoration of wholeness.

In its work the Commission employed over 60 staff members and received depositions from more than 4,000 people, including a few members of the military who were troubled by their conscience. It also relied heavily on the documentation of the human rights groups that had worked under severe risk throughout the Pinochet years to document and record the abuses. Of these groups, the two most significant were the *Vicaría de la Solidaridad* associated with the Roman Catholic Church and the Association of Relatives of the Disappeared Detained. International NGOs like Amnesty International, Americas Watch, and the International Committee of the Red Cross also provided information from their records, while the Commission also gained access to official files, including autopsy reports and judicial transcripts of previous investigations.[38]

The 887-page report was released in March 1991, less than a year after the Commission had started its work. It was published in full in the Chilean newspaper *La Nación,* and President Aylwin presented it in a television broadcast during which he apologized on behalf of the state and asked the pardon of the victims. A personal copy of the report, along with a card signed by Aylwin, was also sent to each of the victims' families. Over half of the report was devoted to a detailed description of the repression, including a day-by-day chronological account of abuses that the Commission had been able to uncover and document. The second volume consisted of a listing of the 2,279 victims identified by the Commission, with brief biographical details about the background and circumstances of the death or disappearance of each of the victims.[39] A typical entry read:

SARAH DE LOURDES DONOSO PALACIOS
Disappeared Detainee. Santiago, July 1975.
　　Sara Donoso, 25 years of age, single, student of nursing at the University of Chile and worked in a consulting office subordinate to the Ministry of Health. She was an activist in the Socialist Party, where she carried out tasks associated with its Central Directorate. She was detained on July 15, 1975, at her workplace by agents of the *Dirección de Inteligencia Nacional* (DINA). Since that date the whereabouts of Sara Donoso are unknown.[40]

The report also included chapters on proposals for reparations and methods to prevent future human rights violations based on submissions solicited from international human rights organizations and Chilean political parties, churches, and trade unions. The reparation proposals included both symbolic measures for restoring the good name of victims, such as the erection of monuments to honor their memory, and material measures such as financial compensation and educational and welfare benefits for the relatives of the victims. In its recommendations regarding preventative measures, the report advocated the ratification of international human rights treaties, creating a permanent ombudsman's office to which citizens could appear against any perceived human rights abuse, reinforcing the independence of the judiciary, and generally promoting through education and other means a culture of respect for human rights.

Unfortunately, the publication of the report did not elicit as much public attention and debate as had been hoped. The truth was that only a relatively small sector of society, albeit a significant one, had been directly affected by the torturing, the killings, and the disappearances. Moreover, while few disputed the facts of the abuses that were presented, the report's historical interpretation of the Pinochet period was challenged. In particular the military insisted that a state of internal war had existed in Chile in 1973, which helped to account for their punitive measures against those threatening class war. Public discussion was also limited by events that took place shortly after the report's release. On 1 April 1991 a right-wing senator, Jaime Guzmán, was assassinated, and this diverted attention away from the human rights violations committed by the right to concern about the threat posed by left-wing violence. As a consequence the Commission's goal of furthering political reconciliation was undermined.

Despite this, Congress proceeded to act upon the recommendations contained in the report, and in February 1992 a law was passed unanimously in parliament that granted compensation to families of the victims recorded in the report.[41] Congress also established the National Corporation of Reparations and Reconciliation and charged it with two main tasks: to complete the work left unfinished by the Rettig Commission, and to administer the compensation scheme.

The Rettig Commission had worked under a very tight time frame, completing its investigations and report in nine months.[42] The Corporation was therefore instructed to complete the investigations of cases that the Commission had been unable to finish within its life span, investigate further grave violations of human rights that had come to light since the Commission had completed its work, and continue the search for the bodies of the disappeared. In 1996 when it submitted its final report, the Corporation had identified a further 123 disappearances and 776 extrajudicial killings or deaths under torture—bringing the total of unlawfully killed and disappeared under the military regime to

3,197.[43] By this stage the investigators had realized that the search for the bodies of many of the disappeared would be fruitless, given that in many cases they had been cast into the sea. However, even if the bodily remains could not be uncovered, the investigators sought to establish the final destiny of the disappeared—what had actually happened to them.

Roberta Bacic, an academic and human rights activist, was one of those working with the Corporation whose job it was to investigate disappearances and search for unmarked graves—not just to discover the truth but also to establish the eligibility for compensation of the relatives and family of the victims.[44] There was a lengthy and painstaking procedure to pursue when there was no body to be found. A birth certificate would suffice to establish that the person had actually existed. Then the details on the birth certificate would be checked against the record of death certificates—after all, plenty of people desert their families to start up a new life elsewhere. The next stage was to check official files to see if any record existed of the person since the alleged disappearance: Had there been any applications for renewal of identity documents, passports, or anything like that? The next stage was to explore the official records—death certificates, prison and police files, court documents and the like—paying particular attention to records of death in "suspicious circumstances," and trying to cross-reference these with newspaper reports of terrorist incidents of the time. A news item about five terrorists discovered dead would alert the investigators, if it corresponded with the dates when relatives and friends had last seen the disappeared person. But even after all this research to establish that the person had existed and had disappeared, the investigators still had to try to uncover evidence of the involvement of the military and state security personnel in the disappearance.

For people like myself, with no direct experience of this kind of work, it is hard to imagine the stress and the pain involved. In fact, according to Roberta Bacic, the Rettig Commission and the subsequent Reparations Corporation had been unwilling to employ human rights activists, as they feared it might prejudice claims to objectivity in the pursuit of truth. However, they soon found that people from outside the human rights field, who were unaccustomed to the horror and the trauma revealed in such investigations and particularly in the interviews with the relatives of the victims, could not cope with the distress occasioned.[45] Roberta tells of one such poignant and painful case. A woman had waited 16 years for her son to return. She had been in the house when the police had come, and they had told her they just wanted to ask him a few questions. Then, in 1991, she came to Roberta in a distressed condition, berating herself for being a bad mother. She had seen a television program on torture, and she realized that in wanting her son back she had been wishing him a life of suffering in which he would have to endure the pain and humiliation of torture. A good mother would have wanted her son to have died immediately, to spare him. This woman was broken. She had organized her whole life around waiting for him to return, and now she knew this would never happen.[46] Of course, investigators could not remain unaffected by such tales of horror and tragedy, and they, too, needed counseling and support to continue with their work.

In many ways the Chilean law on compensation for the relatives of the victims of human rights violations was very progressive, especially for a conservative Catholic country. The rights of the unmarried partners of victims, and the children of such relationships, were recognized, and the Corporation eventually included as victims those who had been driven to suicide because of their suffering at the hands of security personnel. But compensation was paid only to the relatives of those who had been killed or driven to take their own life. There was no compensation for survivors, no matter how damaged they might have been as a consequence of their experiences in captivity. Moreover, while the relatives received health care and educational benefits, the financial element within the compensation package caused unforeseen problems within certain communities of indigenous people in Chile. A number of these people had been targeted by the security services because of their involvement in the agrarian reform program of Pinochet's era. As a consequence, the families and relatives of the victims were awarded compensation. But within these indigenous communities everything was shared—no one person had more than another; and now these people, enriched by their compensation package, were breaking the established pattern of community life. Furthermore, unaccustomed to such financial resources, many compensation recipients ceased to work and spent their time getting drunk.[47] The lesson to be drawn would seem to be that in seeking means to honor and acknowledge the sacrifice of those who paid such a high price in the struggle against dictatorship, one needs to be very sensitive to the cultural milieu and to the heterogeneity of different communities. What is right for one community will not necessarily be appropriate for another.[48]

A more fundamental criticism of the work of the Commission and the Reparations Corporation made by human rights activists within and outside Chile was that in the pursuit of truth and social peace as a basis for reconciliation, justice had been forsaken. No one could be compelled to give testimony. The evidence submitted by individuals was not made public. And no individual perpetrators of human rights violations were identified in the reports. As a result, some would even claim that the real beneficiaries of the Chilean "cleansing exercise" in revealing the truth about the abuses of the military regime were the perpetrators of those same abuses—the military.

The response to such criticisms has been that in a situation where the military had not been defeated as such, but had handed political authority over to a civilian government while retaining all their coercive power as a military and security force, the new regime had done all that it could, given the constraints it faced. Subsequent actions by the military would seem to support such a contention. Thus, on 28 May 1993 military personnel in armored vehicles took to the streets of Santiago in a show of protest against the threat of prosecution within a civilian court against one of their officers for human rights violations.[49]

To be fair to Aylwin's government, draft legislation was prepared that embodied what became known as the Aylwin Doctrine: that all cases of human rights violations covered by the 1978 Amnesty Law should be fully investigated and only then should the perpetrators be granted amnesty. This interpretation was rejected by the Supreme Court and failed to gain the endorsement of all the parties in Aylwin's ruling coalition. In fact the only successful prosecution of perpetrators of human rights violations before 1978 was of General Manuel Contreras and Brigadier Pedro Espinoza for the assassination of Letelier and his associate in Washington, D.C. in 1976. Because of the international ramifications of this case, and in particular its impact on Chilean-U.S. relations, it was excluded from the 1978 Amnesty Law, and in 1993 Contreras and Espinoza, the former chief of operations of the DINA, were charged and sentenced in a civilian court to seven- and six-year prison terms, respectively. In 1995 these verdicts were confirmed by the Supreme Court. Concerned with the implications of this development, Pinochet emerged to deliver a speech to a group of businesspeople in which he advocated amnesia: "The only thing left, my friends, is to forget. And you forget not by reopening a court case, by throwing someone in jail. No, F-O-R-G-E-T. That is the word, and to achieve that both sides have to forget."[50]

The Letelier case raised the hopes of many that justice might be done in the case of their relatives who had disappeared or been killed by the military, particularly when such violations took place during the 12 years of Pinochet's rule that were not covered by the 1978 Amnesty Law. There have been a number of successes, with some 20 people convicted for crimes committed after 1978.[51]

In their pursuit of justice, the families of the victims have struggled to combat amnesia, and in 1998 several legal suits were filed against Pinochet himself. There seemed little hope of success, given that he claimed immunity from arrest in his capacity as a senator-for-life. However, an investigation of the charges was launched and in June 1999 warrants were issued for the arrest of a retired general and four subordinates for the kidnapping and execution of more than 70 political prisoners by an elite army unit that Chileans referred to as "the caravan of death." In an effort to repulse this legal offensive, Pinochet's successor as commander in chief declared that judgment of army personnel would only be acceptable if accompanied by legal proceedings against the politicians who brought about the political crisis of 1973.[52]

In their quest for justice, Chilean activists have been encouraged and assisted by international human rights organizations and networks, the same groups that supported them during the years of dictatorship. Indeed, within the international human rights community the human rights abuses committed by the Pinochet regime are considered sufficiently serious to constitute crimes against humanity, and thus the perpetrators can enjoy no immunity under international law.[53]

In October 1998 General Pinochet was arrested while in London for medical treatment, pending a formal request for his extradition to Spain to face charges of genocide, torture, and terrorism issued by a Spanish judge, Baltasar Garzón. A lengthy legal battle followed, and Pinochet was eventually released from house arrest and allowed to return to Chile on the grounds of his diminishing mental capacities and poor health.

As part of his struggle against extradition, Pinochet had appealed to the British people and to their sense of honor, claiming that no good purpose could be served by reopening the wounds of so many years ago: "Virtually a whole generation has gone by since the painful events of 1973. Today, we understand that reconciliation is essential to peace. . . . The opening up of old wounds, bringing back into debate issues where the true facts have long since been forgotten, serves no purpose." He concluded with a statement of faith in his fellow Chileans: "My fellow citizens have come to terms with our nation's past. They are my true judges."[54] The truth is, of course, that a section of Chilean society has not come to terms with their nation's past and they have not been in a position to judge Pinochet, at least not in a court of law. But that might change as, at the time of writing, it became known that just seven weeks after returning to Chile, Pinochet faced the threat of being stripped of his immunity and called to account.

The passions aroused within the Chilean expatriate communities around the world and within Chile itself by the saga of Pinochet's arrest and detention in Britain gave evidence that the history of those years of tyranny continued to live on. As Roberta Bacic commented at the time:

> All the activity and argument demonstrates that the topic is neither forgotten nor forgiven, and that Chilean society has not been reconciled. No law can achieve that and the process of facing and dealing with our own history has to be dealt with. It cannot be achieved by judicial decree. What do we have to do as a society to restore healthy relationships? Who is responsible for this? How can victims and perpetrators coexist without having at least recognised the harm which has been caused?[55]

Conclusion

In this chapter we have encountered a number of significant issues and problem areas associated with truth commissions. These center around the broad question of whose truth, and how much of it, should be uncovered. We have seen how the decision to restrict a commission's mandate to investigating extrajudicial killings can leave a whole range of human rights abuses unexamined. We have also seen how the decision not to name names and identify the perpetrators of abuses deprived the victims and their families of one of the most important forms of redress—the public naming and shaming of those directly responsible for their injuries, pain, and loss. We have also seen how some people became convinced that the real beneficiaries of the truth commission process were the military and security personnel responsible for the abuses—they were "cleansed" without being punished. This is not just the jaundiced view of embittered victims. Two close observers of the truth commission processes in Latin America have concluded that for successor regimes such commissions are "an attractive option, either as a first step opening the door to other actions or as a relatively cost-free way to meet popular demands for an accounting and then close the book on past violations. While the rhetoric of commissions has highlighted the former conception, the reality has been closer to the latter."[56]

In the conclusion to her excellent book *The Haunted Land,* Tina Rosenberg contrasted what she called the Latin American "regimes of criminals" with the "criminal regimes" of pre-1989 Eastern Europe. According to her analysis the perpetrators of human rights abuses under the military juntas should have been put on trial: "The crimes were horrible, limited in number, illegal at the time of commission, and had clearly identifiable authors."[57] But, as we have seen, the new democracies lacked the power to pursue justice through to the courts. As in Spain, the new regimes could not be sure that the military, who still had their weapons, would remain in their barracks if they saw their colleagues being prosecuted and punished. In contrast, the totalitarian regimes of Eastern Europe relied less on terror, especially after the death of Stalin, and more on corruption and the mass complicity of the civilian population. As a result the most appropriate means of coming to terms with such a past would appear to have been along the path of truth commissions. These could have clarified just how the repressive regimes relied on the preparedness of the population to "live within the lie," to use Vaclav Havel's phrase, revealing the degree to which the victims were also the very pillars on which the regimes depended to survive. However, as we shall see in the next chapter, the successor regimes in Eastern Europe proved themselves more interested in purges and trials than the history lessons of truth commissions.

Notes

1. See Weschler, *A Miracle, A Universe,* p. 75. One of the problems with this type of reporting of human rights abuses and the naming of alleged perpetrators is that the accused are denied any means of challenging the public record and clearing their name as they would in a court of law.
2. Servicio Paz y Justicia, *Uruguay Nunca Más.*
3. Quoted in Rosenberg, "Overcoming the Legacies of Dictatorship," p. 134.
4. See Carmen Feijoó, "The Challenge of Constructing Civilian Peace," pp. 72–94.
5. Fisher, *The Mothers of the Disappeared,* p. 30.
6. Fisher, p. 54.
7. Fisher, pp. 81–82.
8. See Fisher, p. 121.

9. It was felt that a congressional commission of enquiry would carry far more weight, backed as it would be by the majority within the legislature. Nobel Peace Prize–winner Adolfo Pérez Esquivel refused to sit on the Commission because of this criticism. See Kritz, p. 328.

10. Quoted in Fisher, pp. 131–132.

11. This fear that the military might be provoked into another coup was real, given the history of Argentina. Since 1930 the military had seized power six times and had ruled for longer than their civilian counterparts. See Mignone, Estlund, and Issacharoff, "Dictatorship on Trial," pp. 335–336.

12. See Garro and Dahl, "Legal Accountability for Human Rights Violations in Argentina," in Kritz, pp. 359–363.

13. This targeting of those responsible for anti-state violence alongside those responsible for the worst abuses of the "war against subversives" reflected Alfonsín's acceptance of the "twin devils" thesis—that both leftist guerrillas and rightist military personnel shared responsibility for bringing about the years of military rule and the abuses of state power during those years.

14. See Mignone et al., pp. 126–127.

15. *New York Times,* 28 December 1986.

16. *New York Times,* 24 February 1987.

17. It is worth noting that his popularity declined significantly after these pardons, one indication that the majority of Argentinians believed they should have stayed in jail. See Jelin, "The Politics of Memory," p. 49.

18. Alfonsín, "'Never Again' in Argentina," pp. 15–19; quoted in Kritz, p. 378.

19. Kritz, p. 381.

20. *The Guardian,* 20 January 1998.

21. Quoted in *The Guardian,* 11 June 1998.

22. http://www.wamani.apc.org/abuelas/ingles.html.

23. Quoted by Michael McCaughan in *The Guardian,* 12 September 1998.

24. See report by Jean de Vandelaer in *Peace News,* September 1998, p. 10.

25. http://www.desaprecidos.org/arg/victimas/eng.html.

26. http://www.desaparecidos.org/arg/tort/eng.html.

27. Michael McCaughan, "Argentina's Troubled Past Unearthed in Courts," *Irish Times,* 11 July 1998.

28. See Valenzuela, "Chile," pp. 159–206.

29. By 1979 an estimated 28,000 Chileans had gone into exile. See Constable and Valenzuela, *A Nation of Enemies,* p. 149.

30. Constable and Valenzuela, p. 20.

31. By 1992 the number of disappearances during the Pinochet regime was estimated to be 1,102, while the number of extrajudicial executions and deaths by torture was put at 2,095—a total of 3,197 deaths. See Amnesty International, *Chile,* AMR 22/16/98.

32. See, for example, Pearce, "Impunity and Democracy," pp. 45–56.

33. On the day after the fall of Allende, when Pinochet declared a state of siege and hence the right to exercise emergency powers, the president of the

Supreme Court expressed his delight at the junta's pledge to "respect and enforce" the law. Quoted in Constable and Valenzuela, p. 117.

34. For example, of nearly 9,000 *habeas corpus* writs brought before the civilian courts of Santiago by individuals and human rights organizations during Pinochet's rule, only 30 were accepted. Americas Watch, *Human Rights and the "Politics of Agreements,"* p. 73.

35. Alwyn, a lawyer, had been broadly sympathetic toward the coup at the outset.

36. English translation of Supreme Decree No. 355, *Report of the Chilean National Commission on Truth and Reconciliation, vol. 1,* p. 5.

37. In the final report, perpetrators were identified as being either agents of the state or members of the opposition, and it was made clear to which military branch or political group those responsible for particular crimes belonged. See Weissbrodt and Fraser, "Book Review," pp. 621–622.

38. Throughout the years of Pinochet's rule the UN Commission on Human Rights and the Inter-American Commission on Human Rights of the Organization of American States monitored the human rights situation in Chile and issued a number of reports. See José Zalaquett, "Introduction" *to Report of the Chilean National Commission* (English edition), p. xxvii.

39. The Commission had originally identified just over 3,400 cases as requiring investigation. See *Report of the Chilean National Commission* (English edition), p. 15.

40. Quoted from Weissbrodt and Fraser, p. 619, footnote 84.

41. It was estimated that 7,000 relatives of victims would benefit, including the unmarried partners of victims and their offspring. In addition to health and educational benefits, families were to receive the equivalent of around $380 per month, which was to be divided in fixed percentages among the family members. See Weissbrodt and Fraser, p. 619, footnote 82.

42. There is an argument that truth commissions should be appointed and complete their work within a relatively short time following the succession of a civilian regime, because during this early period the new regime typically enjoys its strongest legitimacy, and concern about the abuses of the previous regime remains high. See Hayner, "Fifteen Truth Commissions—1974 to 1994," pp. 597–655.

43. Amnesty International, *Chile,* AMR 22/16/98, p. 1.

44. The following section draws upon notes and minutes of meetings addressed by Roberta Bacic. The meetings were (1) Committee for Conflict Transformation Support, London, 30 January 1999 (CCTS); (2) MA Seminar, Department of Peace Studies, University of Bradford, 18 March 1999 (MA); (3) Nonviolent Action Research Group, Bradford, 18 March 1999 (NVARP).

45. Bacic, NVARP.

46. Bacic, NVARP. Compare the pain of this mother with that of the parents in Ariel Dorfman's poem, "Hope," in which they derive solace from the report of a recently released prisoner that he had recognized the screams of their son as he was being tortured—at least this meant that their son was still alive! Dorfman, *Widows and Last Waltz in Santiago,* pp. 185–187.

47. Bacic, CCTS.

48. This issue raises the fundamental problem within liberal democracies of managing the tension between the values of equality and respect for difference. Chile adopted the egalitarian path—all victims were equal, and hence their relatives should all receive equal compensation. This meant that Allende's widow received the same as the widow of a landless laborer.

49. The *Boinazo* protest (named after the berets worn by the military) resulted in the Supreme Court ruling in favor of military jurisdiction over the case, and eventually proceedings against the officer concerned were dropped (Amnesty International, AMR 22/01/96, p. 10).

50. Pinochet, 13 September 1995, quoted in Amnesty International, AMR 22/01/96, p. 12.

51. For example, on 30 October 1995 the Supreme Court confirmed prison sentences against 16 members of a special police unit found guilty of the 1985 abduction and murder of three members of the Chilean Communist Party. On 6 December 1995, the court also confirmed sentences imposed on a former army officer for his involvement in the assault on two young people during a protest demonstration in 1986 who were doused with petrol, set alight, and abandoned in a roadside ditch. One of them died and the other was disfigured for life.

52. See report in *The Guardian,* 10 June 1999. For details of Arrellano's activities, see Constable and Valenzuela, pp. 37–38.

53. This was the principle established within the Statute of Nüremberg International Military Tribunal, Article 7.

54. *The Guardian,* 9 November 1998.

55. Bacic, "Reflections on Responsibility, Impunity and Hypocrisy," p. 8.

56. Popkin and Roht-Arriaza, 1995, p. 83.

57. Rosenberg, p. 403.

5

The Post-1989 European
"Cleansing" Process

In 1989 the authoritarian state socialist regimes of Eastern and Central Europe began to fall, and popularly elected governments commenced taking up the reins of power. Then a series of debates began at all levels of society about what should be done with the leaders and the agents of the prior regimes, especially those citizens who had acted as secret police informers.

As we have seen, especially in the chapter on occupied Europe, dealing with collaborators raises all kinds of issues about degrees of complicity and guilt in relation to the abuses committed on behalf of state security. Consider the following reflection by a European who is all too familiar with this morally murky world.

> I've scoured hundreds of files. There were so many different kinds of collaboration and reasons for collaborating. Some people informed . . . out of ideological conviction. . . . With some the motivation was petty jealousy or small-time revenge. Some were just born informers; in many ways these were the worst—the twisted ones. Some collaborated for material gain, or to advance their careers—so as to be able to travel abroad, for instance—or not to have their careers dashed. There were some who were blackmailed into collaborating. . . . Some people were put under terrible pressure while serving jail sentences for various political crimes . . . Some did it out of love—so as not to blight a child's education, or so as to be able finally to visit a family member stranded abroad. Some who signed went on to do terrible damage to the lives of their neighbours or co-workers. Others signed and did virtually nothing, offering no information of any import whatever.

This could be a description of collaborators in continental Europe during World War II, but in fact the speaker was at the time the head of the Independent Commission appointed after the 1989 revolution in Czechoslovakia to listen to the appeals of those who had been charged with acting as "conscious collaborators" during the years of communist rule.[1]

It is evident that strong comparisons can be made between the life experience of those who lived under German occupation in Europe during World War II and those who lived under the regimes of the Warsaw Pact countries after that war had ended and been superseded by the Cold War, and not only with regard to the different and complex motives that led people to collaborate. In both periods people lived under authoritarian and repressive regimes that were guilty of abusing the human and civil rights of their citizens with the brutal suppression of real and imagined opponents. Both sets of citizens had reason to fear the agents of the state security apparatus that monitored so many aspects of everyday life. In both periods citizens enjoyed few, if any, autonomous spaces within which they could meet or communicate free from state supervision and control. Both sets of societies were characterized by programs of property expropriation and the imposition of centralized command economies that were subject, in the final analysis, to the controlling interest of an external imperial power—the Third Reich and the Soviet Union.

The brutality of "actually existing socialism," as the late Rudolph Bahro labeled the regimes, waned radically in the years following Stalin's death in 1953 and the subsequent denunciation of his crimes by Khrushchev in 1956. The repression took on a less visible and less arbitrary form. In essence the societies were based on the most radical division of labor—between those whose role it was to govern (the party apparatchiks and state functionaries) and those whose job it was to work. This was the contract—the forfeiture of political pluralism and civil liberties in return for a basic standard of living and economic security. Those who challenged the contract were, by the late 1950s, more likely to be denied the means to work than to disappear into the gulag, while their children would be denied educational opportunities. These consequences were less traumatic than summary execution, but were sufficiently powerful a set of sanctions to cause most people to keep their heads down and get on with life as best they could.

As was remarked with reference to living under occupation in Europe during World War II, most people focused on survival—

eschewing any temptation to become a hero or a martyr. The same can be said for those living under the regimes of the Soviet-dominated bloc, and it was upon this form of acquiescence that the regimes depended for their survival. In other words, most people accommodated themselves to the regimes, turning away from the public realm and focusing upon their private lives. Like Vaclav Havel's greengrocer who would place a notice in his window proclaiming "Workers of the world unite!" simply because it was just one of those thousand little things that guaranteed him a relatively tranquil life in harmony with society, people accommodated themselves to the realities of life. But in acquiescing to the dictatorship of ritual, they were not only the victims of the regime but also its support. It was not necessary for people to actually believe in the system, according to Havel, "but they must behave as though they did, or they must at least tolerate them in silence . . . they must live within a lie. They need not accept the lie. It is enough for them to have accepted their life within it and in it. For by this very fact, individuals confirm the system, fulfill the system, make the system, are the system."[2]

Depending as they did upon the acquiescence of citizens, the regimes could also rely on the forceful intervention of the USSR and Warsaw Pact allies if matters got out of hand, as they did in Hungary in 1956 and Czechoslovakia in 1968. But then in the 1980s Mikhail Gorbachev came to power in the Soviet Union and introduced his new "Sinatra doctrine," promising his Warsaw Pact allies the right to "do it their way" and develop their own responses to the economic crises they confronted.

Poland and Hungary were the first to put Gorbachev's new departure to the test. In Poland, under martial law since 1981, a series of strikes in the summer of 1988 caused the discredited government to seek accommodation with the opposition Solidarity movement. In June 1989 parliamentary elections were held in which Solidarity won a sweeping victory in all the seats it was allowed to contest—except for one in the upper house that the communists retained. Such a devastating defeat cast the Communist Party into terminal decline, although a compromise formula allowed it to retain control of key ministries in the new government. The Hungarian Communist Party followed a similar trajectory—from repression to attempted accommodation to collapse, after Party reformers invited opposition parties to engage in talks, which resulted in free parliamentary elections in March 1990 in which the opposition parties won 85 percent of the seats. In Bulgaria it was a similar tale of street protests, leading to a political crisis as repression failed to quell the demands for democracy. The Bulgarian Socialist Party relinquished its monopoly of power and general elections were held in June 1990. In these elections, contrary to the pattern elsewhere in Eastern Europe, the communists won a majority of the seats and were returned to power.

In the German Democratic Republic (GDR) hard-liners controlled the Socialist Unity Party and refused to contemplate reform. But during 1989 many East Germans began to seek their fortunes elsewhere—taking advantage of the easing of travel restrictions, particularly in Hungary, to cross over to West Germany via Austria. While this was taking place, the authority of the state was being challenged by increasingly massive nonviolent demonstrations. In October the old leader Honecker resigned, but the exodus and mass demonstrations continued; following a million-strong demonstration in Berlin on 7 November 1989, the wall dividing the city was opened up. A week later a new coalition government was formed, headed by a reform communist, but the demonstrations continued, and in March 1990 free elections were held and resulted in a landslide victory for the Christian Democrats and their allies, who subsequently negotiated the end of East Germany as a separate state.

In Czechoslovakia the regime held out against a growing wave of protest and dissent led by the Civic Forum and Public against Violence throughout 1989, until a student-led protest march of 17 November was brutally attacked by security forces. Rumors spread that a student had been killed, and broad sections of the population were galvanized into resistance. During the following week there were nightly demonstrations in Wenceslas Square. Of particular significance was the success of a two-hour general strike of 27 November that convinced the regime that its main bastion of support among the working class had eroded, and before the end of the year Havel had been chosen as the new president, with free parliamentary elections to follow.[3]

Havel, as we have seen, was only too well aware of the manner in which totalitarian rule had been grounded in the cooperation and complicity of everyday people going about their lives. Consequently, on taking office he argued that while the violations of human rights should not be forgotten, their perpetrators should be forgiven. There should be no witch-hunt, because very few could claim to be completely free of responsibility for the years of systemic abuse and repression. This was one possible approach to the question of how the stain of the past might be cleansed to strengthen the new democratic political culture, without tearing the new system apart with new conflicts. After all, who was guilty, and who was qualified to judge culpability, in a society where everyone collaborated with the system to some degree? These were the kinds of questions that confronted the new generation of political leaders as they took up the reins of power throughout Eastern Europe in the early 1990s. In this chapter we will explore how Czechoslovakia and Germany approached the dilemma through their own forms of purge, concluding with an examination of the Polish experience, which was closer to the Spanish model of public amnesia.

Factors Influencing the Mode of
Dealing with the Legacy of the Totalitarian Past

Before moving on to the case studies, it is worthwhile to make a few observations regarding the factors influencing the means chosen by the three states to effect a closure on the totalitarian past as a means of strengthening the new democratic order. Key among these is the speed and the manner of the transition.

In Czechoslovakia and the GDR the old state structures collapsed almost completely and very quickly. The transition from the old to the new was not a negotiated process as such. The old regimes had lost their capacity to rule and enforce their will. Of crucial significance here was that they had lost control of the instruments of repression and physical violence—the military and the state security agencies could no longer be relied upon to quash the demonstrations. As a consequence the new regimes were free to deal with the legacy of human rights abuse, and the perpetrators, as they saw fit. They were not constrained, as were the successor regimes to the juntas in Latin America, by the threat of an enraged military emerging from the barracks to deal a decisive blow against the fledgling democracy.

In Poland, on the other hand, the conflict between the state and the Solidarity movement had been more protracted, its intensity waxing and waning in cyclical fashion over the years. At the end, the actual transfer of power was a negotiated process, with the communists retaining control of the key ministries of Defense and the Interior. In such situations, as with Hungary and Bulgaria where the changeover was also negotiated and protracted and where the members of the old regime still had some cards to play and could lay down certain conditions for the peaceful transfer of power, the chances of the new political elites implementing full-blooded purges were low.

I have already mentioned Samuel Huntington's distinction between three types of transition with different consequences for processes of democratization: transformation, when elites take the initiative to bring about change; replacement, when the initiative is solely that of the opposition; and transplacement, when democratization comes about through joint action by government and opposition. Using this terminology, according to the reading of history presented here, the transitions in Czechoslovakia and East Germany can be depicted as forms of replacement, whereas in Poland, Hungary, and Bulgaria the process was more akin to transplacement.[4] As a general rule, we can say that to the degree that a mode of transition from a repressive old regime to a new democratic order involves coordinated action on the part of personnel from the old regime and their successors, then it is more likely that the new regime will resort to the Spanish pattern of dealing with the past—public amnesia.[5]

The Czechoslovak Experience[6]

Compensation and Restitution

On taking office Vaclav Havel moved quickly to counter one of the legacies of the communist regime—political prisoners. He granted amnesty to more than 20,000 of them. In April 1990 the Federal Assembly passed the Law on Judicial Rehabilitation that provided for the annulment of all verdicts where the conviction had been for political crimes, and by the end of 1991 more than 200,000 citizens had been rehabilitated. Former prisoners were also allowed to turn to the courts for compensation for lost wages, the costs of defense, and for any fines incurred as a consequence of their prosecution and conviction under the old regime.

But the Law on Judicial Rehabilitation did not address the situation of those who, without going to court, still suffered for their convictions. The Confederation of Czechoslovak Political Prisoners estimated that 1.5–2 million had suffered in some way for political crimes under the old regime—people who had been dismissed from their jobs, students who had been expelled from college, farmers who had had lost land, people who had their businesses forcibly nationalized, and families who had suffered housing discrimination because of their political or religious beliefs. So, in February 1991, the Law on Extrajudicial Rehabilitation was passed by the federal parliament, aimed at providing for the rehabilitation and compensation of those who were not convicted or sentenced by a court but who suffered as a consequence of political persecution. Virtually all state institutions made arrangements for the rehabilitation of former employees who had been dismissed for political reasons, thus enabling many to return to their former professions and also reclaim their pension rights. However, this left unaddressed the issue of compensation for property that had been forcibly expropriated in the years following the communist accession to power in February 1948.

Initially the new government had not considered providing redress for confiscated property under forced collectivization of agricultural land and nationalization of enterprises. But once the former prisoners and other survivors of political persecution began seeking compensation for their punishment, which had often included confiscation of property, then it became clear that rehabilitation must include some form of compensation, if not restoration of forfeited property. The first property restitution law was passed in June 1990 relating to the return of some of the properties confiscated from the Catholic Church during the early 1950s. This was followed in October 1990 by an act relating to some 70,000 small businesses that had been nationalized by the state between 1955 and 1961, and in May and December 1991 the Land Restitution Laws provided the original owners with the opportunity to reclaim land that had been collectivized.

In all these cases claims had to be lodged with the courts, with the result that they became completely overwhelmed by the number of cases brought before them, in a situation where new laws were being introduced at a rapid rate. Moreover, there was a desperate shortage of qualified and experienced judges due to the number who either resigned or were dismissed as part of the purge, or lustration process, that followed the collapse of the communist regime.[7]

Lustration

The term "lustration" derives from the Latin *lustratio*—meaning purification by sacrifice. In usage it came to refer primarily to the ritual cleansing of Roman troops on their return from campaigns. Thus, whatever they had done on the battlefields, they could became clean troops of the republic once again.[8] The current use of the term refers to the practice of barring former secret police agents and collaborators from public office for a certain period of time. Czechoslovakia pursued this practice as the main thrust of its efforts to cleanse the country from the taint of what had gone before and mark the commencement of a new democratic era.

As we have seen, Havel knew how the machinery of the old regime could colonize people, turning them into unwitting accomplices in the repressive apparatuses of the state. Thus, despite having been imprisoned on numerous occasions himself, he urged his fellow citizens to be tolerant. Speaking on New Year's Day in 1990 he referred to the way all had been implicated in the maintenance of the totalitarian system:

> None of us is merely a victim of it, because all of us helped to create it together. . . . We cannot lay all the blame on those who ruled us before, not only because this would not be true but also because it could detract from the responsibility each of us now faces.[9]

Many other senior figures in the new regime shared this attitude. Indeed, for the first six months of the new order the secret police were left untouched. As a consequence many key files were destroyed and rumors grew that the entire process of November and December 1989 had been manipulated by the security agencies. Because of these rumors parliament established a commission to investigate the events leading up to the collapse of the old regime, including the violent attacks on demonstrators on the night of 17 November. (It was named the 17th November Commission.)

But others were unable to share Havel's magnanimity. There were too many people who had suffered under the previous regime, and there were too many of their former persecutors still around enjoying the fruits of loyal careers as direct instruments of state repression. This was not right, it was not just, it was not fair. So the momentum grew for the exposure of the many thousands of individuals who had acted as informants and had collaborated with the Czechoslovak state security police.[10] This movement was fueled not just by the anger at the impunity enjoyed by the perpetrators of abuses, but also by the feeling that, if left untouched, these people could continue to abuse their positions of authority and undermine the foundations of the new democratic order that was being established.

It was in this climate that during the run-up to the June 1990 general elections almost all the political parties asked that their candidates be vetted to avoid any disruptions to campaigning by unfounded allegations and revelations. The screening was implemented by the federal Ministry of Internal Affairs, which at that time was the only body with legal access to the records. In other words, the vetting was being done by people who had worked for the former secret police! Indeed, there were several scandals involving false allegations against politicians, and calls were raised for firmer regulations governing the whole process.

As a consequence, on 18 January 1991 the federal parliament resolved to instruct the 17th November Commission, which was composed of representatives from all the political parties, to vet the state security files and identify former agents who were now members of parliament and government officials. Such people were to be confronted privately with the charges, and given the opportunity to resign. If they refused they would be publicly denounced.[11]

At this point it is important to note that right from the start the debate about lustration took place in the context of political power struggles, while being presented as a moral crusade. One of the major problems with any kind of purge, including lustration, is that what should be a fair, honest, and transparent process can become tainted by political rivalries and sectional interests as competing parties struggle to lay claim to have their "truth" about the past officially sanctioned in order to undermine the position of their rivals, and thereby legitimate their own political interests and standpoints.

In March 1991 the Commission reported to parliament that 17 deputies had been found to have collaborated with the secret police. Of these, five had resigned but the others denied the charge. The names of these 12 were read out, to be broadcast throughout the country by the mass media that was in attendance for the occasion. Several of those named subsequently sued for defamation, including the well-known human rights activist Jan Kavan. The Commission also announced that they had identified 13 deputy federal ministers and one full minister (Deputy Prime Minister Vaclav Vales), along with 57 government officials.

Meanwhile, outside of parliament, there were various ad hoc screening processes going on, and the demand grew for a more thorough and systematic house-cleaning process and the "de-Bolshevization" of public life. With right-wing politicians taking the lead, the Federal Assembly approved the Lustration Law on 4 October

1991.[12] It provided for the systematic screening of government agencies and offices and the subsequent dismissal of any who were found to have been members of the state security apparatus or registered with the secret police as agents, or who had "knowingly collaborated" with the secret police. Also targeted were all former Communist Party officials above a certain rank, all members of the party's own militia, and those who had been students at various state security colleges. Such people were to be barred from holding any public office above a particular rank within the civil service, military, judiciary, and the media. The ban, which was to run for five years, also applied to academics in higher education and management positions in state-owned enterprises.[13]

The law stated that all those in posts or about to be appointed to senior state positions were required to submit (1) a certificate, issued by the Ministry of Internal Affairs, affirming that they did not work for the state security service; and (2) a personal affidavit that they had never occupied a senior position within the Communist Party, had not been a member of the People's Militia, and had not attended one of the proscribed colleges. The employers of those who failed to produce such documents were obliged either to fire them or transfer them to a less senior position.

Those certified as former employees of the secret police or as their informants had no right of appeal. Those adjudged to be conscious collaborators, who came to be referred to as "Category C," were allowed to appeal to a special commission, and it was only at that hearing that they would be allowed to view the security files in which their name appeared. Those who objected to the Commission's ruling could appeal their case in the civil courts. The Independent Commission, under the direction of a former human rights activist, Jaroslav Basta, came into existence in February 1992 and was quickly swamped. By October of that year 3,000 people had lodged appeals, of which the Commissioners had only been able to rule on 600; of these 600 only 15 were adjudged to have been conscious collaborators.[14]

There was considerable unease about the implications of the Lustration Law within human rights circles in Czechoslovakia, particularly with regard to its short-circuiting of proper legal procedure and the basic tenets of natural justice. There were at least five main objections.

1. The failure to respect the presumption of innocence. The onus was upon people to prove they did *not* work for the secret police or were *not* communist officials.

2. Limited rights of appeal. There was no right of appeal against the judgment, except for those who disputed their categorization as conscious collaborators.
3. The retrospective nature of the legislation. So many of those responsible for the abuse of human rights were simply doing their jobs. What they did was perfectly legal by the laws that were in effect at the time; technically speaking, they had committed no crime. As Tina Rosenberg has observed, ". . . the crimes of the communists were bureaucratized. . . . the perpetrators often wielded pencils or computers instead of machine pistols. . . . And tapping a telephone, unlike murder and torture, was perfectly legal. . . ."15
4. The introduction of the principle of collective guilt. The law entailed banning broad categories of people from holding certain positions, not because of what they had done but because of their beliefs and their membership in certain organizations or because their name appeared on a list or in a file. Furthermore, in judging and sentencing people according to the principle of collective guilt, there was no way of allowing for gradations of culpability. Presumably there were informers who never passed on anything that was damaging to others, but their punishment would be the same as that handed out to their controllers and employers.
5. Overreliance on secret police files. Thousands of people faced stigmatization and humiliation just because their name appeared in a secret police file, a report that could be inaccurate or fabricated so that an agent could meet his or her quota.16

Underpinning a lot of the concern was the fear that the lustration process was being driven by partisan political interests. Thus, all 41 deputies of the right-of-center Civic Democratic Party in the federal parliament voted for the bill, while all the deputies of the Communist Party opposed it. This raised a question regarding the nature of the new democratic order that was emerging. In seeking to cleanse the system of the tainted officials from the totalitarian era, were the new democrats manipulating the law to suit their own purposes, just like in the old days? Had the lustration process become just one more tool in the armory of political factions seeking to discredit their opponents? There were certainly grounds for believing so, as the case of Jan Kavan illustrated.

Jan Kavan

In 1990 the international pacifist organization War Resisters International held a conference on nonviolent resistance and social defense in Bradford, UK. It was a typical West Yorkshire early April; I remember one morning if you looked out of one side of the conference building there was a blue sky, and through the windows on the other side you could see the snow falling—much to the bemusement of the international participants. One of these was suffering from the cold, and apparently he was just recovering from a serious heart condition, so like a good host I went home to dig out an old sweater for him. The next day he headed back to London with my father's old sweater. I felt quite honored, staunch provincial that I was (and remain), for this was Jan Kavan, the founder of Palach Press and a key figure in a network of Eastern European dissidents who had become closely associated with Western peace activists during their years of exile. I had heard quite a bit about him from my dear friend Michael Randle. Michael had begun to smuggle human rights literature into Czechoslovakia on behalf of Jan in 1971, using the same mode of concealment that he had used to transport the Soviet spy George Blake out of Britain to East Germany a few years earlier in 1966. When Michael, along with Pat Pottle, was eventually brought to trial for helping Blake to escape, Jan Kavan, by then a Civic Forum MP, appeared as a defense witness. That trial took place in June 1991 at the Old Bailey, England's senior crown court. Back in Prague, Jan Kavan was facing his own trial.

A student leader during the Prague Spring of 1968, by 1969 Jan Kavan had settled in London where he became active channeling literature, funds, and other forms of assistance to his fellow dissidents in Czechoslovakia. He also traveled widely on behalf of the movement, raising funds and spreading awareness about what was happening in his home country. He returned to Czechoslovakia just before the final collapse of the communist regime in 1989, and was elected to the Federal Assembly as a member of Civic Forum. However, in February 1991 he was summoned to the offices of the 17th November Commission where he was informed that his name had shown up in the files. He was accused of being an informer and was given 15 days to resign.

What the files revealed was that during 1969–1970 he had held over 40 meetings with a state security agent based at the Czechoslovak embassy in London. Kavan claimed he had no idea that this man had been an agent. Kavan knew the man as the education attaché, and met with him in his own capacity as the authorized representative of Czechoslovak students stranded in Britain after the 1968 invasion. To the dismay of the commissioners, he refused to resign, and on 22 March his name was read out in parliament as a secret police collaborator. There followed years of seemingly fruitless struggle as he tried to clear his name.[17]

Initially he appealed to the Interior Ministry, and in February 1992 the Ministry declared him clean, but a few days later the Interior Minister announced there had been a mistake; in fact the files showed that Kavan was an informer. Jan then took his case to the newly established Independent Commission, where his case dragged on for months with the Interior Ministry refusing to release documents. Eventually, in mid-October 1992 he was informed that he had been deemed guilty of conscious collaboration, this verdict having been reached by a majority vote of the commissioners and without his ever having attended any of the hearings to present his own case.

Jan Kavan then lodged an appeal against this ruling with the Prague Municipal Court, which eventually ruled, in September 1994, that there was no evidence that he had ever consciously collaborated with the security police. The Interior Ministry promptly lodged an appeal, promising to divulge new and damaging evidence. This they never did and eventually, on 16 January 1996, the Appeals Court ruled against the Ministry. Jan Kavan's public reputation was restored.

That year there were general elections and he ran as a Social Democrat candidate and regained his old seat, becoming his party's spokesperson on foreign affairs. By 1998 the government of Vaclav Klaus was increasingly weakened by charges of corruption and financial scandals, and in June of that year new elections were held. The Social Democratic Party became part of the subsequent coalition government, and Jan Kavan was appointed Foreign Minister. Shortly after taking up office he threw a party in the Cernin Palace in Prague, for Michael Randle and all the other leftists, peaceniks, dissidents, and friends who had supported him over the years.[18]

He had needed support. For five years he had been vilified and pilloried in the media as a hypocrite and a liar, as someone who had posed as a dissident and human rights activist when all along he had been a secret police agent. It reminded some of the witch-hunt against suspected communists and their fellow-travelers led by McCarthy in the United States in the 1950s. It reminded others of the plight of Joseph K in Kafka's *The Trial*. To understand why this became a *cause célebre* and one of the central nodes around which the debate about lustration in Czechoslovakia took place, it is not sufficient to point to Jan Kavan's complex character and his stubbornness in refusing to submit; we must also return to the pre-1989 days of life under the communist regime.

As has been remarked, this was a difficult time and the bulk of people made their own accommodation with the regime in order to enjoy a quiet life. There were not many heroes or martyrs in Czechoslovakia after 1968. Even the Charter 77 human rights petition had less than two thousand signatures prior to 1989.[19] This is the reason why, according to some informed observers, there was such a clamor for lustration after the 1989 revolution rather than for a truth commission. The publicly proclaimed rationale for this program was the need to cleanse society of all those who had morally compromised themselves. But, as we have seen, most people compromised themselves. They did not make any overt protest against the repression of the regime. They lived in silence and, according to former opposition activist Jan Urban, interviewed in the early 1990s, "all the current noise surrounding lustration is simply a way of keeping silent about that silence."[20]

After World War II the most vocal in their demands for the punishment of collaborators were frequently those who had the most to fear from too deep an investigation into the history of those years of occupation. In a similar vein, it would seem that the vindictiveness of the Czechoslovak lustration program in general and the treatment of Jan Kavan in particular was driven, at least in part, by a desire to divert attention away from the generally shared culpability, especially of those who were the most fervent in their demands for a cleansing. As Jan Kavan's brother observed to Lawrence Weschler, "It is those who never lifted a finger to oppose the old regime who are pushing for these purges, demanding the publication of all those lists. The nice thing about a list is that if you're not on it you can consider yourself pure."[21]

A slight variant of this analysis has also been proposed. As advocates of nonviolent resistance have argued for many years, even repressive regimes rest in the final analysis upon the cooperation of their subjects. For decades the Czech and Slovak people had acquiesced to communist rule. Then, for a few weeks in 1989 they held nonviolent demonstrations and, lo and behold, the edifice crumbled. How, then, to cope with the shame of not having done anything before? Here one can begin to understand the appeal of the image of a demonic secret police apparatus that had agents everywhere and manipulated and intimidated people into submission. To validate such a narrative, to excuse the fear, it was necessary to reveal the full extent of the security service's reach.[22] If there is any validity in this kind of analysis, then it is not too difficult to see how the former dissidents might become particular targets, insofar as they were people who did put their bodies on the line, who did "walk the talk," and who often paid the price for so doing. They could act as a living reprimand to all those who could have done more.

This observation leads to a third dynamic that drove the lustration program and helps to explain the witch-hunt against Kavan and others. It has already been observed that the right-of-center Civic Democratic Party (ODS) of Vaclav Klaus was at the forefront in pushing through the Lustration Law in October 1991. Subsequent to that, the right-wing tabloids and journals associated with this party were particularly virulent in condemning Jan Kavan. There is an explanation for this. In the pursuit of political power, the ODS, the leading advocate of the rapid transition to a free-market economy, was handicapped because none of its prominent members possessed any oppositionist credentials from before the fall of the old regime.[23] Among the competition were a number of parties that could boast quite impressive oppositionist pedigrees dating back to the spring of 1968. Therefore, as deliberate strategy, the ODS sought to undermine their political rivals by claiming that the dissident movement had been thoroughly infiltrated, and hence controlled, by the secret police. Ergo, the dissidents had in reality been collaborators. This was the revisionist historical myth that the ODS promoted as part of its electoral strategy. The case of Jan Kavan presented them with a wonderful opportunity to delegitimize the dissidents and substantiate their own reading of the past. The strategy seemed to work, for in the elections of 1992 the ODS emerged as the leading party and very few of the former dissidents were reelected.

The general point here is that no purge or lustration process takes place in a power vacuum. When a political movement takes up the issue and runs with it to advance its own particular interests, and when significant sections of the population are susceptible to such an appeal for their own reasons (shame, guilt, resentment), then there is every likelihood that what might have started out as a controlled process will escalate beyond the boundaries that most of us would deem acceptable in a liberal democratic state. This certainly happened in Czechoslovakia. Thus, although lustration was only meant to apply to senior positions, by the winter of 1992, with the election campaign at its height, there

were reports of head cooks in elementary schools and other public sector workers being dismissed from their posts because their names had
appeared in the files. During the same period rightist newspapers were
printing lists containing thousands of names of alleged informers,
names drawn from files that were supposed to be confidential. Many of
the more than 150,000 people whose names appeared on such unvetted
lists would have lost their jobs, without any form of recompense or
right of appeal—all due to the "public pressure" for a moral cleanup!

So, we return to the basic dilemmas associated with any collective
attempt to ensure that those who abused the human rights of their fellow citizens in the past should not continue to enjoy the fruits of
impunity in the future. How can you maintain control of the cleansing
process? How can you prevent it from becoming the vehicle for the furtherance of particularistic interests and ambitions? How can you seek
justice without risking the distortion of history? How can you pursue
justice without deepening the divisions in society? There are no easy
answers. In the next section we shall see how Germany, with its considerable financial and economic resources, coped with the problems
posed by the legacy of repressive rule in the former German Democratic Republic.

Germany

As with Czechoslovakia, the transition in Germany was relatively rapid,
with the old regime collapsing under the combined pressures of economic crisis, the hemorrhage caused by the exodus of its citizens to the
West, and the challenge of mass nonviolent demonstrations that reached
their peak on 7 November 1989, when an estimated 1 million people
went out onto the streets of Berlin, causing the authorities to open up
the Brandenberg Gate in the wall that divided the two halves of the city.

The dismantling of the state security police, the Stasi, was one of
the prime objectives of the opposition movement, and efforts were
made to prevent the destruction of the Stasi files. Even so, during the
period between the resignation of the old guard of Honecker in October
1989 and the first free elections of March 1990, which resulted in the
formation of a Christian Democrat government, the old security apparatus remained in place and a significant amount of archival material was
shredded and destroyed, despite the best efforts of grassroots groups.

The files took up some 200 kilometers of shelving, chronicling the activities of around 6 million people, the bulk of them East Germans but also including reports on more than 2 million West Germans. In a state where the regime had never been popular and every citizen was considered a possible security risk, the Stasi was the shield and the sword of the ruling Socialist Unity Party. The Minister of State Security, Erich Mielke, headed a full-time staff of about 90,000. Around 3,000 were channeled into important positions in public life, the military, and the economy. There were more than 2,000 employed to check the mail, while 1,500 spent their days monitoring phone calls. A further 4,000 were devoted to espionage activities beyond East Germany's borders—especially West Germany.[24] But by far the largest proportion, some 20,000, were involved in running a vast network of around 175,000 informers and collaborators, about 1 in 90 of the population. Over 15,000 of these informers were recruited as adolescents to act as classroom spies in schools and colleges throughout the country.[25] This all-embracing penetrative network of internal spies and the infrastructure that supported them dwarfed the spy apparatus of the Nazi regime. In 1941 the full-time staff of the Gestapo numbered less than 15,000.[26]

As we have seen in the cases of Czechoslovakia and occupied Europe during World War II, there was no single motive that led people to inform on their neighbors, colleagues, and, in some cases, their own family members. Some did it out of a sense of national duty, others because of weakness and greed, some were blackmailed, and others made the painful choice to collaborate with the regime to transform it. As one activist with a human rights group, who had also been a Stasi informer since the early 1970s, told Tina Rosenberg, "I was influencing the government through the information I gave them. . . . The ideas and way of life of the Peace Circle were an example of how the whole society should change. How do you make that a reality? One way to do it is through open dissidence, and the other way is through government channels. I was on the inside and the outside at the same time."[27] I have friends who are members of the Labour Party in Britain who use a similar argument.

What was to be done with such people? The debates that took place after the events of November 1989 were informed by a sense that the groundwork for the totalitarianism of postwar East Germany had been laid by the failure to fully address and come to terms with the complicity of the German population with the Nazi regime. The purges in the Western Zone had been halfhearted and virtually abandoned following the Cold War division of the postwar world, whereas the East German regime felt able to claim that in pursuing a thorough purge of Nazi officials, they had also purged whatever burden of guilt they might have carried, and the last thing the GDR regime had wanted was a debate about the responsibility of the individual citizen in relation to totalitarianism. So, the dominant feeling this time around was that they should do it properly. The past needed to be unveiled, confronted, and worked through if the foundations of a new democratic political culture were to be laid. And no one can fault the Germans for not investing in this effort; they tried a bit of everything—trials and prosecutions, a truth commission, and lustration.[28]

Trials

By 1997, roughly 150 trials had been held of former East German border guards and security officials in connection with the deaths of some 265 attempted escapees to the West. Most of those charged were acquitted, but 46 guards were convicted on charges of manslaughter, most of them receiving suspended sentences. One guard, however, received a sentence of six years imprisonment after it was revealed that he had shot and killed an escapee who had already been apprehended.[29]

These trials raised a number of thorny moral and legal issues. First, there was the old concern about the fate of the *lampistes,* the functionaries who get punished for carrying out the orders and policies of the big fish who escape prosecution. Second, there was concern voiced about the legality of the whole judicial process. The Unification Law only came into effect on 3 October 1990 when the provinces of East Germany became part of the Federal Republic of Germany. Before that date West German law did not apply in the East. The guards had shot people in line with their orders and in accordance with East German law that declared unlawful border crossing a criminal act, which the guards thereby had a duty to prevent. Therefore, it was argued, their prosecution was a case of ex post facto justice—the punishment of acts that were not criminal at the time they were committed.[30] Others argued that wicked laws should not be obeyed, especially when they contravened universal human rights, such as the right to life and freedom of movement. Whatever the legal arguments and the moral judgments, the fear began to grow that East German officials were being subjected to victor's justice and that the new Germany was in danger of resorting to the habits of the old one, twisting the law to suit its own ends.[31]

This was certainly the view presented to the courts by those senior officials of the old regime who were brought to trial. Although a significant proportion of them were deemed unfit to stand trial on the grounds of ill health, a number were convicted.[32] Thus, in 1997 began the trial of Egon Krenz, East Germany's last leader, and two of his senior colleagues. While his codefendants admitted their moral guilt but maintained their juridical innocence, Krenz refused to recognize the court. In January 2000 he was eventually jailed for six and a half years, still claiming that his conviction was unconstitutional as he was subject to East German law during the period when he held overall responsibility for the "shoot-to-kill" policy practiced against those trying to flee to the West.

In fact, relatively few people in East Germany suffered direct physical injury at the hands of identifiable individuals. As in Czechoslovakia (and elsewhere in the Warsaw Pact countries), the abuse of human rights was bureaucratized. It was the system that damaged people, albeit a seemingly impersonal and objective system that depended on individual functionaries doing their duty to sustain it.[33] Trials focus on the crimes of individuals, and are not best suited to unveiling the truth or promoting justice with regard to a structure of repression within which the perpetrators were officials sitting at their desks following normal procedure day after day. Hence, to come to some understanding of the systemic nature of state repression in the former GDR, the federal parliament in March 1992 established a commission of inquiry to investigate human rights abuses committed between 1949 and 1989.

Truth Commission

Germany was the only Eastern European state to sponsor a truth commission. The *Enquetekommission* was composed of 11 private citizens and 16 members of the Bundestag, drawn from all the political parties represented in the federal legislature. Its chairperson was the human rights activist and pastor Rainer Eppelman. Unlike the South African Truth and Reconciliation Commission considered in Chapter 6, the focus of the Commission was not the criminal activities of individuals. According to Ulrike Poppe there had been some discussion about establishing a commission to tackle areas relating to individual culpability, but this was eventually rejected for a number of reasons: no one in Germany could command the authority of a Desmond Tutu and there was the feeling that perpetrators would not admit responsibility when the federal parliament had already ruled against amnesties.[34]

The Commission aimed to write the authoritative historical analysis of government policies and the methods used to retain power, including the role of the West German government in helping to sustain the system. The tribunal proceeded to hold hearings throughout the former GDR on different aspects and structures of its totalitarian regime, including the Stasi, the justice system, the prisons, and the churches. It had access to all the available archives, except for the foreign ministry, and it commissioned more than 750 research papers. According to one of its researchers, "The report will serve as background for judges. The real task is not to pass judgement but to clarify what went on. Then you can understand what a cog in the machine each person was."[35]

A shortened version of the final report was published in 1994 and the fuller version of more than 15,000 pages was issued the following year. But if one of the aims was to get people to examine their own complicity with the system, then it has to be said that the report failed to reach the very people at whom it was targeted. The hearings were only reported in the more serious newspapers and few people outside of political circles paid any attention to the report, even if they were aware of its existence. This should not be too surprising; after all, why should we expect people to read accounts that, among other things, explore and analyze their own systemic complicity in structures of repression?

What did get people's attention was the third string in the German approach to unveiling the past—the lustration system.

Lustration

In late 1991 the federal parliament of unified Germany approved the Act Concerning the Records of the State Security Service of the Former German Democratic Republic. The act had two main provisions: the screening of all employees within the state sector of the former GDR and the opening up of the security files to private citizens.

With regard to the cleansing of the government agencies, the law granted the right to request background checks on employees, and allowed for them to be deemed unfit to work for a unified service. The underlying theme was that those who had either been employed directly by the security services or had worked for them as informers, and had thereby conspired against fellow citizens, were unsuitable people to continue occupying positions of trust and public responsibility in the new order. All public employees were required to complete a questionnaire; these were then submitted to local personnel review boards, which made recommendations to the appropriate ministries. The result was that thousands of teachers, judges, police officers, and other state employees were revealed to have worked for the Stasi in some capacity and lost their jobs.

Many lives were ruined in this way, and the more people suffered, the more resentment grew in certain quarters. The feeling was that East Germany was being colonized by the West. People were being banned from their jobs to create employment opportunities for the flood of professionals who could not find jobs in West Germany. As a consequence, those who were fired did not feel so much shame or repentance regarding their role under the old regime as self-pity and anger. They were victims of a West German witch-hunt. They were being punished, not for what they as individuals had done, but to help the victors deal with a surfeit of qualified people searching for employment.[36]

The actual files of the Stasi, all 6 million of them, were placed under the custodianship of the Protestant pastor Hans Joachim Gauck. By the end of 1996, 1.7 million requests had been made to the Gauck Authority by public and private employers seeking to screen job applicants and employees. In addition, more than 1 million private citizens had applied to see their own files during that same period.[37] Of these, probably about 45 percent discovered that there were no files on them, but for the remainder the results of their inquiry could be traumatic.[38] Perhaps the best-known case is that of the Wollenbergers, a couple active in peace and human rights circles. When the wife, Vera, read her file she made the horrendous discovery that her husband had been informing on her since the day they had met. A similar case was that of the woman who had served five years in jail for attempting to escape to the West. The person who had betrayed her was her partner, who had wished her well that very morning as she left their home.[39] As Rainer Eppelman confessed, "After reading your file you are wiser, but poorer."

Undoubtedly, many who took the risk of reading their file felt relief; at least now they knew, for good or ill, whether or not their friends and neighbors had been true. Now they could get on with life. Apparently, there was some discussion at the time of unification that the files should remain sealed, but this option was rejected by the East Germans. People had a right to know who had been informing on them. There should be no covering-up, no attempt to cast the past into oblivion, as happened after World War II. The best way to effect a closure on the past was to bring it out into the open. If you like, the best way to close the files was to open them.

The danger with opening up access to the files, of course, was that innocent people could suffer (and they did). Thus, in Germany there were plenty of cases of people being "outed" in sensationalist journalistic exposures on only the flimsiest of evidence.[40] And, of course, there were suicides, and lives and relationships were shattered.

Once again the doubt is raised about making facile distinctions between victims and perpetrators. How does one judge someone like Manfred Stolpe? A leading figure in the Lutheran Church who became Brandenburg's premier, he defended his involvement with the Stasi by arguing that he had to work with them to work against them and to influence the political leadership. Certainly, those of us who have never lived under occupation or under totalitarianism should hold back from casting judgment; we have never had to make the agonizing choices that others have had to make.

Adam Michnik, the onetime Polish Solidarity activist and intellectual, was one who articulated the concerns of many about the inherent logic of purges and cleansing exercises. In an interview with Lawrence Weschler he explained:

> First there is a purge of yesterday's adversaries, the partisans of the old regime. Then comes the purge of yesterday's fellow-oppositionists, who now oppose the idea of revenge. Finally, there is the purge of those who defend them. A psychology of vengeance and hatred develops. The mechanisms of retaliation become unappeasable.[41]

In the final section of this chapter we will examine how Poland sought to eschew the path of revenge in its attempt to exercise a closure on the communist past after the fall from power of the Polish Workers Party (PZPR) and lay the foundations for a new democratic and pluralist future. On the basis of the Polish experience it would appear that for bygones to be bygones, certain structural conditions need to be present, particularly with regard to the balance of forces in existence during the process of transition.

Poland

The transition in Poland fitted Huntington's ideal-type model of transplacement—the negotiated transfer of power in a situation where the opposition was strong enough to force the regime to agree to new power sharing arrangements and where the old elite still held sufficient power to ensure that they retained control over key institutions.

The Polish "negotiated revolution" was formalized at the Round Table Talks of April 1989. In the subsequent elections the Solidarity leadership was astounded by their victory, achieved even though they were only permitted to contest 65 percent of the seats for the lower house, the *Sejm*. Indeed, they were so surprised that one of their first impulses was to tone down the triumphant mood and assure their communist "partners" that they remained committed to the Round Table agreements. As the first noncommunist prime minister, Tadeusz Mazowiecki, advised, "Pushing the PZPR into opposition and forcing it into conflict would be a trap for all of us and the country. There is no opposition in any other country which has control of the army, the secret service and still is only in opposition."[42]

At the same time, the legitimacy that Solidarity enjoyed as a consequence of its mobilization of anticommunist opposition for so many years, and that was reflected in the popular vote, gave its leadership the strength to call upon the public to let bygones be bygones. The priority for the new government was to deal with Poland's economic crisis, and this project could only be strengthened by a process of national reconciliation involving, in the words of Mazowiecki, the drawing of "a thick black line" under the past and starting afresh. The model he had in mind was, of course, the Spanish one.

However, as the economic hardships suffered by the Poles increased, so did the criticism of this forgive and forget policy. So, while in 1991 only 38 percent of those polled favored the dismissal of former communists from public posts, by March 1992, 64 percent of those asked were in favor of some form of lustration process.[43] This demand for a cleansing of the state and related institutions was encouraged by right-wing groups and political factions, who were keen to point out how many of the old guard retained elite positions. Whether in public office or private enterprise, they argued, the old apparatchiks constituted a continuing threat to economic liberalization and democratization. But this very strength of the former communists, particularly in the legislature, ensured that the five coalition governments that held office between 1989 and 1993 all failed to pass or implement a lustration policy. Then, the December 1993 elections resulted in victory for the Democratic Left Alliance, which was dominated by the Social Democratic Party, the successor to the PZPR, who strengthened their call for national reconciliation. So, the years passed in postcommunist Poland without any official policy or measures for dealing with the past beyond letting bygones be bygones.

The debate about lustration only reemerged in 1996 when allegations that Prime Minister Olesky had collaborated with Russian agents resulted in his resignation. Various political factions then began to push their own lustration proposals, and eventually in 1997 the president, himself a former communist minister, signed a lustration act into law. It proposed screening state officials, including the president, deputies, judges, and prosecutors. They would be asked to declare whether or not they had been secret service agents or collaborators before 1990. Their declarations would be made public, and those suspected of lying would be investigated by a special commission of judges and could be banned from office for 10 years.

Of course, it is one thing to pass a lustration measure; it is a different matter to carry it out. The Poles soon ran up against the obstruction of the judiciary. Perhaps not surprisingly, the members of the judiciary were decidedly unenthusiastic about implementing a policy that targeted themselves, among other groups, for lustration, when so many of them had been integral props of the old regime.[44] As a consequence, the law was amended in November 1998, allowing cases to be brought before a special Lustration Prosecutor, who was empowered to instigate inquiries of those suspected of making untruthful declarations. Such people, if found to have been lying, faced a 10-year ban from public office.

One of the well-founded fears about this measure was that it allowed any member of the legislature to initiate proceedings—leaving the system wide open to abuse and political manipulation. It was resolved to launch a National Remembrance Institute, modeled on the Gauck Authority. According to its proponents it would promote the "moral purification of the nation" by allowing people access to their files and facilitating the prosecution of those guilty of crimes during the communist regime.

It is too early to determine how the lustration policy will work in practice, but certainly the evidence of the whole cleansing debate in Poland since the fall of communism would indicate that the supposed pursuit of justice will continue to be driven by factional political considerations. As in each of the case studies examined in this chapter, during a period of radical political transition that takes place within a fractured society, the different political factions and groupings will seek to manipulate the past, laying claim to a particular version of history to establish their political identity and strengthen their position in the competitive struggle for political advantage and power. In the process, not only does historical truth get distorted, but the cause of reconciliation is frustrated, as old wounds are aggravated and new divisions created.

In the next chapter we shall see how the South Africans tried to handle the tensions between unveiling the truth about the apartheid system and identifying those responsible for perpetrating human rights abuses during the apartheid years, while averting the threat of a bloodbath and promoting reconciliation in one of the most deeply divided societies in the world.

Notes

1. Jaroslav Basta, quoted in Weschler, *Calamities of Exile*, pp. 110–111.
2. Havel, "The Power of the Powerless," p. 45.
3. Romania was the main exception to this general pattern of nonviolent protest from below, accompanied by a loss of confidence by the political elite as their authority evaporated, leading to political pluralism and free democratic elections. Ceaucescu's intransigence led to armed clashes between demonstrators and security forces. Eventually forced to flee his palace in Bucharest, he and his wife were captured and summarily executed on Christmas Day 1989.
4. See Huntington, *The Third Wave*. Huntington presents a different reading from that presented here. He classed the changeovers in Hungary and Bulgaria as transformations, Poland and Czechoslovakia as transplacements, and East Germany as replacement.
5. A policy that the former Polish prime minister Tadeusz Mazowiecki depicted as drawing a "thick line" between the new and the old, to start afresh.
6. In 1990 Czechoslovakia changed its name to the Czech and Slovak Federal Republic, then on 1 January 1993 officially divided into two countries, the Czech Republic and Slovakia.
7. See Smith, "Decommunization After the 'Velvet Revolutions' in East Central Europe," p. 89.
8. See Stinchcombe, "Lustration as a Problem of the Social Basis of Constitutionalism," p. 246. It is interesting to note that in Mozambique fighters returning to their villages after the conclusion of the civil war have been subjected to a similar cleansing ritual.
9. Quoted in Weschler, *Calamities of Exile*, p. 106.
10. The old regime had relied on a network of 140,000 informers to spy on a population of 15 million. Smith, p. 88.
11. A similar screening process was carried out at the republican level at the request of the Czech and Slovak National Councils.

12. The vote took place in the immediate aftermath of the scare caused by the failed August coup against Gorbachev, which enabled the rightists to get their bill through without too many amendments.

13. See Pehe, "Parliament Passes Controversial Law on Vetting Officials," pp. 5–9.

14. Paulina Bren, "Lustration in the Czech and Slovak Republics," in Kritz, *Transitional Justice,* pp. 555–557. The verdict of the Commission could be appealed in the civil courts.

15. Rosenberg, *The Haunted Land,* p. 336.

16. The secret police had tens of thousands of agents, and it has been estimated that there were as many as 140,000 informers. The People's Militia also had tens of thousands of members, and during the years of the communist regime tens of thousands must have acted as party officials at the district level or above. All these faced a banning order.

17. The following is based on the account presented in Weschler, *Calamities of Exile.*

18. The final ironic twist in the tale is that Jan Kavan, who had been active in the European Nuclear Disarmament movement during the late 1970s and 1980s, was the minister who presided over his country's entry into the ranks of NATO in 1999.

19. This contrasts with the situation in Poland where millions had participated in the Solidarity movement, especially during 1980–1981.

20. Quoted in Weschler, *Calamities of Exile,* p. 114.

21. Weschler, *Calamities of Exile,* p. 115.

22. In the words of Jaroslav Basta, "That's why it has become better to speak of this demonic, omnipresent StB apparatus, with its treacherous agents everywhere who held us all down and now needed to be revealed and expunged—better that than admitting the truth, which was one's own lack of courage." Quoted in Weschler, *Calamities of Exile,* p. 114–115.

23. Vaclav Klaus, who was to become prime minister, had worked quietly and comfortably at the Economic Institute of the Academy of Sciences, never joining the Communist Party but never raising his voice against their rule.

24. Figures from "Destasifying Germany," *The Economist,* 1 December 1990, pp. 21–27.

25. *The Guardian,* 13 February 1997.

26. Ash, *The File,* p. 74.

27. Rosenberg, *The Haunted Land,* p. xiii.

28. One explanation for the range of initiatives pursued by the Germans in attempting to come to terms with the 1949–1989 period is the financial resources that were available to the state. The budget for the Gauck Authority for 1996 was DM 234 million, about £100 million.

29. Figures from *The Guardian,* 25 August 1997.

30. For a discussion of this point see Adams, "What is Just?" pp. 272–314.

31. One of the most glaring travesties of justice was the sentencing to six years imprisonment of Markus Wolf, the former head of foreign espionage for the Stasi, on charges of bribery and treason.

32. The old leader, Erich Honecker, who had been welcomed as a visiting

head of state in West Germany in 1987, had been arrested in January 1990, but was released within 24 hours on the grounds of ill health. Whisked off to Moscow, he was returned in 1992 but once again it was decided he was too ill to face trial. Released and given a passport, he took himself off to Chile. Some nine years later, of course, the Chilean dictator Pinochet was declared too infirm to face trial in Europe and was allowed to return to his homeland.

33. The image of bricks in the wall comes to mind, as the only time I visited Berlin was in 1991 at the time of the Pink Floyd's "The Wall" concert.

34. Ulrike Poppe in discussion at conference *Burying the Past,* Oxford, September 1998.

35. Quoted in Rosenberg, *Haunted Land,* p. 354.

36. A poll of August 1993 indicated that 65 percent of East Germans supported an amnesty for Stasi informers. Kritz, *Transitional Justice,* p. 598.

37. By the end of 1996 the Gauck Authority employed around 3,000 full-time staff to maintain files, pursue research, and deal with inquiries.

38. This estimate is based on the figures presented in Ash, p. 198.

39. Ash, p. 197.

40. In February 2000 the entire list of people who were on the Stasi payroll was released to the Internet, with some 5 million site visits while it was on the Web. *The Guardian,* 24 February, 2000.

41. Weschler, "A Reporter at Large," p. 127.

42. Quoted in Misztal, "How Not to Deal with the Past," p. 35.

43. Misztal, p. 36.

44. The judges had already shown their resistance to punishing the perpetrators of past human rights abuses by ensuring that prosecutions against the perpetrators of criminal abuses barely progressed. Thus, it was not until October 1997 that the first successful prosecution of one of those responsible for the slaughter of nine miners at the Wujek coal mine in 1981 was achieved. See *The Guardian,* 3 November 1997.

6

South Africa: Amnesty in Return for Truth

As South Africa moved toward the 1990s it became increasingly apparent that the rule of a privileged white minority over the disenfranchised majority of the population could not be sustained in the face of mounting international condemnation and internal resistance. The apartheid system could no longer withstand the onslaught of escalating social conflict and the costs of international economic sanctions and diplomatic isolation. On 2 February 1990, President F. W. de Klerk lifted the ban on the African National Congress (ANC) and the other nationalist movements and organizations that had been struggling for freedom. Ten days later Nelson Mandela was finally released from prison and there began the tortuous process of negotiating the framework for a common future. As violence continued in streets and townships throughout the country, the old elite sat down with their erstwhile enemies in an effort to chart a path toward a new democratic nonracial South Africa. It was not easy, and it was a year before de Klerk's National Party agreed to the formation of a constituent assembly, and another year was to pass before the first meeting of the formal all-party talks of the Conference for a Democratic South Africa was convened in December 1992.

Within a year of this first meeting an Interim Constitution was agreed upon by all the parties, and this came into force on 18 December 1993. Fully democratic elections were held for the first time in South Africa in the last week of April 1994, and Nelson Mandela was duly inaugurated as president two weeks later on 10 May.

A key factor in enabling this process to take place so swiftly was the "sunset clause" in the Interim Constitution that protected the jobs of the police and military and other state employees against the threat of a purge following the transfer of power to majority rule, and promised amnesty to the perpetrators of politically motivated violations of human rights. Without this concession there would have been no negotiated settlement. It was a price that had to be paid, and it is worth quoting this final clause at some length.

> This Constitution provides an historic bridge between the past of a deeply divided society characterised by strife, conflict, untold suffering and injustice, and a future founded on the recognition of human rights, democracy and peaceful coexistence and development opportunities for all South Africans, irrespective of colour, race, class, belief or sex.
>
> The pursuit of national unity, the well-being of all South African citizens and peace require reconciliation between the people of South Africa and the reconstruction of society. . . .
>
> In order to advance such reconciliation and reconstruction, amnesty shall be granted in respect of acts, omissions and offences associated with political objectives and committed in the course of the conflicts of the past. To this end, Parliament under the Constitution shall adopt a law . . . providing for the mechanisms, criteria and procedures, including tribunals, if any, through which such amnesty shall be dealt with at any time after the law has been passed.[1]

South Africa, like Argentina and Chile, faced the dilemma of how an emerging democracy could deal with the legacy of the gross human rights violations committed under the previous regime, when many of those responsible for such abuses remained a powerful force in the land and continued to occupy some of the key positions in the transitional coalition government and in the state security forces. Under such circumstances it was clear that criminal prosecution of the culpable could never be a serious option, at least not as long as the paramount concern was to avoid further bloodshed and lay the foundations for a new society and a new moral order. As the deputy president of the Constitutional Court, Judge Ismail Mahomed, observed, "If the Constitution kept alive the prospect of continuous retaliation and revenge, the agreement of those threatened by its implementation might never have been forthcoming."[2]

There were other, more pragmatic considerations as well. To pursue the torturers and murderers through the courts in pursuit of justice would have placed an intolerable strain on the judicial system, and the financial costs of mounting a series of prosecutions would have been prohibitive, particularly in a country scarred by gross social and economic inequality that was crying out for attention.

But if the prosecution of the perpetrators was impractical and too threatening to the fragile peace that had been achieved, then the alternative model of a blanket amnesty was equally unthinkable. The obscenity of apartheid and the terrible crimes committed in its name could not be swept under the carpet. To do that would have been an unacceptable insult to the dignity and the memory of all those who had suffered in the struggle for freedom. As the new minister of justice, Dullah Omar, acknowledged, "I could have gone to Parliament and produced an amnesty law—but this would have been to ignore the victims of violence entirely. We recognised that we could not forgive perpetrators unless we attempt also to restore the honour and dignity of the victims and give effect to reparation."[3]

Truth Commissions:
The Weaknesses of the Latin American Models

As we have seen, the successor regimes in Latin America tried to steer a path between vengeance and amnesia by means of truth commissions. But we have also seen that truth commissions took place in the context of a blanket amnesty, which the new regimes felt constrained to respect. Thus, the authorities could do little to challenge or undermine the culture of impunity that had fueled the horrors of the military dictatorships. We have also seen how the efficacy of such truth commissions was seriously weakened by certain key restrictions placed upon them.

The legitimacy of the Latin American commissions was undermined from the start because, in general, they were appointed by presidential decree rather than by the legislative assembly. This helped foster the suspicions of some that the prime aim of such commissions was to consign the painful past to the dustbin of history as quickly and painlessly as possible. Such suspicions were strengthened by the restrictions on the mandates of the truth commissions. Thus, in Uruguay, Argentina, and Chile the mandate of their commissions was confined to the investigation of disappearances and unlawful killings, thereby excluding consideration of torture, assault, and illegal imprisonment that did not result in death.

Another weakness of the Latin American commissions was that they lacked the power to subpoena witnesses or to seize relevant documentation. Suspicions about their "cleansing" function were strengthened further by their failure to identify the perpetrators by name. The argument against identifying individuals who were accused was that it would be equivalent to publicly indicting people without due legal process. But for the surviving primary and secondary victims of human rights abuses, the failure to identify the perpetrators denied them any means of making the culpable acknowledge the pain and anguish they had caused.

For all these reasons, the Latin American experience highlighted the weaknesses of the truth commission method of dealing with the legacy of abuse committed under the previous regime. There was too little justice, too little truth, and hence, although social peace was maintained, there was no solid foundation for reconciliation. This was the lesson that was communicated to the South Africans by Latin American human rights activists when the South Africans were trying to devise their own means of dealing with the painful past of the apartheid system—a method that would not provoke the bloodbath that many feared, but that would acknowledge the competing historical narratives within a divided society and facilitate reconciliation.

Toward a South African Model

In 1992 a group of South Africans under the auspices of the Institute for Democracy in South Africa began to study how other countries had dealt with this issue. They held two conferences during 1994 in which they reviewed the lessons to be learned from the different approaches adopted during the transitions from dictatorship to democracy in Latin America and Eastern Europe.[4] These conferences were supplemented by a series of workshops and symposia held throughout the country that looked at the concept of a truth and reconciliation commission for South Africa. Reports of these deliberations were fed into the parliamentary committee responsible for drawing up a bill to present to the South African legislature.

So here we see the first divergence from what might be called the Latin American model—the effort to stimulate public debate about the truth and reconciliation process, and to involve as wide a range of people as possible in the consultation exercises that would inform those charged with drafting the relevant legislation. From the start an effort was made to convince the people of South Africa that this was *their* truth commission and not a cynical exercise in executive cleansing. More than 127 hours were spent discussing the details of the bill in committee before it was presented to parliament. The Promotion of National Unity and Reconciliation Act, which established the legal framework for the South African Truth and Reconciliation Commission (TRC), was signed into law by President Mandela on 19 May 1995.[5]

Structure and Functions of the South African Truth and Reconciliation Commission

The Act provided for the appointment of 17 full-time commissioners, who were to complete their work within a two-year period.[6] They were charged with four key functions:

1. To establish as complete a picture as possible of the causes, nature, and extent of the gross violations of human rights committed from 1 March 1960 to a chosen cut-off date, 10 May 1994. Nelson Mandela was inaugurated as president on this day, which symbolized the irrevocable break with the old South Africa.
2. To facilitate the granting of amnesty to those who applied for it and who complied with the requirements established by the Act.
3. Allow the victims/survivors of violations to relate their own accounts of their experiences, make known the fate of victims, and recommend reparation measures.
4. Compile a comprehensive report including recommendations to prevent future violations of human rights. In light of these core tasks, the Commission was to be composed of three separate committees: a Human Rights Violation Committee to conduct hearings for the victims/survivors; a Reparation and Rehabilitation Committee to make policy recommendations on the basis of these hearings; and an Amnesty Committee, composed of legal officers, to hear amnesty applications.[7]

The Act allowed for the president to appoint the commissioners in consultation with the cabinet. In keeping with the commitment to transparency and public involvement in the official process of "truth recovery," nongovernmental organizations, faith communities, political parties, and other bodies were invited to nominate candidates. Eventually, 299 names were submitted and in November 1995 a "long shortlist" of them began appearing in public before a panel appointed by the president.[8] After three weeks of interviews, a short-list of 27 names was submitted to the president, from which the final appointments were made. The chairperson was to be Archbishop Tutu, and his 16 co-commissioners were drawn from the major communities of South Africa: Afrikaner, English, Black, Indian, Colored. There were six women and eleven men on the Commission.

Despite efforts to ensure the representativeness of the Commission, the Inkatha Freedom Party (IFP) continued its opposition, and the old National Party (along with parties to its right) expressed the view that there were insufficient members of the Commission in whom they had trust. Underpinning such reservations was the fear that the TRC would turn out to be little more than the pliant tool of its political masters, serving to present a veneer of legitimacy for an ANC witch-hunt of the white establishment and the persecution of their political rivals in KwaZulu-Natal. This suspicion of its relationship with the ANC was to persist throughout the life of the Commission. But in 1995 the commissioners did not let these concerns worry them; they hit the ground running, embarking on a sustained countrywide round of public meetings and encounters coordinated with the support of civil society groups and faith communities, all aimed at raising the level of public awareness about the TRC and encouraging folk to come forward with their stories. For example, the Durban office distributed some 100,000 leaflets throughout KwaZulu-Natal containing basic information about the Commission and how to make a statement to it in an effort to counter the widespread suspicion of the TRC engendered by the Inkatha Freedom Party, whose leader, Chief Mangosothu Buthelezi, had expressed the view that "the IFP would be digging its own grave, if it cooperated with the Commission."[9]

The Human Rights Violations Committee

Volunteer statement takers were recruited from all sections of society. It was their task to go out into the communities to elicit the stories of those who had suffered gross human rights violations, to listen and gather the fundamental information to pass on to the Commission. In total, more than 20,000 statements were taken. Those wishing to record their story would go to one of the TRC offices or a reception center in the outlying areas. The Investigation Unit would seek to corroborate the accounts, and then a selection of deponents would be invited to testify before the Human Rights Violations Committee. In fact, for the majority of the deponents the interview with the statement taker was their only face-to-face contact with the Commission; only one in ten actually testified in the public hearings.

This decision to hold the hearings in public was a significant departure from the Latin American model, and the first hearings were held in the Eastern Cape in April 1996. This was the area where whites and indigenous people had fought the first wars over land; it was the birthplace of black resistance and the place where many of the black political leaders had been born, including President Mandela himself. It was an appropriate location to launch a new struggle—for reconciliation. During these first sessions efforts were made to ensure that victims/survivors who testified were drawn from as wide a political spectrum as possible, that their stories related to the broad span of the 34-year period the Commission was mandated to cover, and that they included young and old, women as well as men—all so that the process could be shown to be broadly representative and inclusive.

In the ensuing months the public hearings on human rights abuses took on a pattern as the Commission covered the country. Usually, the hearings convened in a local civic center, church hall, or similar venue. Counseling was available to those about to undergo the grueling experience of recalling their experience of loss and pain on a public stage. Sitting facing the commissioners, with a community briefer, a friend, or a relative alongside as support, the witness—more often a woman than a man—would tell her or his story, with the commissioners asking the occasional question for clarification.[10] After 10 or 20 minutes the tale was told and the person would make way for the next witness.

The main aim of these hearings was to allow the victims/survivors to bring out into the open what had been hidden and suppressed under the conspiracy of the apartheid system. It was driven by the therapeutic model of the emancipatory consequences of truth telling. To quote Desmond Tutu, "We must deal effectively, penitently, with our past or it will return to haunt our present and we won't have a future to speak of."[11] This imagery of individual and collective healing through uncovering the pain of the past was compounded by a medical model that portrayed the past as a poisonous wound that needed to be lanced and exposed to the fresh air if true healing was to occur.

These were the models that informed the decision to hold the proceedings of the commission in public, and to subject them to comprehensive media coverage. During the life of the TRC, South Africans were bombarded with television pictures of tearful witnesses and exposed daily to newspaper reports of human rights violations. Pamphlets and posters were circulated urging people to come forward with their testimony, reminding them that "The Truth Hurts, But Silence Kills." A particularly important role was allocated to the radio, with its ability to communicate to people of all languages, literacy levels, and political persuasions wherever they might live. The aim was not just to uncover the past but to broadcast it—literally as well as metaphorically—to as many South Africans as possible, to ensure that the stories of the victims and the survivors entered the public domain, making it impossible for anyone to claim ignorance of the extent of the abuses that had occurred during the decades of state-organized racism. In this effort to promote the widest degree of public involvement in the truth and reconciliation process, the Commission also made use of the electronic media with its own extensive website and regular updates on proceedings that were sent out around the world by electronic mail.

A number of observers have pointed out that in South Africa there were relatively few direct perpetrators of human rights abuses, but a huge number of people who benefited from the structural violence of the apartheid system that impoverished, oppressed, and damaged so many of their fellow citizens. These were the people at whom many of the broadcasts were targeted.[12] But these beneficiaries of the apartheid system were the very folk who failed to come forward and participate directly in the truth commission process. They remained bystanders. But being a bystander during times when crimes against humanity are being committed carries its own forms of political, moral, and metaphysical culpability.

As part of the effort to involve those who shared some of the political and moral guilt for the evils committed in the name of apartheid, and to extend the domain of truth telling beyond the confines of the Commission hearings, a Reconciliation Register was opened, with books kept at various locations where people could go and sign them as a personal symbol of regret for their past culpability and their commitment to a new beginning. It was also possible for people to make entries in the Register via the Internet.

The apartheid system depended for its existence on the individual and institutional bystanders, those who benefited from the system and did nothing to undermine it. The Commission was mandated to attempt to uncover the "antecedents, circumstances, factors and context within which gross violations of human rights occurred." Therefore, in what was another new departure that distinguished the South African model from the Latin American truth commissions, Archbishop Tutu and his colleagues held a number of special institutional hearings, which examined the role of business, the media, the health sector, the faith communities, the trade unions, and the judiciary in the apartheid system.[13] These hearings revealed the extent to which the different sectors colluded with the status quo of racial division and exclusion during the apartheid period. Special hearings were also held on youth, military conscription, and prisons, in addition to a series of forums that focused on the experience of women activists. There were also special "event" hearings in which particular episodes during the period of history covered by the Commission were highlighted as illustrative of broader patterns of human rights abuses.

The TRC also differed from other truth commissions with regard to the breadth of its interpretation of gross violations of human rights—the causes, nature, and extent of which it was charged with mapping. Instead of restricting themselves to killings, disappearances, and torture, the commissioners decided to extend their mandate to cover a fourth category—"severe ill-treatment." Moreover, in the recording of the statements of those who had suffered either directly or indirectly from such gross violations, it was decided that in the interests of transparency and openness, the names of the alleged perpetrators should be made public. This decision was roundly condemned in certain quarters as being contrary to one of the basic principles of natural justice (that both sides of a case should be heard) as the accused were not allowed to cross-examine the witnesses who had identified them as perpetrators. Indeed, during its first year of operation, the Commission faced a number of legal challenges from people who had been identified as perpetrators of human rights abuses in the testimony of victims/survivors, and on 30 April 1996 the Supreme Court ruled that the TRC was required to give "proper, reasonable and timeous notice" to anyone who might be implicated or "prejudicially affected" by evidence presented to the Commission.[14]

Amnesty in Exchange for Truth

The biggest difference between the Latin American and the South African models related to the issue of amnesty. As we have seen in Argentina and Chile, their truth commissions took place within the context of a broad amnesty devised by the very people responsible for the human rights abuses. For the survivors of such abuse these amnesties constituted a travesty of justice and an insult to the lives and the memory of those who had suffered. Blanket amnesties, it was felt, strengthened the culture of impunity and hence undermined the foundations of the new democracy with its core principle of accountability.

Amnesty for the perpetrators of gross human rights abuses was the price the architects of the South African model felt they had to pay to uncover the truth, but they were well aware of the fundamental weakness in the Latin American experiments, and determined to incorporate into their program a number of conditions designed to ensure a degree of accountability and disclosure from perpetrators that general amnesties sidestepped. Central to the South African approach was the rubric "amnesty in return for the truth." There was to be no collective amnesty; it had to be applied for on an individual basis and it would only be granted in exchange for a full disclosure of the details and circumstances relating to the crime for which the amnesty was being sought. In other words, the perpetrators of human rights abuses could escape the threat of prosecution only if they were prepared to reveal the full extent of their criminal activities. They did not have to express regret or remorse. They did not have to apologize, but if they were to be free from the fear of prosecution then they needed to admit to their crimes and, moreover, convince the Amnesty Committee that these had been political in nature and were not committed out of personal malice or for personal gain.[15]

To increase the pressure on perpetrators to apply for amnesty and thereby acknowledge their responsibility for past abuses, the South Africans imposed a time limit—initially of 12 months from the launch of the TRC—for people to come forward. Once this deadline was passed, perpetrators faced the likelihood of a court case and a prison sentence. The original deadline for applications was set for 14 December 1996, but due to delays in setting up the infrastructure necessary for the hearings to commence, it was extended to 10 May 1997. By that time, some 7,700 amnesty applications had been received.

As one of their conditions for supporting the truth commission legislation, the Nationalist Party had insisted that the Amnesty Committee be headed by a judge and that its decisions be subject to review by a court of law, not by the rest of the Commission. The Amnesty Committee, composed of three judges and two commissioners, both of them legal practitioners, did not meet for a public hearing until late May

1996. One reason for the delay was the number of legal challenges to its role and mandate that it faced. From the ranks of those who feared the consequences of being identified as perpetrators came the objection that amnesty had been promised in the final clause of the Interim Constitution, and therefore the power of the Committee to refuse to grant an amnesty was unconstitutional. Then from some of the victims and their families came the challenge to that part of the legislation that would deny them the right to pursue criminal proceedings against any perpetrator who had been granted an amnesty.[16]

One of the Committee's first tasks was the design of an amnesty application form, which was then distributed to all the prisons, magistrates, courts, and TRC offices. Initially the Committee targeted possible applicants already serving custodial sentences, but later sought to attract applications from representatives of other groups who had played a significant role in the conflict, either as agents of the apartheid state or as members of the freedom movements. Most of the applications that did not involve the gross violation of human rights were dealt with in chambers; the remainder involved a public hearing in a setting that was more courtlike than the "victim-friendly" ambience of the human rights violations hearings. There were lawyers involved, who enjoyed the right of cross-examination of witnesses, and this meant that the proceedings went quite slowly. Furthermore, as a body whose decisions were subject to judicial review, the Committee needed to obtain all the relevant official documentation, such as court transcripts and the like, relating to the cases coming before it to arrive at an informed and fair decision. To strengthen its investigatory teeth, the Committee had the power to subpoena people to appear before it, and to search and seize documents and artifacts.[17]

Despite such powers, the Committee was very aware of the limitations it faced, not least the fact that in its efforts to uncover the darker truths behind the violations of the apartheid era it was dependent on perpetrators emerging from under the cloak of secrecy and silence to acknowledge and confess their guilt. In this regard there was a significant difference in the response of the police to the amnesty process compared with that of the military. Large numbers of security police grasped at the possibility of amnesty. This was due not to some collective change of heart, but to the efforts of the Transvaal Attorney General, whose pursuit of killers and torturers in the force drove a string of officers to seek the safety of the Commission. No comparable flow of amnesty applicants came forward from the ranks of the military, with the former minister of defense, General Magnus Malan, urging them to boycott the TRC after he had been acquitted on a murder charge. More than 400 ANC leaders and cadres submitted applications, including Thabo Mbeki, who was deputy president at the time, but this was only after Tutu threatened to resign from the Commission after a provincial leader of the ANC insisted that there was no need for ANC combatants to apply for amnesty because they had been fighting a just war against apartheid.[18]

In its report the TRC concluded that gross human rights violations had been committed during the period of its mandate by all the major parties to the conflict, and that culpability extended beyond the direct protagonists of the state security agencies and the liberation movements to the main organizations and institutional networks of civil society. Everyday people going about their normal lives, working within the health, education, welfare, and other sectors of society, were all deemed to have contributed to the maintenance of an unequal and fundamentally violent system of minority racial rule. Thus, with regard to the complicity of the faith communities, the report observed: "The failure of religious communities to give adequate expression to the ethical teaching of their respective traditions, all of which stand in direct contradiction to apartheid, contributed to a climate within which apartheid was able to survive."[19] Some of the applications to the Amnesty Committee reflected this awareness of what Jaspers would have termed political and moral guilt. Apparently, an Eastern Cape artist applied because she felt she had not reflected the atrocities of apartheid in her paintings. Six black youths requested an "Amnesty for Apathy": "We neglected to take part in the liberation struggle. So, here we stand as a small group representative of millions of apathetic people who didn't do the right thing."[20]

Reparations

The prospect of amnesty and freedom from prosecution was the main carrot used in South Africa to encourage perpetrators to come forward and confess to their crimes. From the perspective of the victims and survivors, however, the state was offering absolution to those responsible for heinous crimes, and depriving those who had suffered of the opportunity to seek justice by making the perpetrators pay the consequences of their actions. In an effort to compensate the victims for their suffering and for depriving them of the chance to pursue the guilty through the courts, the Promotion of National Unity and Reconciliation Act provided for a Reparations and Rehabilitation Committee within the Commission. Its task was to recommend appropriate measures "aimed at the granting of reparation to, and the rehabilitation and the restoration of the human and civil dignity of the victims of violations of human rights." The Committee's report ranged from the detailed computation of the level of financial grants to be made to victims, to the advocacy of far-reaching changes in the provision of the means to satisfy the basic needs of the deprived and excluded sectors of South African society.

In taking this broad perspective and acknowledging the need for structural change and reconstruction in South Africa as a necessary foundation for any sustained reconciliation process, the TRC was to be applauded. However, it is one thing to produce a set of recommendations, but it is far more difficult to marshal the political will and the fiscal resources to implement them. Given the persistence of gross inequalities in South Africa, the gap between the rhetoric of reconciliation and the practice is painfully apparent.

For various reasons to be discussed below, the South African truth and reconciliation process caught the interest and attention of the world's media, but in attempting to evaluate the strengths and weaknesses of this process it is important to remember that it constituted just one strand, however significant, in a broader process of transformation toward the vision of an open, democratic, and pluralist South Africa.

The Limitations of the
South African Truth and Reconciliation Process

The struggle against apartheid caught the attention of the world to such a degree that by the 1980s it had become the most celebrated cause in the world, one that people of all faiths and political persuasions embraced. As South Africa became more ungovernable, the fear of a bloodbath grew. But then there was the breakthrough of Nelson Mandela's release and the talk was of forgiveness and reconciliation, with the new president leading by example. Throughout the world people wanted the truth and reconciliation process to succeed. After all, if a society as fractured as South Africa could reconstitute and redefine itself as a nation, without bloodshed and terror, then here could be the transitional model that might be followed by other divided societies throughout the world.

For many outside and within South Africa the most obvious symbol of this model was the TRC, so much so that it was hard to avoid the impression that the TRC was *the* transformation process, its high visibility overshadowing other dimensions of the peace-building process. And at the heart of the TRC was the charismatic figure of Archbishop Tutu. It was Tutu, sitting at hearings with his cassock and his crucifix, under the banner "Truth—The Road to Reconciliation," who came to symbolize the South African truth and reconciliation process. Indeed, one of the criticisms made was that due to his prominence and centrality it was his vocabulary of redemption and reconciliation, forgiveness and healing, that came to dominate the process, leaving little space for the harsher language of justice and retribution.

Thus, among the black majority the main criticism was of the amnesty provisions that allowed perpetrators to walk free. Tutu was the key articulator of an alternative conception of justice in his efforts to justify the process. In his writings and talks he returned repeatedly to the principles of restorative justice embodied in the concept of *ubuntu*. At the heart of this was the basic insight, shared by so many spiritual traditions, of the thread of interdependence that links us all. Hence, to the extent that we treat others as if they were less than fully human, so we dehumanize and impoverish ourselves. From this perspective, then, it is in all our interests to try to restore social harmony once it has been fractured. Therefore, to forgive others and welcome them back into our common human household is not altruistic, it is the highest form of enlightened self-interest, insofar as it affirms the humanity of the other, and hence of ourselves, and thereby helps restore community.[21]

The weakness of this argument, at least from the perspective of many, was that the core element of restorative justice—the restoration of what had been lost—could not apply to South Africa. What had been lost could never be replaced.

The hard answer to such people was that their pain was part of the price that had to be paid for the political settlement that paved the way for the new regime. The architects of the TRC were clear that the search for justice in the sense of making the perpetrators pay for their crimes would have been counterproductive. In effect, to insist on retribution would have been to insist on the perpetuation of violence. The TRC was the result of a political compromise, and for the sake of peace it was necessary to allow murderers to walk free. As Desmond Tutu subsequently admitted:

> We have had to balance the requirements of justice, accountability, stability, peace and reconciliation. We could very well have had retributive justice, and had a South Africa lying in ashes—a truly Pyrrhic victory if ever there was one.[22]

Another argument put forward by the defenders of the TRC was that it was necessary to relinquish the quest for retribution for the sake of truth. One of the main failings of the Argentinean and Chilean truth commissions was that they never found a way of drawing the perpetrators into the truth-telling process. In the South African model, by a mixture of threats (the risk of prosecution) and offers (amnesty in return for confession), at least some of those responsible for gross violations of human rights were brought into the process. Of course, it remained a cause of regret and anger that more did not avail themselves of the opportunity to apply for amnesty, but the harsh reality was that for too many of them the threat of prosecution remained too remote to coerce them into confession.

In contrast with the criticisms from the black majority about the amnesty provisions and the lack of justice, the main criticism of the truth and reconciliation process coming from the white minority was that it was too much like a witch-hunt of whites in general and the Afrikaans population in particular. There was a basic suspicion, never satisfactorily overcome, that the TRC was a tool of the ANC. Critics could point to the TRC's composition, with all but two of the commissioners alleged to be pro-ANC.[23] The Afrikaans press voiced a similar suspicion regarding the composition of the TRC staff. That there was some substance to such charges was evidenced by the report that in one of its early rulings the Amnesty Committee awarded amnesty to seven out of twelve applicants—all were black ANC members. Four of the five who were refused were white right-wingers. Only after the intervention of the deputy chair of the Commission was the ruling revised and amnesties granted to the four whites.[24] Former President F. W. de Klerk was particularly strong in his condemnation of the TRC, alleging that its investigations were targeted "almost exclusively against those associated with the former government, and its behaviour at times appears to be increasingly aggressive and prosecutorial . . . little is said, written or reported about the abuses perpetrated by those who were opposed to the government."[25]

De Klerk was one of the senior figures from the apartheid regime who consistently denied any personal involvement in or knowledge of atrocities, attributing them to "rogue officers" acting beyond their purview. In its efforts to challenge such protestations of innocence the TRC was hamstrung by the fact that so many of the relevant files had been shredded by a security force that remained virtually intact, even after the change in government. As a consequence, the bulk of the confessions came from middle-ranking operatives, those who had—quite literally—blood on their hands, while their senior officers and political masters stayed silent. The refusal of senior figures to come forward and acknowledge their responsibility for the crimes of their subordinates, and the failure of the TRC to force them into the open, led some to suspect that a deal had been struck during the transition to majority rule—that the uncovering of the truth would stop short of revealing the full complicity of the former political elite.[26]

Despite such suspicions, and however partial the history uncovered by the Commission, there was sufficient evidence revealed to ensure that no South African could ever again deny the atrocities committed. This was a major achievement. As a South African advocate remarked, "It's certainly an imperfect process. It's not going to achieve complete reconciliation, it's not going to discover the whole truth. But a great deal of truth has been uncovered. I think whites have been rather shaken to hear day after day of the abhorrent atrocities committed in their name, and it certainly has done a lot to mould white opinion."[27]

But if, for the white minority, the most significant aspect of the work of the TRC was the unveiling of an authoritative account of the horrors of South Africa's past, for many among the black majority the Commission's report only confirmed the history with which they were familiar. And for too many of the primary and secondary victims of apartheid the resentment and hurt persisted. This continuing anguish was expressed by one mother at the amnesty hearing of her son's killer: "I am not forgiving them. They are not asking forgiveness from us, the people who've lost their beloved ones; they are asking forgiveness from the government. But what they did they did to us."[28]

The TRC process was designed to promote reconciliation at the national level, hence the publicity surrounding the Commission's hearings. It was born out of political compromise and its prime concern was to restore the moral order on a national basis. It was in the national interest that amnesty was offered to perpetrators. The needs and concerns of individuals were secondary. But this focus served to reveal a disjunction between the macro and micro levels. Thus, the massive media coverage in some ways served to increase the trauma of many of those who suffered under apartheid, exacerbating their pain and suffering rather than helping their wounds to heal. The experience of many was that reconciliation was a process that was taking place at some level far removed from their own lives and experience. As one respondent in a survey conducted in the rural community of Grabouw in the Western Cape complained, "We have seen reconciliation on television with the TRC, but here in Grabouw we have not had anything like that."[29]

There was a poignant cartoon published in the *Rhodes Journalism Review* that showed Desmond Tutu accompanied by a black victim in a wheelchair and a white perpetrator, the three pursued by a horde of media personnel. Tutu is consulting a map in a perplexed fashion as he stands on the edge of a precipice labeled TRUTH. Across the gap, just too far to leap, is another peak called RECONCILIATION.[30] It expressed graphically the achievement of the TRC and its limitations. It was strong on the truth dimension of its project, but the pursuit of its broader objective of promoting reconciliation was far more problematic.[31]

The Need for Reconstruction and Reconciliation

Clearly it was beyond the capacity of any single body to make reconciliation happen. Reconciliation might be a desired end point but above all it is a process. It is not an occurrence, and it is certainly not an event that happens on a television screen. Reconciliation cannot be legislated or proclaimed from above. It is a process that can be extremely painful and takes place between people who seek to get beyond the hatred and the division of the past and move toward a shared future. At the heart of such a process is the preparedness of people to begin to consider re-creating some kind of human community with those that were once enemies.

But this is not an easy process. Outsiders have no right—no right whatsoever—to expect the victimized to forgive those who abused them. What can be done is to create the situations where people can begin to come to terms with their pain and move toward that stage where it no longer dominates their lives. For this to happen they need safe spaces where they can tell their stories, give expression to their anguish and anger, and be assured that they are being taken seriously. Only then can they begin to engage in the sustained dialogue with their former enemies that is necessary for reconciliation to progress.

The realization that South Africans needed a much broader and deeper process than that initiated by the TRC if reconciliation was to take place led various civil society groups and networks to initiate their own community-based programs. In this, a particular responsibility fell upon the faith communities. As the dean of St George's Anglican Cathedral in Cape Town acknowledged, "within the context of our church there are both those who might be called 'perpetrators' and those who are 'victimised,' because the church in many ways reflects the society in which we live and all those people are contained in the self-same community."[32] Individual parishes therefore took upon themselves responsibility for facilitating processes of healing and reconciliation within their congregation and wider community. This was mainly through creating situations, either in small groups or in front of the assembled congregation, where people could tell their stories. Many also developed outreach programs to work with young people, helping them to understand and come to terms with the painful history of the apartheid system.

One of the better-known civil society initiatives was the "Healing the Memory" project launched by Anglican priest Michael Lapsley of the Trauma Centre for Victims of Violence and Torture in Cape Town. Using various mediums, including drama and painting, the workshops sought to challenge the participants to ask certain basic questions of themselves: What have I done? What was done to me? What have I failed to do? On the final day, workshop participants would use modeling clay to create symbols of their hopes for the future. The aim was to create a process through which people were helped to transform themselves from victims into survivors, and from survivors into victors. Reflecting on the workshops, Michael Lapsley explained:

> Through these stories of hope, pain, joy, anger, fear, we draw people's feelings into understanding issues of peace, justice, reconciliation and healing. This is how the human story of the heart unfolds. It becomes a universal story. . . . There is no evidence in the history of the world that societies were able to successfully bury their past. . . . Look at slavery, or the experience of the Afrika[a]ner in the British concentration camps. Those memories never healed. People that continue to see themselves as victims actually become the victimisers. For this generation it is extremely important to confront the past and wrestle with it, to not be consumed by it in the future.[33]

Such grassroots efforts, along with initiatives such as victim-offender mediation programs, can have a significant impact on people's lives. But the acknowledgment of the trauma and the abuses of the past, including apologies from perpetrators, constitutes only one component of the reconciliation process. If the process of reconciliation in South Africa is to take root and progress, then something more is required. Those who were oppressed and powerless under apartheid and still suffer the consequences of that history require some degree of justice if a sustainable peace is to be reached, and justice requires some degree of restitution and social reconstruction.

As we have seen, the most painful and difficult part of the truth and reconciliation process for the victims of human rights abuses was to see the perpetrators walk free. The victims were denied justice in the narrow retributive sense, and nothing could restore or make up for the loss of a murdered child or family member. These were the people who told their stories at the human rights violations hearings and gave their evidence at the amnesty applications. But Mahmood Mamdani has claimed that in focusing on such narratives the TRC served to highlight a partial view of apartheid, leaving unaddressed what he termed the banal reality of racism as experienced by the bulk of the South African population. In his words the TRC looked at apartheid "through narrow lenses, through the experiences of a tiny minority of political activists on the one hand and stage agents on the other—of perpetrators and victims . . . so defined as to exclude the vast majority of South Africans."[34]

For the majority of apartheid's historic victims, their everyday experience was of the humiliation of the Pass Laws, the injustice of forced removals, the inadequacies of Bantu education, the inequity of black poverty set against white wealth. This was the mundane reality of apartheid, the fundamental racial division between haves and have-nots that permeated all institutions and areas of life.

To its credit the TRC did try to open up this dimension of apartheid with its special institutional hearings. What was brought out in those hearings was the degree to which so many white South Africans were beneficiaries of the structural inequalities and hence bore a degree of political and moral culpability for the injustices of the system.[35] Moreover, in the interim constitution it was recognized that national unity required reconciliation *and* reconstruction of society.

The big question facing South Africa is how can new relationships based on a shared vision of a common future be forged between the beneficiaries of years of racial domination and the historic victims of that oppression? If South Africa is to move along this path of reconciliation, then something more than truth is needed. An acknowledgment of past evils and a proclaimed commitment to forge a shared future rings hollow if it is not accompanied by some effort to remedy the effects of those evils. In other words, reconciliation requires some degree of justice: restitutive justice. Without it, the South African reconciliation process will remain a false and partial phenomenon. The significance of this form of justice in the overall reconciliation process has been illustrated wonderfully clearly by the following morality tale told by Reverend Mxolisi Mpambani at a meeting at the University of Cape Town in March 1998.

> There were two friends, Peter and John. One day Peter steals John's bicycle. Then, after a period of some months, he goes up to John with outstretched hand and says "Let's talk about reconciliation."
> John says, "No, let's talk about my bicycle."
> "Forget about the bicycle for now," says Peter. "Let's talk about reconciliation."
> "No," says John. "We cannot talk about reconciliation until you return my bicycle."[36]

In this tale we see the effort to obtain a "cheap" reconciliation: the attempt to end the conflict and restore the relationship, but without restitution. Once again, the victim is being asked to become reconciled to loss, and this is no basis for a sustainable settlement.

But in a country like South Africa, how do you make restitution in a manner that will not cause new wounds, that will not deepen the conflict and will not threaten increased violence? It is one thing to try to compensate the primary and secondary victims of gross human rights violations with cash payments, educational scholarships, access to health care, the construction of memorials, and other forms of material and symbolic reparations. But how do you address the issue of reparations for the vast majority of the South African people who were not affected directly by the torturers and murderers, but who suffered under the banal everyday reality of apartheid? How can the violence and the damage done to these people's lives be redressed without a major shift in the distribution of wealth and property in South Africa?

A fundamental component of the political compromise of 1993 was the agreement that property relations should be left untouched, and there were valid arguments to support such a commitment at that time.[37] However, there can be little doubt that unless some moves are eventually made to bridge the gap across the racial divide between haves and have-nots in South Africa, then the political and social order is going to come under severe threat.

It is clear to all that the TRC could never be a panacea that would fix everything that was wrong with South Africa. At the same time there can be no question that it has been a significant component in a complex process that is still unfolding. Perhaps in a few years we shall be able to look back and see the TRC as a crucial stepping-stone between the political accommodation reached by the elites and a broader process of social reconciliation between the former beneficiaries and victims of the old order. For this to happen, however, it is important that decision-makers realize that while uncovering the past and acknowledging the truth can be important constituents of the social healing process, reconciliation requires more than truth, it requires a modicum of justice—not necessarily in terms of the punishment of the perpetrators of evil but in the constructive sense of action to reduce socioeconomic inequality. As this is not likely to happen without grassroots pressure from below, it is equally important that all the educational work of the TRC and civil society groups with regard to the promotion of a culture of respect for human rights should be sustained, so that when people do mobilize to create a new future for South Africa, they will pursue their vision by democratic and nonviolent means, thus minimizing the risk of the country descending into the kind of violent conflict that could destroy all hopes of reconciliation.

Notes

1. Quoted from *Truth and Reconciliation Commission*, pp. 1–2.
2. Quoted in Tutu, *No Future Without Forgiveness*, p. 26.
3. *Truth and Reconciliation Commission*, p. 3.
4. The papers from these two conferences were published. See Boraine et al., *Dealing with the Past;* Boraine and Levy, *The Healing of a Nation?*
5. During the final vote in the National Assembly the Inkatha Freedom Party abstained, while the rightist Freedom Front voted against the measure. Krog, *Country of My Skull*, p. 10.
6. The life of the commission was later extended to three years because of the volume of work. It presented its final report in October 1998, but the Amnesty Committee continued its work through 1999.
7. As part of its commitment to a democratic process, details of the Commission's terms of reference were published in booklet form in all eleven main languages of South Africa.

8. The interviews went on for more than three weeks. The core question asked was "What would you do if you discovered information that implicated the highest positions in the new government?" Krog, p. 18.

9. Initially, the IFP established its own rival structure, the Commission of Enquiry into Violence, but began to cooperate with the TRC after it was pointed out to them that victims of violence would not receive reparations unless they made depositions to the Commission.

10. A permanent feature of the hearings was the box of tissues on the table, leading some cynics to label it the Kleenex Commission.

11. Quoted in Frost, *Struggling to Forgive,* p. 23.

12. According to the vice-chairperson of the Commission, Dr. Alex Boraine, the decision to open up proceedings to the scrutiny of the public and the mass media was intended to ensure "transparency and also a strong educative opportunity so that healing and reconciliation is not confined to a small group but is available to all." Boraine, "Alternatives and Adjuncts to Criminal Prosecutions."

13. The *Enquetekommission* in former East Germany did hold comparable institutional hearings.

14. People who were going to be named by victims were alerted ahead of time and invited to make a written representation or appear in person at a subsequent meeting of the Commission.

15. Whether or not a particular act was deemed to be associated with a political objective was to be decided according to certain criteria that included the motive of the perpetrator, the context of the acts, the nature of the target or victims of the act, and whether or not the crimes were committed in the execution of an order or on behalf of a political organization or institution.

16. The challenge brought by the family of Steve Biko, Case No. CCT17/96 in the Constitutional Court of South Africa, attracted particular attention.

17. In one amnesty hearing it was revealed that former Prime Minister P. W. Botha had personally given orders for illegal killings and bombings. He refused to appear before the Commission, ignored subpoenas, and was eventually charged with contempt in a provincial court presided over by a black magistrate. His sentence was eventually quashed on a technicality.

18. At one stage there was the bizarre phenomenon of the Commission appealing to the courts against a decision by its own Amnesty Committee to award a collective amnesty to ANC leaders. The Promotion of National Unity and Reconciliation Act made no allowance for such a corporate amnesty where no specific crimes were itemized. See Tutu, p. 187.

19. Final Report, Truth and Reconciliation Committee, vol. 5, ch. 6, para. 156. See http://www.polity.org/govdocs/commissions/1998/trc/5chap6.htm.

20. Krog, p. 122.

21. For discussions of *ubuntu,* see Tutu, pp. 34–36. See also Frost, p. 25.

22. Tutu, p. 27.

23. Two of the commissioners had some sympathies with the National Party, one of whom criticized the final report of the Commission for relying on "improper material" and uncorroborated oral evidence. There were no pro-

Inkatha members on the Commission. See Muller, "Facing Our Shadow Side," p. 16.

24. Reported in Krog, p. 118.

25. Quoted in Andrew O'Hagan, "Soul-Searching in South Africa," *The Guardian*, 26 November 1997.

26. See, for example, "Burying South Africa's Past," *The Economist*, 1 November 1997, pp. 23–24.

27. Quoted in Victor Mallet, "Truth, Not Reconciliation," *Financial Times*, 30 October 1998.

28. Joyce Mtimkhulu, quoted in "Burying South Africa's Past," *The Economist*, 1 November 1997.

29. Quoted in Spies, "A Safe Space," p. 15.

30. *Rhodes Journalism Review*, issue 14, 1997.

31. This is not to deny that there were strong criticisms made of the "truth" uncovered by the TRC.

32. Reverend Rowan Smith, address to public meeting, "Transforming Society Through reconciliation: Myth or Reality?" Cape Town, 12 March 1998.

33. Michael Lapsley, quoted in "Healing the Memory," *Track Two*, v. 6, nos. 3 and 4, 1997, p. 46.

34. M. Mamdani, address to public meeting, "Transforming Society Through Reconciliation: Myth or Reality?" Cape Town, 12 March 1998.

35. It could of course be argued that the white minority were themselves also victims of apartheid, insofar as they were damaged by the racist structures within which they led their lives. As Commissioner Wynand Malan argued, "Trying to posit perpetrators versus victims in this country is an over-simplification . . . I am both perpetrator and victim. I am both beneficiary and victim in different ways, and I think that goes for the majority of people . . ." "Transforming Society Through Reconciliation: Myth or Reality?" Cape Town, 12 March 1998.

36. M. Mpambani, "Transforming Society Through Reconciliation: Myth or Reality?" Cape Town, 12 March 1998. See also Krog, p. 109.

37. There was a genuine fear of the impact of flight of capital from South Africa with the onset of majority rule. There is a continuing fear among many whites that although they were innocent bystanders during the apartheid years, the pursuit of restitution for the sake of reconciliation will cause them to become a new class of victims.

7

Palestine: Collaboration and Its Consequences— A Worst-Case Scenario?

In the case studies examined up to this point, the successor regimes have all pursued one or more strategies to deal with the legacy of human rights abuse and shameful behavior on the part of certain sections of society. Whether the approach has been driven by the search for retrospective justice, as in the case of the purges and trials that followed the liberation of occupied Europe after World War II or after the collapse of some of the state socialist regimes of Eastern Europe in 1989; or whether it has been primarily focused on unveiling the truth and allowing victims' narratives to be expressed and acknowledged as in Argentina and Chile after the juntas and in postapartheid South Africa; or whether it has been a negotiated pact of oblivion as in the case of Spain after Franco, in each case there has been a conscious policy and a sustained effort to implement it, whatever the weaknesses in design and execution.

In this chapter, in contrast, I want to focus on what has occurred in the embryonic state of Palestine to illustrate what can happen in a society where the relevant authorities have so far not only failed to establish any coherent strategy for dealing with those who have been accused of betraying the national struggle by collaborating with the Israeli occupiers, but have undermined any efforts by civil society groups to develop their own approaches to healing the wounds and divisions within the "national home." The result has been the incidence of the worst kind of lynch law, abuse of human rights, and a burgeoning culture of revenge.

Clearly, in trying to understand why the Palestinian leadership has failed to generate any kind of coherent attempt to tackle the legacy of "traitors in their midst," one has to take account of the particularities of

Palestinian history, the nature of the liberation struggle, the failure of the peace process with Israel to progress, and the nature of Palestinian culture. But despite the peculiarities of the Palestinian case, the lessons remain.

Background

On 28 September 1995 Israel and the Palestine Liberation Organization (PLO) signed an interim agreement on the transfer of control of the main population centers of the occupied West Bank to the Palestinian Authority (PA). This accord came two years after the original agreement, or Declaration of Principles, signed in Washington in September 1993. Since that time the peace process has faltered and all but collapsed on a number of occasions. By November 2000, with the outbreak of the "Al Aqsa Intifada" more than 250 Palestinian lives had been lost in an ongoing bloody battle with the occupying Israeli forces and a lasting peace settlement seemed further away than ever. Despite this, most people agree that the only workable peace agreement is one that recognizes the reality of two peoples and two states, with Jerusalem as a shared capital. Thus, at some point within the not-too-distant future, a Palestinian state will come into existence. It is not certain where its borders will be, it is not clear whether it will be able to exercise normal statelike sovereignty over its airspace, and it is highly unlikely that it will enjoy complete autonomy over defense-related issues.[1] However, as Mark Heller has observed, "A semi-independent state already exists, resembling recognised states in some respects but different from them in others. . . . this semi-state will continue to exist even if no permanent-status agreement is reached. And its formalised independence will inevitably be incorporated into any agreement that is reached."[2]

Whatever the territorial borders of the Palestinian political entity that eventually comes into being, it will continue to face huge problems of social, economic, and political reconstruction after decades of Israeli occupation. It will also face the challenge of healing the divisions within the Palestinian community created in and through the long years of occupation. One problem in particular has been crying out to be addressed—the fate and future of all Palestinians who collaborated with the Israelis during the years of occupation.

The concern felt by the Israeli authorities over the fate of their informers and agents was indicated by their insistence, in both the 1995

Taba or Oslo II Agreement and the earlier Cairo Agreement of 1994, that the safety of Palestinian collaborators be guaranteed until a solution was found.[3]

Unfortunately the PA has failed to develop or implement any consistent policy or strategic approach to this problem whatsoever. The result has been a chaotic mix of self-help justice by those seeking vengeance against alleged collaborators, the pursuance of personal and family feuds under the guise of purging the traitors, the persecution of political opponents and members of rival political factions for alleged collaboration, various forms of blackmail, and the ad hoc arrest, torture, and prosecution of a host of Palestinians under the umbrella charge of acting as an informer for Israeli intelligence by one or more of the burgeoning Palestinian security forces. As a consequence, human rights have been violated in the name of justice; rumor and hearsay have triumphed over historical truth in the absence of any kind of authoritative approach to uncovering the pains of the past; and the process of in-house reconciliation among Palestinians has been stillborn, while cycles of violence have intensified.

Before going on to document the extent of this failure, we need to establish the nature and the extent of Palestinian collaboration with the Israeli occupiers to obtain some sense of the scale of the problem.

Throughout the years of occupation, the provision of various kinds of services, permits, and licenses to Palestinians was often made conditional upon the applicant agreeing to "return the favor" by providing information or other kinds of services to the Israeli authorities. The result has been that Palestinians who collaborated in some way with the Israeli security agencies exist in every village and institution in the West Bank and Gaza Strip. Obviously, the bulk of these operated undercover, so estimates of their number vary considerably. One Palestinian lawyer interviewed in October 1995 estimated the figure to be in the region of 6,000–7000, extrapolating on the basis of roughly 18 collaborators who he knew existed within his own village of 30,000 inhabitants. In contrast, a well-informed human rights worker put the total figure in excess of 40,000,[4] while a senior political activist familiar with the Gaza Strip estimated that there were at least 30,000 collaborators in the Gaza Strip alone, approximately 4 percent of the population.[5] If this was the case, and the pattern was replicated throughout the West Bank in addition to the Gaza Strip, with a combined population in the region of two and a quarter million, we would arrive at a total figure approaching 90,000 collaborators!

The truth is that no one knows how many collaborators there are or have been, but it is clear that a substantial and significant proportion of the population have in one way or another "served the enemy" at some stage during the long years of occupation. To begin to understand this phenomenon we can periodize the analysis: before the Intifada, during the Uprising, and since the establishment of the PA.

Palestinian Collaboration Before the Intifada

To understand why the phenomenon of Palestinian collaboration with the Israeli occupiers has been so widespread, it is important to take account of a number of contributing factors that were present during the first 20 years of occupation, from 1967 to the outbreak of the uprising in 1987.

One crucial factor relates to the lack of any clear and unambiguous directives provided to the inhabitants of the occupied territories concerning the appropriate relationships to be adopted with the Israeli occupiers. Unlike the liberal democracies of Western Europe occupied by the Germans in World War II, when the West Bank and Gaza Strip were occupied by Israel in 1967 there was no legitimate Palestinian government in existence. Even after the establishment of the PLO and its recognition as the legitimate representative of the Palestinian people, it failed to lay down clear directives for the inhabitants of the West Bank and Gaza Strip as to how they should relate to the occupiers.

As a result, the majority of the Palestinian inhabitants of the occupied territories before the outbreak of the Intifada in 1987 experienced considerable confusion as to how they should behave toward their occupiers, and were unclear about the borderline between steadfastness and treachery. This dilemma was compounded by the dependency of the Palestinians upon the Israeli occupiers. As a consequence of the relatively undeveloped state of the Palestinian economy and infrastructure at the time of the Israeli occupation in 1967, and the subsequent Israeli policy of undermining any autonomous Palestinian development in the fields of health care, education, welfare provision, and, most crucially, the economy, Palestinians became increasingly dependent upon Israel for their livelihood as the years of occupation passed. In light of this relative powerlessness and the lack of unequivocal guidelines from any authoritative source concerning the proper relationship with the occupier, it is easy to understand how many Palestinians found themselves obliged to cooperate with the Israelis in ways that, in other circumstances and with the benefit of hindsight, might be classed as collaboration.

Thus, in the years before the Intifada as many as 150,000 Palestinians worked in Israel each day, particularly in agriculture and the construction industry. Others worked for Israeli contractors in building the settlements that grew to house over 140,000 Israelis upon land expropriated from the Palestinians. Drawing on the classification of different types of collaboration presented in Chapter 2, we could categorize such people as accommodationists, people who saw no alternative means of livelihood other than working for the enemy.

This dependency also helps to explain the vast number of Palestinians who, from time to time, passed on information to the security services. Whoever needed a permit, a license, or any other documentation or service that lay within the domain of the Israeli administration was put under considerable pressure to inform on their neighbors and workmates. This practice of reciprocating favors becomes more readily understandable when one places it in the context of certain aspects of the Palestinian social structure that the Israelis were able to exploit. Historically, Palestinian society has been riven by horizontal and vertical fissures. People were divided not just along economic or class lines, but by communal loyalties to their religion, their village, and, most important, their family and *hamula*, or clan. The whole system was permeated by a network of patron-client relationships that stretched from the level of the village to the notable families of the Palestinian economic, social, and political elite via a series of brokers or go-betweens. In pursuit of their interests, Palestinians, whether they were peasants or professionals, were accustomed to approaching an intermediary to petition on their behalf, or else addressing their request directly to someone with influence in the appropriate circles.

The key characteristic of all such relationships was that it was a form of exchange. But the service obtained was not a right that the client could demand, it was a favor that had to be requested. And if the favor was granted, or if the go-between was successful in the brokerage, then the expectation was that the service or favor would be reciprocated in some way. Into such a system the Israeli occupiers were able to insert themselves, as a new and extremely influential layer of patrons, people who were in a position to grant favors and provide services for those who chose to petition them. And in return, as would be expected under such a system, they required certain forms of reciprocity. Herein lay the roots of the actions of thousands of Palestinians who informed on their fellow citizens, the ordinary villagers and urban dwellers who acted as small-scale informers *(mukhber)*, monitoring the activities of neighbors and colleagues. Once again, most of them might be classified as accommodationists, as they provided such services to the enemy because they felt that their own welfare and that of their families required it; they had no realistic alternative.

However, the constituency of clients catered to by the Israeli authorities was not confined to the relatively powerless of Palestinian society. They also targeted the erstwhile patrons of such people, seeking to co-opt the established local leaders of Palestinian society, such as village *mukhtars* and clan elders. Traditionally, the prestige enjoyed by such people depended to a considerable degree on their ability to provide essential services for their clients. Once the Israeli administration was installed, the ability of Palestinian patrons to meet the expectations of those who petitioned them depended crucially upon the goodwill of the officers in the civil administration. The Israelis thus became the patrons of the patrons, and the degree to which a local *mukhtar* could successfully perform his role as a go-between, obtaining permits and licenses for his constituents, depended ultimately on the quality of his relationships with the occupation authorities. Thus, one can identify another layer of Palestinian collaboration, the conditional collaborators who cooperated with the occupiers in the belief that they were serving the wider interests of their own community. Invariably, it was common knowledge that such people acted as informers, but it was accepted that generally the information they passed on was never of life-or-death significance. For the most part their collaboration was viewed as a necessary evil. Without their services, life would have been a lot more difficult for many Palestinian families trying to survive under occupation.

Among the ranks of the conditional collaborators one should include also the Palestinian civil servants and public officials who continued in office under the Israeli administration on the grounds that this was their professional duty and that the community needed their services.

While such conditional collaborators might have approached their dealings with the Israeli security services with distaste, others sought to derive personal benefit from their relatively privileged access to the occupation authorities. This was encouraged by the Israelis, and eventually it culminated in an effort to sponsor a collaborationist organization that was intended to undermine the influence of the PLO within the territories. This project involved the establishment of the Village Leagues in the early 1980s, when the prestige of the PLO was particularly low after its expulsion from Beirut following the 1982 Israeli invasion of Lebanon. The Israelis sought to invest certain conservative rural figures with considerable local powers, building upon the traditional tension between urban and rural dwellers in Palestine, and so weaning significant sections of the population away from their identification with the PLO.[6] In this they were only marginally successful, but there is no doubt that in a few localities, such as the Hebron area, the local leaders of the Village Leagues enjoyed considerable influence.[7]

Among the leading figures within the Village Leagues, there might well have been a few who believed that the long-term interests of the Palestinian people would be best served by bodies other than the PLO, and who saw their involvement with the Village Leagues in that light. Such people could be classed as collaborationists, patriotic traitors motivated by a deviant commitment to the welfare of their community. However, it would appear that such an altruistic stance was relatively rare. The majority were motivated by pure self-interest, and were referred to as profiteers (*'amil*) by their fellow Palestinians. Many had acted as informers for the Jordanians before 1967, and subsequently came under Israeli control. Under the patronage and protection of the Israeli security services, such people were able to exploit their compatriots, lining their own pockets and enjoying their status. One of the most odious forms of treachery with which some of them were associated was the sale of Palestinian land for Israeli settlements. Using their position within the community, they would trick or intimidate residents into signing away their property, which was then sold to Jewish dealers and developers.

In contrast with the quality of information passed on to the Israeli authorities by accommodationists and conditional collaborators, much of which was background knowledge, the unconditional collaborators approached their task in a far more active manner, seeking out information directly related to the immediate security concerns of the Israelis, infiltrating resistance groups, and identifying key activists. On the shoulders of such spies (*jasus*) lay the responsibility for the imprisonment and death of many who were active in the resistance.

Indeed, some became collaborators while imprisoned for resistance or criminal activities. There they joined the ranks of what Palestinians called "birds" (*'asafeer),* their role being to obtain the confidence and trust of new detainees and obtain details about the prisoners' resistance activities. This information would then be passed on to the Israeli security services.[8]

As in occupied Europe during World War II, the unconditional collaborators were hated and despised by most of the Palestinian population, but also they were feared. They acted as if they were above the law. Indeed, many of them were involved in criminal or antisocial activities ranging from theft and extortion to drug dealing and prostitution.

Collaboration During the Intifada

The Intifada has been depicted as a mass movement of civilian-based unarmed resistance against the Israeli occupation. At the heart of the uprising was an effort to undermine and transcend the structures of dependency that had tied Palestinians to Israeli rule. As such, it had an impact upon every aspect of life under occupation, not least the situation of collaborators.[9] It was directed and coordinated through a network of neighborhood committees under the guidance of a Unified National Command (UNC).

During the first couple of years of the uprising there was a remarkable feeling of national solidarity. As part of this sense of unity, the hand of forgiveness was extended even as far as the unconditional collaborators in their midst. Thus, 29 March 1988 was set aside as a "day of repentance" when collaborators were invited to "return to the national consensus on pain of the punishment due to them." Special gatherings were held in mosques for those who sought forgiveness for past sins and were prepared to vow to forsake collaboration.[10]

For those who spurned the possibility of reconciliation and rehabilitation, life became increasingly difficult. The surge in collective self-confidence that accompanied the uprising meant that people were no longer afraid of the traitors in their midst, especially since so many neighborhoods and villages were virtual "no-go" areas for the Israeli soldiers. In the most highly organized communities collaborators faced a graduated scale of sanctions, starting with a social boycott, followed by assaults on their property and person by the local strike forces. If this proved insufficient pressure to persuade them to repent or leave the neighborhood, then their homes and property would be firebombed. The ultimate sanction, assassination, was resorted to only after consultation with the Palestinian leadership outside the territories, and would be carried out by special hit squads.

The reluctance to resort to killing the unconditional collaborators was due to a number of factors. Certainly during 1988 and the first half of 1989 there was a real desire to provide them with every opportunity to return to the national fold. The UNC also wanted to avoid providing the Israelis with any opportunity to make propaganda about alleged PLO intimidation and so-called terror campaigns. There was also the desire to avoid the tragic deterioration that had characterized the Palestinian revolt of the late 1930s, which was torn apart by internecine conflicts between feuding clans and political groupings, with false charges of collaboration being leveled to discredit rivals and legitimize their elimination.

By the summer of 1989 this nightmare had become real. Before April 1989 the number of Palestinians killed for alleged collaboration, according to Israeli figures, was around 60. Most Palestinians felt comfortable with this, in the belief that the collaborators had received the appropriate punishment, arrived at through a just process in which they had been given every reasonable opportunity to repent. However, as spring turned to summer, the number of slayings increased dramatically. It was obvious that the fate of alleged collaborators was no longer being determined through any kind of due process involving graduated sanctions and referral to the outside leadership. Rather, local strike forces were kidnapping suspects, interrogating them, and killing them. They were acting as prosecutors, judges, and executioners. By the spring of 1990 more Palestinians were being slain by their fellow citizens than by the occupying forces.

The killings were part of a general decline in law and order within the Palestinian community that became apparent from mid-1989 onward. In part this was due to the unprecedented levels of economic hardship suffered during this period, but it also reflected an erosion of the capacity of the UNC to control and direct the young activists, who had been growing increasingly frustrated at the lack of tangible achievement in the struggle to throw off the Israeli yoke. A crucial factor in the creation of this political vacuum had been the mass arrests of the middle-level cadres of experienced activists who had been in a position to control the young hotheads of the streets.

The situation continued to deteriorate from the latter half of 1989 onward. What had started as a selective cleansing process directed by recognized political authorities deteriorated into a murderous, out-of-control purge, in which the fundamental human rights of suspects were blatantly and brutally abused. The increase in the killings is revealed by the following figures. During the first year of the uprising, 20 suspected collaborators were killed. During the second year, 1989, 150 were killed.[11] During subsequent years, up to 30 November 1993, the average number of Palestinians killed on suspicion of collaboration remained between 150 and 200 a year.[12] These relatively high numbers were the result of a twofold process: the intensification of the struggle against collaborators on the part of the strike forces and a broadening of the category of people deemed to be collaborators and deserving execution. Thus, in addition to the informers and the land dealers who were generally acknowledged to be traitors, the label of collaborator began to be applied to anyone who was suspected of undermining the national struggle. Included within this category were all kinds of deviants who contravened not just the criminal law but the established moral code of Palestinian society. Hence, the targets included not only pimps and pornographers, prostitutes and drug dealers, but also those suspected of such "immoral behavior" as adultery and homosexuality. The professed justification for such moral totalitarianism was the fear of *isqat,* the extortion and blackmailing of the moral deviants for the purpose of recruiting collaborators.

One outcome of this morality policing was that any woman who appeared to step beyond the narrow bounds of appropriate conduct within Palestinian society risked being denounced as a security threat or collaborator. According to one human rights report, "Women who did not behave as expected became vulnerable to attacks by Palestinian activists. These attacks included pouring acid on their bodies, throwing stones at them, threats, and even rape."[13]

In addition to the hundreds of women who were physically intimidated and attacked as punishment for their alleged "immoral" behavior, it has been claimed that over one hundred Palestinian women were killed on suspicion of collaboration during the six years of the Intifada up to December 1993. Of the 107 recorded deaths, 81 took place in the Gaza Strip, which undoubtedly reflected the relative strength of the Islamic factions.[14]

As part of their efforts to justify the killing of collaborators, and to convince the public of the guilt of particular suspects, groups would make audio and video recordings of confessions, which were then distributed throughout the underground communication networks that permeated Palestinian society during the Intifada. For people suspected of minor acts of collaboration, various forms of social boycott would be employed to isolate and stigmatize them, with a view to pressuring them into changing their ways. Other forms of exclusion included house arrest, being excluded from the family home, or being separated from the family for a set period. Breaking such exclusion orders would expose the suspect to more severe sanctions. Suspected collaborators were also subject to various forms of physical assault, ranging from physical beatings to shooting in the legs and, apparently, in the case of some men considered guilty of the moral corruption of young women, castration.

In an effort to restrain the activities of the masked youths, the Palestinian leadership in the occupied territories arranged for the safe passage of known collaborators from their village or neighborhood and relocation to an area close to Qalqilya, adjacent to the border with Israel. Collaborators who had put themselves beyond the pale, but sought redemption, would be asked to atone for their sins. They might be instructed to kill their Israeli "handler," or kill other collaborators as evidence of their sincerity in seeking readmission to the "national house." For others, the alternatives were starker: the choice between being remembered as a traitor or as a martyr. It has been alleged that a number of suicide bombers killed in raids against Israeli targets were collaborators, seeking to wipe the slate clean and atone for their treachery with their lives.

The other option available to collaborators was resettlement within Israel. During the Intifada a few hundred collaborators and their families relocated to one of the two protected villages established by the Israelis for collaborators, Fahmeh in the West Bank and Dahaniyeh in the Gaza Strip.[15]

The Circumstances of
Collaborators Under the Palestinian Authority

Unlike the experience in liberated Europe after World War II, the establishment of the PA was not accompanied by a mass purge of collaborators. This was due to a number of factors, not least the very real limitations on the powers of the PA with regard to functional authority and territorial control. Thus, as we have seen, while negotiating the various agreements that have marked the different phases of the putative peace process between Israel and the Palestinians, the Israelis have insisted that the Palestinian authorities refrain from prosecuting or persecuting "Palestinians who were in contact with the Israeli authorities." Moreover, even though the Palestinian justice minister claimed in 1995 that "collaborators must be arrested and put before the Palestinian court," the authority of the Palestinian judicial system with regard to security matters has not run beyond the population centers that lie within the control of the PA, the areas designated as Zone A under the various agreements.

During the early years of the PA, Palestinians in general were prepared to leave the apprehension and punishment of collaborators to the security forces. There was no large-scale incidence of revenge attacks. The general pattern seems to have been that as the Israelis withdrew from the main Palestinian population centers within Zone A, a token number of suspected collaborators was arrested to encourage others to surrender and pledge allegiance to the PA.[16]

A number of outright unconditional collaborators who could expect little mercy at the hands of either the Palestinian authorities or the Palestinian people relocated to Israel where, according to reports, they were made to feel unwelcome within their new neighborhoods, despised and discriminated against by both Arabs and Jews.[17]

A number of those who remained within the territories—no one knows how many—were recruited by one of the wings of the Palestinian security services. In the harsh world of state security there is an obvious logic in the Palestinian agencies concerned with internal security drawing on the expertise of experienced informers, rather than relying on untrained novices for information gathering and surveillance purposes. This is all the more understandable when one considers the pressure on the PA from Israel and other powers to monitor and control the activities of Palestinians opposed to the peace process in order to minimize the risk of violent assaults and bomb attacks against Israeli targets.[18]

Clearly the risk is that if people do not see justice being done, but rather the opposite—treachery being rewarded—they will take the law into their own hands. This has fed into the general sense of lawlessness that pervades the territories under the control of the PA, and the community resentment against the privileges enjoyed by former collaborators has contributed to the general seepage of legitimacy from the PA. This was brought home to me in 1995 when a former Intifada activist told me of his disgust at the manner in which one Gazan resident, a

well-known collaborator who had grown rich on the basis of the services he had performed for the Israelis, had ingratiated himself with the
new Palestinian regime by making large donations of money and land to
worthy causes. As a result he had been "rehabilitated" and enjoyed a
position of considerable influence under the PA. I was told that evidence of his new status was provided when Arafat had his photograph
taken alongside the hospital bed where the ex-collaborator was recuper-
ating after a failed attempt to assassinate him.[19] Since then, the standing
of the PA has been further diminished by revelations of wholesale corruption, financial malpractice, and the widespread abuse of basic human
rights.[20]

Here are two extracts from the files of a Palestinian human rights
agency that illustrate the manner in which the charge of collaboration
has been used by the Palestinian security services to abuse and violate
the human rights of those who fall into their clutches. The first is from
the testimony of a Gazan fisherman arrested in 1997, indicating the
manner in which personal enmity can lead to the arrest and torture of a
father of three children.

> I was accused of having connections with the Israeli intelligence. I
> hope that whoever has this document interrogates Abu . . . because he
> was a collaborator during the occupation. There was an enmity
> between him and me when he asked me during the occupation to put
> all those who were chased by the army in the launch. When I asked
> him for the money he threatened to put me in jail. He now works for
> the Palestinian . . . Force. I was forced to confess due to all the torture
> I was under.[21]

The second is taken from the testimony of a Gazan merchant accused of
acting as an informer for the Israelis.

> The General Intelligence accused me of buying rotten foodstuffs and
> bringing it to Gaza and spoiling the economy. I was accused of watch-
> ing the PA and collaborating with Israel, of transferring news to
> Israelis in the U.S. I was also accused of taking an Israeli ID and giv-
> ing information in return. During the interrogation I was told to buy
> my freedom for 100,000 Jordanian dinars. I was forced to confess due
> to the torture I was under.

One of the painful ironies to emerge from such accounts is that the people doing the torturing learned their "craft" as political prisoners of the

Israeli security services. Indeed, many refined their techniques in Israeli prisons, practicing on others what they had suffered at the hands of their interrogators. Here is an extract from a 1996 press release from two Palestinian human rights organizations after three Palestinian prisoners died in Israeli prisons after being tortured by their cell mates:

> Under the guise of "interrogating suspected collaborators" Palestinian prisoners are torturing fellow prisoners in the Megiddo military detention center in Israel. According to reports, the torture includes burning detainees with cigarettes, beatings with electrical wires, sleep deprivation, denial of food, placing objects under the detainees' nails, wrapping up feet and hands in plastic bags and igniting them, severe beatings, and torture methods used by Israeli interrogators—body-hangings, prolonged sitting in contorted positions and body-shakings. Afterwards the prisoners are subjected to humiliating and degrading treatment by the prisoners as they are forced to shave their heads, clean the tents and constantly make coffee for the detainees. Most of the torture victims are the younger prisoners under 20 years old.[22]

The abuse of due process extends beyond the torture of suspects to summary execution. Thus, in June 1997 three Palestinians alleged to have sold land to Israelis were kidnapped. They were bludgeoned to death and their corpses were left on public highways in the West Bank. It was presumed that the executions had been carried out by people associated with the Palestinian security services.[23]

When "justice" is administered summarily and without regard for the human rights of the suspect, then it feeds into a culture of violence. Sometimes this takes a completely perverted form that makes you want to weep. In August 1996, Palestinian police arrested three brothers who had killed their 22-year-old sister by forcing her to drink poison. She was married to a collaborator who had fled to Israel, and the brothers murdered her to defend their family honor![24]

In the absence of any due process, of course, people have no formal means of clearing the family name, no right of appeal, no recourse to law, and can be driven to seek their own vengeance. In 1998 Dr. Iyad Sarraj of the Gaza Community Mental Health Program pleaded for an end to the cycle of killing that had grown under the PA. He told of a young man called Yousif whose father had been stabbed to death on suspicion of being a collaborator during the Intifada. Seven years later Yousif was arrested and sentenced to death by a Palestinian military court for the killing of a Palestinian officer, the man who had killed his father. Dr. Sarraj went on to give two more illustrations. One was of a child who had witnessed the killing of his mother some years earlier. When he was old enough he joined one of the security forces, searched for the killer, and murdered him. The other case I shall quote at length as it illustrates the manner in which the sociopolitical order can be undermined by the failure of the Palestinians to develop an appropriate program for dealing with the problems posed by collaborators, showing how acts of violence can lead to cycles of revenge attacks and counter-violence that can spread through the community like a contagious disease.

> A few months ago Lieutenant Hassona was driving home in Deir al-Balah when he was stopped by a pedestrian and hit with a barrage of bullets. He died instantly. His killers were three neighbours from the Bheissi clan who were taking revenge for the killing of their son, Ibrahim, a few years earlier. Lieutenant Hassona's leaders had instructed him to kill Ibrahim because he was a spy. Ibrahim was a teacher and was shot dead in front of his pupils. . . . The killing of Hassona alarmed his comrades, other Fateh hawks . . . who are now officers in the Palestinian Preventive Security Forces. Two hundred of them went to the scene of Hassona's murder and threatened to wipe out the entire Bheissi clan. . . . Only a last minute intervention by police averted a massacre. A military court was rapidly formed and within three days people were sentenced to death and twelve others to various prison sentences. All the condemned were from the Bheissi clan. . . . The military judge defended the speedy trial and the sentence as important elements in appeasing the burning rage of the security forces and showing that the Authority can protect its own.[25]

Conclusion

It seems clear that there is a desperate need for a deep cleansing and healing operation within Palestinian society as a necessary component of the wider process of reconciliation and reconstruction required to heal the growing rift between the Palestinian "semi-state" and its citizens, and to counter the growing fragmentation and tribalization of Palestinian society. Iyyad Sarraj is one of a number of Palestinians who have called for just such a program.

> The legacy of the Israeli occupation and the Intifada is heavy and serious, and our tradition of revenge and our culture of violence are deeply rooted. The solution is not in military courts or in tribal *solha*

(reconciliation). It will take much more. . . . We need a community *solha,* an acceptance of grief and recognition of guilt. We need to begin the process of healing ourselves. We need scholars, leaders and concerned people to launch an initiative. And we need courage. But above all we need a state authority that applies the laws and acts as an example for us. People have to feel that they are equal before the law and that they are protected by the law, rather than by family or party connections.[26]

Of course any program for promoting community reconciliation within Palestinian society has to take account of the Israeli-Palestinian conflict that remains the unhealed wound at the heart of the Middle East. Various civil society initiatives to promote understanding and mutual tolerance between Israelis and Palestinians have been under way for decades, but these all take place in a context where the Israeli state has proven itself unwilling to risk any sign of weakness and has consistently sought to determine the pace and the substance of the peace process from its own position of strength. This asymmetric relationship has been replicated in its attempts to ensure the impunity of the perpetrators of human rights abuses among it own occupation forces. Thus, in July 1998 the Likud-led government introduced a bill to deny compensation to Palestinians injured by Israeli security forces. The bill retroactively defined all actions of the forces in the Occupied Territories as "combatant activity" and found these forces to be exempt from civil damage suits, thus ensuring that Israeli forces would not be held accountable for their human rights violations in the territories.

For understandable, if shortsighted, reasons Israel has not only sought to protect its security personnel from claims brought by Palestinians in their own courts; successive governments have also expressed their opposition to attempts to establish an international criminal court before which they might be summoned to account for the multiple violations of international humanitarian law committed during their years of occupying the West Bank, the Gaza Strip, and the other occupied territories such as the Golan Heights. The momentum to establish such a court has been growing in recent years and in the next chapter we will explore the significance of such third-party efforts to assist in pursuing justice, uncovering truth, and promoting reconciliation processes in societies traumatized by protracted and violent conflict.

Notes

An earlier version of this chapter was published in A. Rigby, *The Legacy of the Past: The Problem of Collaborators and the Palestinian Case,* Jerusalem: Palestinian Academic Society for the Study of International Affairs, 1997.

1. The same conditions apply to many states throughout the world, not least to the members of the European Union.

2. Heller, "Towards a Palestinian State," p. 9.

3. In the Cairo Agreement the Palestinian side committed itself "to solving the problem of those Palestinians who were in contact with the Israeli authorities. Until an agreed solution is found, the Palestinian side undertakes not to prosecute these Palestinians or to harm them in any way" (Cairo Agreement, Article XX, para. 4). Likewise, in the agreement of September 1995 the Palestinians vouchsafed that "Palestinians who have maintained contact with the Israeli authorities will not be subjected to acts of harassment, violence, retribution or prosecution" (Article XVI, para. 2).

4. Interview with author, 14 October 1995, East Jerusalem.

5. Interview with author, 15 October 1995, Nablus.

6. See Tamari, "In League with Zion," pp. 41–56.

7. See Hiltermann, *Behind the Intifada,* p. 97.

8. See *Collaborators in the Occupied Territories,* pp. 63–70. See also *Palestine Report,* 15 September 1995, p. 16.

9. See Rigby, *Living the Intifada.*

10. It is not clear how many of the unconditional collaborators took advantage of this opportunity for rehabilitation, but according to one well-informed observer, the number was low—to be counted in tens rather than hundreds. (Interview with Atieyeh Jwabrah, 12 October 1995, Nablus.)

11. *Collaborators in the Occupied Territories,* p. 163.

12. According to Israeli Defense Force figures, 942 Palestinians were killed by other Palestinians on suspicion of collaboration between 9 December 1987 and 30 November 1993. In the same period the Associated Press put the number at 771. See *Collaborators in the Occupied Territories,* p. 9. Much of the material presented in the following pages is based on this excellent report from the Israeli Centre for Human Rights in the Occupied Territories and upon information provided by Bassem 'Eid.

13. Ibid., p. 90.

14. Ibid., p. 90.

15. For a profile of life in Fahmah, see Batrawi, "Collaboration," pp. 10–11. See also Sarah Helm, "Peace Terrifies Arabs Who Sided with Israelis," *San Francisco Examiner,* 21 September 1993.

16. See reports in *Palestine Report,* 24 November 1995, p. 3, and 5 January 1996, p. 1.

17. There have been numerous reports in the Israeli and Palestinian press concerning the problems faced by Palestinian collaborators in trying to adjust to life in exile in Israel. See, for example, accounts in *Al Quds* (Arabic), 25 September 1995, and the Israeli newspaper *Haa'er,* 13 October 1995. In May

1998 the residents of Al Tireh within Israel demonstrated for the expulsion of collaborators from their midst, while the inhabitants of one village within the municipality of Jerusalem refused to accept the children of collaborators in their schools (*Palestine Report,* 11 May and 28 June 1998).

18. An obvious question concerns the relationship that these former agents of the Israeli security services have with their former masters, now that they are members of the Palestinian security agencies. This in turn raises the sensitive question of the relationship between the Palestinian and Israeli security services.

19. Interview with author, Gaza City, 17 October 1995.

20. See, in particular, David Hirst, "Shameless in Gaza," *The Guardian Weekly,* 27 April 1997, p. 8. See also Robinson, "The Growing Authoritarianism of the Arafat Regime," pp. 42–56.

21. I am grateful to Bassem 'Eid of the Palestinian Human Rights Monitoring Group for making copies of these testimonies available to me.

22. Press release from Law (The Palestinian Society for the Protection of Human Rights and the Environment) and Al-Haq, 25 November 1996.

23. *Palestine Report,* 13 June 1997, p. 14.

24. *Palestine Report,* 23 August 1996, p. 14.

25. Iyyad Sarraj, "Kill your neighbour!" *Palestine Report,* 25 September 1998.

26. Iyyad Sarraj, "Kill your neighbour!"

8

Third-Party Intervention

The prime focus of this book has been on the different means adopted by successor regimes to deal with the legacy of a painful past. In reviewing the different approaches it has been clear that governmental and nongovernmental third parties have played significant roles in the development and implementation of the different policies pursued. One of the clearest illustrations of this has been the effort by the Spanish judiciary to prosecute the Chilean dictator Pinochet for the human rights crimes committed against Spanish nationals during the period of military rule in Chile. We have also seen how the South Africans drew upon the experience of the Argentineans and Chileans in developing their own truth and reconciliation commission.

In both of these cases the role of the third parties, while significant, was essentially supportive and secondary to that of the successor regime and its citizens. However, in certain situations third parties have played the primary role in devising and implementing strategies for dealing with the horrors of the past. This chapter is devoted to a consideration of such cases.

Before presenting the case studies, however, we can begin to identify some of the key variables that tend to bring about efforts at "policing the past" implemented by outsiders rather than by indigenous institutions and groups. Generally speaking, we can say that to the degree that a successor regime lacks the material, financial, and human resources to pursue a means of coping with the past other than collective amnesia, the likelihood of outside agencies taking up such a role will be heightened.

Two additional sets of circumstances also seem to be relevant. First,

165

when a society emerges from a protracted period of violent conflict, particularly when the peace settlement has been signed because of mutual exhaustion and outside pressure, then there is likely to be no clear victor and very little trust between the parties to the settlement. In such situations there is little chance of the protagonists coming to an agreement over a joint approach to uncovering the history of the conflict or how to pursue justice against those responsible for criminal acts during the conflict. Both sides would have their own reasons for avoiding such a truth-telling/justice-seeking exercise, given the likelihood that neither had a monopoly on the abuse of human rights during the struggle. Furthermore, neither side would be likely to trust the motives and intentions of the other in such a process. Therefore, in such circumstances, one possibility is to hand the responsibility over to an outside agency or third party that all parties to the settlement trust sufficiently to endorse its involvement. In the case of Guatemala, which is examined below, the United Nations played such a role.

Second, when a country has been wracked by civil war and where charges of indifference, incompetence, and criminal neglect of moral and legal duties have been leveled at the international community for failing to intervene in a manner capable of curbing the slaughter, then pressure can grow for the UN or some other transnational body to establish not only a commission of inquiry into the circumstances surrounding the violations of human rights, but also a criminal court to prosecute those deemed responsible for war crimes and crimes against humanity. During the 1990s two such international criminal courts were established, one focusing on the war in Former Yugoslavia and the other upon the genocidal killings in Rwanda in 1994. Both of these cases are discussed in this chapter. They will be placed in the context of the growing movement for the establishment of a permanent international criminal court, a development seen by many as central to the global struggle against impunity, for it could mean that perpetrators might be apprehended and prosecuted for serious breaches of international humanitarian law wherever such crimes occurred—there would be no more safe havens for war criminals.

Guatemala

The truth commissions of Argentina and Chile examined in Chapter 4 involved investigations appointed by civilian governments following the transfer of power from repressive military regimes. Toward the end of the chapter it was suggested that such truth commissions could be considered relatively low-cost ways to bury significant aspects of the past. This same criticism can be leveled at similar exercises carried out by third parties as part of negotiated settlements to inconclusive civil wars. For example, as part of the January 1992 peace accords that brought an end to 12 years of brutal civil war in El Salvador, during which some 75,000 people were killed, a UN-sponsored investigatory commission was appointed. The three commissioners were eminent people from outside the country, appointed by the Secretary-General of the UN. They were given six months to investigate "serious acts of violence that had occurred since 1980 and whose impact on society urgently demands that the public should know the truth."[1] In their final report, published in March 1993, the commissioners condemned the violence of both sides in the war, but most of their findings dealt with the abuses committed by agents of the state and the death squads. They also identified some of the individuals responsible, much to the anger and disgust of the Salvadoran military. However, nothing came of this as within five days of the publication of the report a general amnesty was passed. It was clear that a deal had been struck and justice was sacrificed for the sake of political stability.

Four years after the conclusion of the civil war in El Salvador, the war in neighboring Guatemala came to an end. There, too, a truth commission sponsored by the UN was agreed upon as part of the peace process.

The civil war in Guatemala started in 1962 with the Rebel Armed Forces (FAR) taking up arms against an increasingly repressive government supported by the United States. It was a particularly brutal war. During more than three decades of fighting and killing that preceded the final peace accord of 1996, an estimated 100,000 people were killed, at least 25,000 disappeared, with around 1 million displaced. Most of these deaths, disappearances, and displacements took place during the late 1970s and 1980s when the Guatemalan army resorted to massacres of whole villages in response to the growing guerrilla threat. Those who escaped fled to the mountains, the cities, or into exile—in some regions half of the villages were abandoned with up to half of the local population killed.[2] For people living under army domination during those years, the atmosphere of fear and mutual suspicion promoted a pervasive "culture of silence." The main means of coping were keeping your head down, "not knowing," or rather knowing what not to know, forgetting, losing your memory, and silence.

During this period regional pressures for peace grew, with the Contadora Group of Mexico, Venezuela, Colombia, and Panama launching their initiative in January 1983. Although they failed to establish peace throughout the troubled states of Guatemala, El Salvador, and Nicaragua, their initiative did lay the foundations for subsequent interventions in 1986–1987 initiated by Costa Rican president Oscar Arias. Within five years the Guatemalan regime had agreed to peace talks with the guerrillas, and after a further five years of negotiations, the final peace accord was signed in Guatemala City on 29 December 1996. This Agreement on a Firm and Lasting Peace brought into effect six previous agreements reached over several years of UN-mediated peace negotiations. One of these was the Agreement on the Establishment of the Commission for the Historical Clarification of Human Rights Violations and Acts of Violence Which Have Caused Suffering to the Guatemalan People, signed in Oslo on 23 June 1994, which set out the mandate and terms of reference for the Historical Clarification Commission (CEH), which began its work in September 1997 by examining the period of internal armed conflict from 1960 to December 1996.

By December 1996, when the peace accord was reached, the guerrillas were down to about 3,500 members, and consequently were in no position to impose their demands relating to the issue of impunity. Hence, they went along with the 1996 Law of National Reconciliation, which established a new amnesty for the perpetrators of human rights abuses, much to the disgust of the civic opposition groups whose rank-and-file members had been targeted by the death squads.[3]

Such human rights and victim support groups had played an important role in monitoring military abuses, identifying clandestine cemeteries, and exhuming the remains of the victims of the death squads. In 1984 the Mutual Support Group (GAM) had organized a 100,000-strong march in Guatemala City and occupations of the legislature and the Justice Ministry to press their demand for a commission of investigation into the disappearances.[4] To counter this pressure the regime had created a tripartite commission composed of a conservative Catholic bishop, a military officer, and an official from the Ministry of Justice. Formed in 1985, it dissolved itself after a short life during which it produced no formal report, complaining that it could not locate any of the so-called disappeared! A year later the Supreme Court appointed a special judge to look into writs of habeas corpus, but when GAM filed over a thousand writs President Cerezo Arévelo broke off relations with the organization and canceled plans for a new presidential commission on the disappeared, claiming "We are not going to be able to investigate the past. We would have to put the entire army in jail. . . . Everyone was involved in violence. But this has to be left behind. If I start investigations and trials, I am only encouraging revenge."[5]

Following the publication of the Argentinean truth commission's report, human rights groups began to lobby for a similar body to be established in Guatemala. But, as the peace negotiations continued in various parts of the world during the 1990s, the influence of these groups waned. The result was that the Commission for Historical Clarification (CHC) agreed upon in June 1994 fell far short of their hopes and demands. Like that of its Salvadoran predecessor, the mandate of this UN-sponsored body was to investigate "past human rights violations and acts of violence that have caused the Guatemalan population to suffer." It also was to consist of three commissioners, although in this case they included two Guatemalans and the former UN human rights monitor in Guatemala. As in El Salvador the commissioners were given a very limited time, 12 months, to complete their investigations into decades of human rights violations. Furthermore, the Commission's powers were very weak. It was to have no right of subpoena and no power to search properties and seize relevant documents. Moreover, it was to operate in private behind closed doors, with the content and the source of evidence submitted remaining undisclosed. In addition, there was to be no identification of individual responsibility for violations, and the material discovered by the Commission's investigators could not be used in subsequent prosecutions.

Disappointed with the limited mandate and tempted to see it as a device to deflect the demands for justice coming from the survivors and the relatives of the victims, certain elements within Guatemalan civil society determined to initiate their own alternative truth commission. If the representatives of the international community were not prepared to uncover the systematic nature of the violence perpetrated against so many Guatemalan citizens, then civil society groups should take up the challenge. And it is in this response that the special nature and interest of the Guatemalan case lies, and what is particularly noteworthy is the crucial support role played by transnational civil society groups and networks in enabling their counterparts in Guatemala to establish their own alternative truth commission.

For a number of years human rights groups in Guatemala had relied upon civil society groups and organizations around the world for financial, moral, and political support. One of the most practical ways this was manifested was through the work of groups such as Peace Brigades International, which provided unarmed bodyguards to accompany human rights activists whose lives were threatened by death squads. With such outsiders alongside them the activists were able to enjoy a degree of relatively autonomous space within which they could pursue their human rights work.[6] Now Guatemalan human rights groups used their links with global civil society networks to obtain the necessary funding and support to launch their own investigatory commission. This was called the Interdiocesan Project for the Recovery of Historical Memory (REMHI) and was the initiative of the Archbishop's Human Rights Office (ODHA).

Assisted by funding from Europe and international aid agencies, REMHI established local offices throughout the country during 1995, using the church's extensive rural networks. The overall project was envisaged as a four-stage process.

1. Consciousness-raising among victims. REMHI delegates went to rural communities and informed people of the nature of the project and encouraged them to participate. Over 700 local *promotores* were recruited and trained to take statements.[7]
2. Collecting statements. Over a period of two years, more than 5,300 testimonies were recorded by the interviewers. While in some villages the REMHI staff had to counter the threats of military officials seeking to intimidate the villagers; in others it was clear that the former guerrillas had been urging people to report only military abuses and forget the crimes committed by the rebels.[8] Not all the testimonies were from victims and survivors; some perpetrators sought the opportunity to obtain some kind of relief from their troubled conscience.[9]
3. Processing and publishing the material. The tapes were taken to Guatemala City for transcription into Spanish and entry into REMHI's database, which formed the basis of the four-volume report *Guatemala, Nunca Mas,* which was published on 26 April 1998. It constituted the first national attempt at investigating the abuses committed during the years of armed conflict and documented over 55,000 human rights violations, with nearly 80 percent of them attributed to the Guatemalan military.
4. Disseminating the results. From the start REMHI staff had

believed that enabling survivors to tell their own stories would create a space where people could experience a new identity and sense of dignity—as citizens, people with rights, including the right to tell their own story and to be taken seriously. Therefore, REMHI organized literacy programs based on the people's own narratives to feed the stories back into the communities they came from. The hope was that in the process of collective truth telling and the reworking of social memory, significant steps would be taken away from the culture of silence and toward a new sense of community.[10] In the course of their work, the REMHI staff came across a number of mass graves throughout the country. Consequently, a significant element of their work was the construction of memorials to commemorate the names of the dead and disappeared.[11]

At the presentation of the report in Guatemala City's Metropolitan Cathedral, Bishop Juan Gerárdi, coordinator of ODHA, spoke of the REMHI project as the unveiling of the painful truth that was a crucial element in the necessary but difficult process of national reconciliation:

> It is a painful truth, full of memories of the deep and bloody wounds of the country. It is a liberating and humanising truth that makes it possible for all men and women to come to terms with themselves and their life stories. It is a truth that challenges each one of us to recognise our individual and collective responsibility and commit ourselves to action so that those abominable acts never happen again.[12]

Two days later, on the night of 26 April 1998, Bishop Gerárdi was murdered. Among the human rights community it was presumed that this was the work of groups associated with the Guatemalan security forces, intended as a warning to others. It was also a brutal reminder that a peace agreement does not mean the end of a conflict, and that a truth commission—whether it be the work of outsiders or insiders—does not constitute the whole of the peace process.

Uncovering the truth might be a necessary dimension of a reconciliation process, but it is not sufficient in itself. Alongside truth there needs to be some form of justice and an end to the killing if people are to come to terms with the horrors of the past and begin to move with their former enemies toward a shared future. Clearly, third parties, whether they be state or nonstate actors, can play a range of roles in supporting these processes. In the Guatemalan case we have seen how the UN sponsored a commission to uncover at least a part of the truth of the civil war years, but this did little to help the bulk of the victims of the violence come to terms with that past. It was the alternative truth commission, supported by outside funds and agencies, that focused more clearly on allowing people to express their own memories and stories, helping them in practical and symbolic ways to come to terms with their individual and collective pain and loss, so that they might live to shape a different future.

But what was missing from the whole Guatemalan process was any movement along the path of justice. In the examination of the South African truth and reconciliation process we saw how the notion of restorative justice encapsulated within the concept *ubuntu* was articulated by Archbishop Tutu and others as an answer to critics who complained about the failure to make the perpetrators pay for their crimes. We can be fairly certain that if South Africa had gone down the path of retributive justice, then the whole future of the country as a multiracial democratic state would have been undermined. But even if such fears were unfounded, there was also the belief that South Africa did not have the necessary financial or human resources to devote to the prosecution and trial of all those accused of human rights abuses. It was not a feasible project, given the circumstances in which South Africa found itself as it emerged from decades of apartheid-driven division and conflict.

In such a situation one possible outcome might have been to hand over the role of seeking justice to an outside body with the resources and the standing to pursue such a task. This is what happened on at least two occasions in the 1990s, when International Criminal Courts were established to prosecute the war criminals of the Bosnian conflict and the Rwandan genocide. In both of these cases, the intervention of the international community arose in part out of a sense of shame and guilt on the part of the major powers that they had not done all that they might have to prevent the occurrence of the war crimes in the first place. The commitment to prosecute the criminals was the least they could do in a situation where the parties to the respective conflicts were either unwilling or unable to pursue justice on their own behalf.

International Criminal Tribunals for Former Yugoslavia and Rwanda

In the early 1990s war returned to Europe, and it was fought with a barbarity not seen for decades. The war in Former Yugoslavia spread from

Slovenia to Croatia in 1991, and then to Bosnia in 1992. There, in continental Europe, concentration camps were established, members of particular ethnic groups or nationalities forcibly deported, towns and villages destroyed, women systematically raped, and civilians targeted in the name of ethnic cleansing. The war was fought without any respect for the rules of war established in the wake of World War II. There was no discrimination between combatants and noncombatants. In fact, the terrorization and expulsion of civilians was the main goal of the military offensives, aimed at cleansing territory of unwanted population groups and communities. During the four-year war it has been estimated that 250,000 died, 90 percent of them civilians. Some 2 million were displaced and 30,000–40,000 women were raped.

There was public outcry against what was happening in Bosnia. Scenes of horror were broadcast around the world and the demand grew that something must be done. Right from the start the major Western powers had sought to broker a sustainable ceasefire by means of diplomatic persuasion and economic pressure, but they were reluctant to send their own ground troops into a war that would undoubtedly cost them dearly in terms of soldiers' lives and where there was no consensus regarding the desired outcome of such intervention other than putting a stop to the killing.

The UN persisted in passing resolutions condemning the atrocities and calling for a ceasefire, but to little avail. In the meantime, disgust with the failure of the major powers to intervene in an effective manner grew. In response, and perhaps as a sop to criticism, a Commission of Experts was appointed to investigate the extent of war crimes in Former Yugoslavia.[13] In its interim report of 9 February 1993, the Commission called for the creation of an ad hoc international tribunal, and on 22 February the UN Security Council adopted Resolution 808, which instituted the International Tribunal for the Prosecution of Persons Responsible for Serious Violations of International Humanitarian Law Committed in the Territory of the Former Yugoslavia Since 1991 (ICTY). Basically, the UN and the international community were saying to the combatants and warlords in Former Yugoslavia, "We may not be willing or able to do anything to force you to stop the slaughter just now, but later we will hold you accountable for your actions."

During this period fears were mounting, particularly among international NGOs, about developments in the small central African country of Rwanda, which had been wracked by violence between its major ethnic groups since the 1950s. The majority Hutus had held political power since the early 1960s but in 1990 the regime was challenged by an invasion from Uganda by the Tutsi-led Rwandan Patriotic Front. In July 1992 a ceasefire was agreed to at Arusha, Tanzania, but the killing and the terror continued.[14] Following further negotiations in Arusha in April 1994, the Rwandan president was assassinated by extremist members of his own party when his plane was shot down as it prepared to land at Kigali airport. His death then served as a pretext to launch a campaign of genocidal terror against political moderates and ethnic Tutsis that resulted in some 800,000 deaths during the spring and summer months of that year. Local officials systematically organized the slaughter, implementing the instructions relayed through national and local radio for the *Interahamwe* ("Those who fight together") to continue the butchery.

While this was going on, UN peacekeeping forces on the ground stood by without intervening, as the world watched on television. In fact, as the slaughter intensified, the UN scaled back its force to a mere token presence, on the grounds that the peace agreement they were there to oversee was no longer valid. Once again the body that was intended to represent the international community had failed to meet the challenges posed by the post–Cold War world. To quote the assessment of one well-informed observer: "the member states of the UN Security Council failed the people of Rwanda: they failed to heed the warning signs of impending genocide; they failed to react promptly and appropriately once the killing started . . ."[15]

In the aftermath of the slaughter the exposure of the complicity of the major powers in the tragedy continued. World leaders offered their apologies and in July 1994 a contrite Secretary-General Boutros-Ghali promised the Rwandan people that the international community had not forgotten them and that those guilty of the atrocities would be rounded up and punished.[16] So it was that within a period of two years the UN Security Council created its second ad hoc tribunal. The International Criminal Tribunal for Rwanda (ICTR) was created by Resolution 955 on 8 November 1994. It was mandated to prosecute "persons responsible for genocide and other serious violations of international humanitarian law committed in the territory of Rwanda and Rwandan citizens responsible for genocide and other such violations committed in the territory of neighbouring states between 1st January 1994 and 31st December 1994."

The Precedent of Nuremberg

The two international criminal tribunals established in 1993 and 1994 were the first since the precedent set by the military tribunals at Nuremberg and Tokyo after World War II, although the idea of an international tribunal to hold individuals responsible for international crimes was widely discussed after World War I.[17]

The allies had made clear at the 1943 London Conference that they intended to prosecute war criminals after they had obtained the unconditional surrender of Germany. Although some urged that the captured German leaders be summarily executed, the dominant view was that putting them on trial would strengthen the rule of law and a culture of respect for the law over that of brute force. Hence, in August 1945 the London Agreement established the International Military Tribunal at Nuremberg and the three main categories of crime it was to enforce: crimes against peace (waging a war of aggression), crimes against humanity, and war crimes. A similar tribunal, the International Military Tribunal for the Far East, was set up in Tokyo to try Japanese officers and leaders.

The Nuremberg Tribunal initially charged 24 individual Germans, but subsequent trials brought to 185 the number prosecuted between December 1946 and April 1949. Of these, 25 received death sentences, 20 received life sentences, 97 received shorter prison terms, and 35 were acquitted.[18] The trials were criticized as travesties of justice on a number of counts. The prime charge was that it was a kind of victor's justice, a politically motivated process. The tribunal was established in the context of the complete surrender of the vanquished, and the victors subsequently drafted the laws, established the court, chose the judges, and selected those to be charged.[19] It was a selective form of justice insofar as no one among the Allies was charged with responsibility for such war crimes as the bombings of Dresden, Hiroshima, and Nagasaki. Moreover, the number of those who were charged was only a fraction of those who could have been indicted. Furthermore, some argued that these individuals were being prosecuted for acts that were more properly attributable to the state. However, this was one of the two key legacies left by the post–World War II tribunals—that the international community can hold individuals personally responsible for heinous crimes, even when committed in obedience to superior orders or in the service of the state. The other precedent established at Nuremberg and Tokyo was the establishment of a category of acts that were so abhorrent that they constituted crimes against humanity as a whole, and that humanity as a whole should take responsibility for bringing the perpetrators to justice. The message was that never again would genocide, wars of aggression, crimes against humanity, and war crimes go unpunished. But that promise was to remain unfulfilled.

Although in the years after Nuremberg the codification of war crimes and crimes against humanity proceeded apace, and the principle of individual accountability took root, there was no advancement in developing the means to enforce the principle.[20] The International Court of Justice at The Hague was restricted by its statute to jurisdiction of disputes between consenting states, while the Cold War rivalries sabotaged any possibility of establishing a permanent international tribunal or court with the powers to indict and try those deemed responsible for crimes against humanity. Both sides had too much to fear from an international body with the power and the legitimacy to prosecute its own nationals, and neither was prepared to consider any erosion of state sovereignty.

However, things began to change with the breakup of the Soviet Union, and the outrages committed in Former Yugoslavia and Rwanda aroused the Security Council to establish the two ad hoc tribunals.

ICTY and ICTR: The Practice and the Promise

As we have seen, there are strong grounds for believing that the establishment of the two tribunals was a political ploy by the UN Security Council members to deflect criticisms that they were not doing enough to curb the atrocities in Bosnia and Rwanda. The tribunals were, if you like, originally conceived for display and show, public symbols to indicate that the international community of sovereign states represented in the UN really did care about the crimes and would not let them go unpunished. This was the promise. The practice was to fall short of the noble intent. But despite the limitations of the tribunals' powers and practice, they have grown into powerful symbols for those campaigning for a permanent international criminal court, and therein lies their deeper significance.

From the start of the war in Former Yugoslavia, the prime concern of the major powers was to obtain a ceasefire and prevent the conflagration from spreading throughout southeastern Europe and beyond.

Eventually, a substantive ceasefire was secured in October 1995, and on 14 December the Dayton Agreement brokered by the U.S. diplomat Richard Holbrooke was signed. This commitment to establishing some kind of peace, in the sense of bringing a halt to the killing, conflicted with the declared commitment to the pursuit of justice embodied in the ICTY's mandate to indict and try the perpetrators of war crimes, genocide, and crimes against humanity, because the warlords who were in a position to deliver a ceasefire were the very people guilty of some of the most horrendous crimes committed during the course of the war. As one observer commented when the UN Security Council declared its intention of establishing a tribunal,

> By preparing war-crimes trials now, [the ICTY] may actually impede the faltering peace negotiations. After all, if the UN is ever to broker a durable peace in the old Yugoslavia, it will need the participation of some of the same politicians and commanders who now direct or tolerate the crimes of murder, rape, torture and ethnic cleansing.[21]

Indeed, in a situation where the Serbs had committed the bulk of the atrocities, but were also the dominant military power in the war, the tribunal was a real obstacle to peace. It was argued that the promise of a general amnesty would be a more appropriate initiative, insofar as it would constitute a powerful incentive for the military and political leaders of the different parties to agree to a peace settlement. There would not be much justice in such a program, but it might well save lives.

As a consequence of this dilemma, the permanent members of the Security Council backpedaled on the implementation of the ICTY. It took 14 months before the chief prosecutor, the South African Richard Goldstone, was appointed to the tribunal, while its budget for the first year was risible. The tribunal had no resources of its own to locate and arrest those who had been indicted; for this it was dependent upon the same states and organizations that were also responsible for implementing the Dayton Agreement. Moreover, it was the policy of the international troops on the ground not to engage in the pursuit of wanted suspects—their declared practice was only to apprehend indicted persons with whom they came into contact! This helped to explain why such arch war criminals as the Bosnian Serb leader Radovan Karadzic and his military commander Ratko Mladic could continue to live in the small town of Pale apparently without fear of capture.

This was all terribly frustrating to Richard Goldstone, and he was very direct in his condemnation, arguing that "if international justice is to be used as a cheap commodity only to be discarded when realpolitik so requires, then it would be preferable to abandon justice and leave victims to seek revenge in their own way."[22] The lack of support for the work of the tribunal was not just motivated by fears of upsetting the fragile peace process by threatening the warlords, it was also driven by a reluctance to reveal evidence of the complicity of international forces in some of the worst atrocities. For example, in July 1995 Dutch blue-helmeted troops in the "safe haven" of Srebenica allowed the Serbs under Mladic to take away and massacre some thousands of Muslim men and boys.[23]

One of the consequences of the lack of political will and the fear of destabilizing the peace process was that those accused who were arrested and transferred to The Hague for trial tended to be relatively low-level personnel. It was the *lampiste* phenomenon once again—the concentration-camp guards and others who actually carried out the rapes, tortures, and killing were apprehended, while their commanders were left untouched.

In Rwanda it was a similar tale.[24] Following the victory of the RPF, somewhere in the region of 120,000 Hutus and members of the *Interahamwe* were arrested and imprisoned to await trial and a possible death sentence for their involvement in the massacres. Meanwhile, the key architects of the genocide escaped across the border to the relative safety of the refugee camps in what was then Zaire, or to President Moi's protection in Kenya.[25] These were the people targeted by the tribunal in Arusha.

But like its counterpart in Europe, the ICTR got off to a painfully slow start. It took a year to open the headquarters in Tanzania. The first indictment was not issued until December 1995, and it was 1997 before the first trial got under way. There have been allegations of corruption, of the accused being denied proper access to defense lawyers, and inadequate witness protection arrangements. By late 1999 only 48 individuals had been indicted, of whom 10 remained at large, and only 5 cases had been concluded.[26] By March 2000 the ICTY had indicted 93 individuals, of whom 28 remained at large. However, in April 2000 one of the most senior Bosnian Serb leaders, Momcilo Krajisnik, was seized from his home in Pale and transferred to face trial at The Hague, leading some observers to conclude that the tribunal was developing its teeth and that the "big three" of Yugoslav President Slobodan Milosevic, Radovan Karadzic, and Ratko Mladic "must know by now that for them there is, ultimately, no hiding place."[27]

Toward a Permanent International Criminal Court

In April 1997 Richard Goldstone, referring to the two ad hoc tribunals, confessed that "if an assessment of their success is limited to a head count of high profile accused apprehended, convicted and punished, the number of suspects in the tribunals is insufficient justification for the expenditure and effort."[28] But he then went on to identify the broader significance of the tribunals—their contribution toward the eventual establishment of a permanent international criminal court.

As we have seen, both tribunals were ad hoc responses by the UN Security Council to the political pressure consequent upon the atrocities in Former Yugoslavia and Rwanda fed by the widespread perception that the international community had somehow failed the victims. The two tribunals remain open to charges of political motivation and selective justice. Why were Bosnia and Rwanda deemed sufficiently significant to justify international criminal tribunals and not Russia's genocidal action in Chechnya or the horrors of Algeria's civil war? Leaving this matter aside, the fact remains, as Benjamin Ferencz has pointed out, "Ad hoc courts, created *after* tragedies occurred, to punish a limited number of crimes committed in a limited area during a limited time, is not an ideal way to assure universal justice."[29]

Whatever their weaknesses, the two tribunals have contributed toward the momentum for the establishment of a permanent international court by demonstrating the possibilities of international enforcement. In 1998, 120 countries approved the Rome Statute calling for the establishment of such a permanent court. The debates and disagreements continue, particularly with regard to the degree of autonomy that its prosecutor should enjoy. There are considerable fears that if the court is made answerable to an unreformed Security Council, it will be dominated by the particularistic interests of the permanent members. Among those who failed to ratify the agreement, the United States refused to contemplate the possibility of any of its military personnel someday facing justice in a non-American court; China remained fearful of a court that might have the power to judge its repression in Tibet; and Israel feared that a clause relating to the settlement of civilian populations in occupied territories and the forcible dispossession and deportation of civilians would be used as a hammer against her.

So the struggle goes on, but the movement is gathering momentum and informed opinion estimates that by the end of the first decade of this millennium, the world should have a permanent international criminal court. But it still leaves a question concerning the relationship between peace, justice, and the possibilities for future reconciliation. While acknowledging that in certain circumstances the international community, as a third party, can intervene more or less effectively to ensure at least a modicum of justice against those guilty of gross abuses of human rights, and granted that this power is likely to increase with time, as national borders become ever more porous under the impact of the different processes that we label globalization, the question still remains whether such a form of retributive justice is the best way to help communities cope with wounds of the past and promote processes of healing as a foundation for the creation of some kind of shared future.

Arguing in favor of such a quest for justice are those who maintain that without the prosecution of, say, Serbs guilty of crimes against humanity, then there will be no way of breaking down the stereotypical image of all Serbs as rapists and torturers. Then we have no less a body than the British Foreign and Commonwealth Office proclaiming: "Justice is a precondition for reconciliation. A society cannot recover from the horrors of war or acts such as genocide if those who have committed atrocities are allowed to remain in office."[30] This might be true. Some form of justice (and not necessarily the kind administered by a criminal court, whether national or international in scope) undoubtedly is a necessary dimension of any reconciliation process. But justice on its own is not sufficient. There needs to be some shared commitment to move forward and let go of the past. This does not mean forgetting the pain, but learning to live with it in such a manner that it does not determine the future. For this to happen there needs to be some degree of confidence that the old days are really gone and will not return. And the only sound basis for that is the development of a new and resilient culture of respect for human rights and for human difference, a culture that is embodied in the everyday routines of life within the family, the school, the neighborhood, and the wider community. This is the focus of the next chapter.

Notes

1. See Popkin, "El Salvador," pp. 198–217.
2. For details of such incidents, see account by Sieder in *Impunity in Latin America*, pp. 62–64.

3. The exceptions to this amnesty were the perpetrators of torture, disappearance, and genocide.

4. GAM had been formed in 1985 by people trying to trace their lost relatives. It was composed predominantly of Mayan women.

5. Quoted in Amnesty International, *Guatemala*, p. 9 (http://www.amnesty.org/ailib/aipub/1998/AMR/23400298.htm).

6. See Mahony and Eguren, *Unarmed Bodyguards*.

7. Approximately two-thirds of these were Mayan and about 35 percent were women. Irma Graciela Azmitia Dorantes, presentation at Northern Kentucky University, 17 November 1997.

8. Paul Jeffrey, "Guatemala," p. 4.

9. This raises once again the problematic issue of distinguishing between perpetrators and victims.

10. Many villagers found it difficult to communicate their experience of violence and abuse in words, so they were encouraged to use other forms of expression, such as painting and other art forms. In seeking to re-present these accounts to the villagers, the *promotores* themselves relied on drama as a particularly effective means of uncovering the wounds in order to heal them. Dr. Edgar Gutierrez, executive director of REMHI, at *Burying the Past* Conference, St. Anthony's College, Oxford, 1998.

11. This included the construction of symbolic graveyards for the disappeared. The Mayans place great emphasis on communicating with their dead, so these were special sites where the bereaved could go to consult with those they had lost. They also trained paralegal workers to help survivors caught up in the bureaucratic maze relating to the disappeared. How can widows remarry when they cannot prove their husbands are dead because there is no corpse?

12. Quoted in "Human Rights Activists Fear Implications of Bishop's Murder," Witness for Peace Online Services, 14 May 1998 (www:/witnessforpeace.org/nwsmay14_98g.html).

13. The Commission eventually produced a report of 3,300 pages providing grounds for indicting several hundred suspected war criminals. It concluded that of all the war crimes committed in Bosnia, 90 percent were carried out by Serbs, 6 percent by Croats, and 4 percent by Muslims.

14. Part of the Arusha Accord allowed for the establishment of a commission of inquiry into past atrocities. Funded from European sources, a commission composed of 10 outsiders produced an initial report in 1993.

15. Sarah Westcott, in Waller, *Rwanda*, p. 70.

16. Ignatieff, *The Warrior's Honor*, p. 77.

17. Article 227 of the Versailles Treaty provided for an international tribunal to try the Kaiser for offending "international morality and the sanctity of treaties." Nothing came of this.

18. Shriver, *An Ethic for Enemies*, p. 248.

19. Chief Justice Stone of the U.S. Supreme Court characterized the tribunal as a "high class lynching party." Minow, *Between Vengeance and Forgiveness*, p. 30.

20. The 1948 Geneva Convention defined genocide and declared it an international crime. The Geneva Conventions of 1949 codified the rules of war,

and in 1950 the International Law Commission on behalf of the UN established the principle that "any person who commits an act which constitutes a crime under international law is responsible therefore and liable to punishment."

21. John Hay, quoted in Pearl, "Punishing Balkan War Criminals," p. 1403.

22. Quoted by M. Klarin, "Crisis Time in The Hague," *Tribunal,* no. 4, June/July, 1996, p. 2.

23. There is reason to believe that the Western powers knew what was happening at Srebenica through the pictures from the U.S. "spy satellites." In February 2000 the Mothers of Srebenica and Podrinja Association filed a criminal complaint with the ICTY against officials of the UN and others for their failure to intervene to halt the massacre. See http://www.domovina.net/complaint.

24. Both tribunals share a similar structure of two trial chambers and one appeals chamber.

25. Many of the "genocidaires" established themselves as leaders in the refugee camps, which became safe havens for some of the most wanted war criminals. In 1997 President Moi came under international pressure to change his position, and subsequently a number of the criminals were arrested. See L. Hilsum, "Rwanda—Refugees and Genocidaires," in Gutman and Rieff, *Crimes of War,* pp. 316–318.

26. Human Rights News Service, *The International Criminal Tribunal for Rwanda After Five Years* (www.publicedcenter.org/rwanda.html).

27. Editorial comment, *The Guardian,* 10 April 2000.

28. Goldstone, "War crimes: Linking peace with justice," p. 12.

29. B. Ferencz, "Getting Aggressive About Preventing Aggression" (www.igc.org/icc/html/ferencz199907.html).

30. FCO Annual report on Human Rights, April 1998, quoted by Ian Black, "Dictators in the Dock," *The Guardian,* 3 June 1998.

9

Toward a Culture
of Reconciliation

In concluding this overview of the different means by which successor regimes attempt to tackle the legacy of human rights abuse and other crimes left by their predecessors, a number of points must be borne in mind relating to the possibilities for eventual reconciliation between victims and perpetrators.

1. The necessary conditions for reconciliation between formerly antagonistic parties can only be realized over time. Moving beyond the divisions of the past is a multidimensional process that can take generations, and the different constitutive elements involved in the journey toward reconciliation can rarely be pursued all at the same time.
2. In the efforts to promote reconciliation it is crucial that the process should not be confined to a narrow strata of society. The different dimensions and values that together contribute to any healing process must be deepened and broadened to encompass all levels of society, creating in the process a new culture of respect for human difference and human rights—what some might term a culture of peace as opposed to a culture of violence.

Reconciliation Takes Time

As we have seen, the means by which successor regimes attempt to come to terms with a painful legacy of conflict and criminal abuse depend very much on the balance of power during the period of transition. Thus, following the defeat of the Axis forces in Europe in 1945, the victors had no qualms about seeking various forms of retributive justice against those who had collaborated with the occupiers and thereby betrayed their fellow citizens. In contrast, wherever the transition has been negotiated rather than imposed, some kind of amnesty is almost inevitable, particularly if the parties to the settlement continue to possess the capacity to shatter the peace. The consequent fragility of the transition process and the vulnerability of the new institutions mean that some form of amnesty is the price that has to be paid for the peace and stability necessary for the new regime to establish itself. After all, why should anyone relinquish power, if as a consequence they will face criminal prosecution and subsequent loss of privilege and position?

But while peace and a general feeling of personal security (all matters of degree) are necessary conditions for sowing the seeds of reconciliation between erstwhile enemies, they are clearly not sufficient in themselves. Drawing on the framework developed by John Paul Lederach, we can identify three other values that need to be present for reconciliation as a process and a condition to reach fruition: truth, justice, and mercy/forgiveness. But these values are invariably in tension with one another.

Perhaps the clearest conflict is between the values of peace and justice. There is a strong argument that before justice can be sought against perpetrators of abuse from a previous regime, the foundations need to be laid for a new order that is free from the immediate risk of violent intervention by those threatened by such a search for justice. Thus, although people might criticize the transition from military rule in countries like Argentina and Chile for the manner in which the perpetrators continued to enjoy impunity, it has to be acknowledged that during the initial phases of such negotiated processes the prime commitment should be to the broadening and deepening of the peace, so that people can grow accustomed once again to living their lives without undue fear of state violence and arbitrary terror. In such situations it is not feasible to pursue peace (in the sense of an end to killing and arbitrary abuse) and justice with equal vigor at the same time.

We have also seen how the threat of indictment and trial against those who violated people's human rights can conflict with the quest for truth. People are unlikely to reveal the full extent of their involvement in, and knowledge of, crimes and abuses without some kind of prom-

ised immunity from punishment—otherwise, why should they incrimi-
nate themselves? We have seen how the South Africans tried to manage
this tension by making amnesty conditional on full disclosure.

But we also know that amnesties for the criminals responsible for
torturing, killing, and damaging their fellow citizens are deeply offensive, not only to the victims and survivors, but also to many bystanders
and third parties. Somehow, we feel, such people should pay for their
crimes in some way. They should not be allowed to continue their lives
as if nothing untoward had happened. So once again we come up
against a clear and painful tension—between the value of forgiveness/
mercy, as institutionalized in amnesties and pardons, and the value of
justice.

Yet these values, which rest so uneasily alongside each other, are
the constitutive elements of reconciliation as a process and a condition.
So those seeking to create or restore social harmony between former
antagonistic parties and sectors of society are faced with a genuine
dilemma of how to manage and cope with such tensions. A number of
hypothetical options offer themselves.

First, the new political leaders can settle for an imperfect process,
lowering their aim from achieving social harmony to that of peaceful
coexistence and an end to the violent conflict. Typically this is pursued
by requiring the victims and survivors of abuse to forfeit their claimed
right to restitution. Like the victim in the bicycle reconciliation story
from South Africa, they are asked to accept their loss and the injustices
suffered for the sake of national reconciliation. Sometimes the painful
pill might be sugared by offers of material compensation and symbolic
reparations as a substitute for, rather than a complement to, retributive
justice.

Second, key figures and opinion leaders can attempt to redefine the
values, and invest new meanings in old terms. They can start to talk
about restorative justice, or *ubuntu*, as a higher value than the vengeful
quest for retribution.

Third, people can acknowledge that processes of reconciliation take
a long time to come to any kind of fruition, recognize that the relationships between the constitutive values are fundamentally problematic,
and realize that the only way forward is to pursue these values in
sequential phases. I want to explore this approach in a little more detail
by means of an ideal-typical model of such a phased reconciliation
process, one that might be pursued in societies emerging out of division

and a history of human rights abuse where the perpetrators still control significant resources that could undermine the stability and resilience of the new regime.

Stage One: Securing the Peace

Peace, in the sense of people being able to enjoy a degree of personal security, is the fundamental grounding necessary for the pursuit of the other values. But it is only a first stage. One of the main points that has struck me during the research and writing of this book has been that no matter how war criminals and others might try to keep the past covered up, the struggle to expose their dirty history continues in one form or another. But this pursuit of truth can only take place in a context where the peace is considered to be resilient enough to withstand efforts to uncover the pains of the past.

As long as people remain vulnerable to gross human rights violations and perpetrators feel able to act with impunity, there is no possibility of any movement along the reconciliation pathway. The prime requirement before all else is that the killing, the arbitrary arrests, the disappearances, the torturing of prisoners, and the illegal persecution of individuals and groups become a matter of history and not an ever-present threat.

Stage Two: Uncovering the Truth

At the heart of reconciliation is the preparedness of erstwhile enemies to anticipate a shared future either with or alongside each other. This requires a profound redefinition of one's personal and collective identity vis-à-vis "the other," a transformation from "us" versus "them" and "victims" versus "perpetrators," toward a new definition and relationship that acknowledges difference but on the basis of a shared identity as survivors and as human beings. But for this to happen, for people to move on so that they are no longer imprisoned within the past, they need to know what happened to their loved ones. Those who have suffered wrongs, trauma, and bereavement need to feel that their pain and loss have been appropriately acknowledged—their truth needs to be heard and validated.

In the first instance, the nature and the degree of truth revealed will be determined primarily by the alignment of forces at the time of the transition. But the kind of uncovering exercise that is finally attained will reflect the changing balance of power within the society. Crucial in this calculus is the increasing resilience of the peace, and the determination of victims and survivors not to relinquish the struggle to broaden and deepen the parameters of publicly acknowledged truth.

Stage Three: Approaching Justice

There is, of course, a fundamental injustice in not knowing what happened to one's loved ones, in not having one's history acknowledged. And justice is another value that needs to be woven into the reconciliation process; in the quest to lay bare aspects of the painful past, a kind of justice can be approached by identifying the perpetrators deemed responsible for abuses and violations. Naming involves shaming, and that is a form of justice that challenges cultures of impunity by making perpetrators pay some kind of penalty for their past actions.

This might not be feasible during the early phase of a transition, as the risk to peace and the new democratic structures from those threatened by such exposure might be too great. However, with the passage of time, as the democratic culture takes firmer root, as the fears of a return to the past decline and people gain confidence in their reclaimed rights, so the struggle to name and shame the perpetrators can continue, along with the insistence that they should make recompense in some way or another for their evil. This can pass from one generation to the next, as we have seen in the case of the *Hijos* in Argentina—the sons and daughters of the disappeared and their supporters who refuse to allow the former torturers and death squad members to live their lives without facing up in some way or another to the enormity of their guilt.

We should also recognize the potential significance of third parties in ensuring that the struggle for justice continues. Thus, Argentinean torturers and murderers responsible for the disappearance and deaths of foreign nationals have found themselves facing international arrest warrants. The case of General Pinochet has been another to catch the headlines. Pinochet was pursued by a Spanish magistrate, placed under house arrest in Britain, and eventually returned to Chile a broken man to face legal challenges to his self-awarded immunity from prosecution.[1] Meanwhile, the movement for a permanent international criminal court continues to gather momentum, and it is perhaps not too far-fetched to believe that someday those guilty of war crimes and crimes against humanity will be unable to stray beyond their safe havens for fear of arrest and the prospect of being brought to trial.

.   But beyond such efforts to pursue some form of justice in the retributive, eye-for-an-eye sense, there is perhaps a more important justice-related quest necessary if people are really to put the past behind them and focus on the future—a sustained effort at restitution and putting things right. If people are to have genuine hope for the future, then it is vital that serious efforts are made to change those structures and circumstances within which folk live their lives that repeatedly remind them of what they suffered. Only when the institutions that embodied and perpetrated the divisions of the past have become a matter of memory will people be in a position to let go of their grievances and pain, relinquish the impulse for revenge—forgive the past, if you like—and begin to anticipate a shared future.

Stage Four: Putting the Past in Its Proper Place

It is a old cliché—"time is a great healer." Certainly, the passage of time allows the past to be reinterpreted, imbued with new meanings. As the perpetrators of past abuses grow older and realize that the world they once knew has changed, they can be moved to regret their crimes and apologize for the pain and grief they caused. Thus, in August 2000 the Guatemalan president, Alfonso Portillo, acknowledged that the government had been responsible for tens of thousands of killings and kidnappings during the civil war, saying: "We have recognised that the state committed human rights abuses. We are doing this today so that the dramatic history we have lived through isn't repeated."[2]

Such formal acknowledgments and apologies can act as powerful levers in the process of laying the past to rest. As Michael Ignatieff has remarked, "Leaders give their societies permission to say the unsayable, to think the unthinkable, to rise to gestures of reconciliation that people, individually, cannot imagine."[3] By acts of apology, opinion leaders can open up the symbolic space where victims and survivors can begin to cast the past in a new light, relinquishing the quest to settle old scores, and begin to focus on the future. In this manner, as the pain of loss ceases to be ever-present, so people are capable of coming to the conviction that they should honor, rather than avenge, the memory of their loved ones by committing themselves to creating a new future rather than perpetuating the cycle of vengeance and violence.

Toward a Culture of Reconciliation

The four-stage process outlined above is, of course, completely hypothetical. There can be no universal prescriptive guide as to how people can begin to move on to escape the tyranny of the past. Moreover, the analysis has been pitched at the macro level of societies emerging out of division and destructive conflict, but societies and communities are made up of individuals, people who are embedded in their primary groups and social networks. What might be portrayed as some kind of collective movement is composed of the sum of the new relationships that people manage to create, not only with their past, but with their neighbors and with their former enemies.

There are no grounds whatsoever for expecting the members of any divided community or society to move as a unitary whole along the pathway to new relationships. We all have our own ways of coping with pain and with hurt. Some advanced souls can forgive the evildoer even as their person or their rights are being violated, while most of us would still be blinded by rage and the desire for revenge.[4] But time is a medium for a kind of healing. Those of us who have lived long enough know that the intensity of hate feelings, the drive for revenge and retribution, can fade with time. We know that eventually it even becomes possible to detect signs of humanity in those we have hated and despised, and with this comes the capacity to distinguish degrees of guilt and culpability. In this manner the bonds of the past can be loosened, and people who once defined themselves as victims can begin to orient themselves toward the future.

But for this to happen, for former victims to begin to envision a new life alongside their former persecutors, they must have some degree of hope—for a future where victim and perpetrator can reclaim their humanity. Such a hope, if it is to be realistic, must be based on a degree of trust that the evils of the past will not return. People must be confident that things are moving in the right direction, and this requires a change in the old structures and institutional arrangements within which people were cast as victims and perpetrators, "us" and "them." In other words, it is vital that the pursuit of the values of peace, truth, justice, and forgiveness is not confined to some symbolic realm removed from the everyday lives of the people at the grassroots. It must be embodied and lived out in new relationships between people at all levels of society. Here I am reminded of the respondent to a survey in South Africa who complained that reconciliation was something she saw happening on the television screen at the hearings of the truth and reconciliation commission; it was not something that people like her experienced in their own communities and neighborhoods.[5]

Some years ago I attended a Peace Studies conference in Austin, Texas. There I met someone who taught a course on genocide, and she explained how she would commence by asking her students to consider the different ways they dealt with people begging on the street, remarking on how some folk avert their gaze, ignoring the presence of the panhandler. The point she was trying to convey was that the seeds of the most horrendous crimes against humanity do not start "out there." They have their origins in the denial of the full humanity of the stranger, the nonrecognition of the other as a human being. That lesson has stayed with me, illustrating as it does the causal relationship between our mundane everyday actions and the mass crimes that are beyond the comprehension of most of us.

So it is that the cultures of violence and vengeance, which reproduce the hatreds and grievances of yesteryear and transmit them from one generation to the next, have their roots in everyday life—in the home, the school, the workplace. And it is at this level that the seeds for a durable reconciliation process must be sown, by means of a counterculture that embodies those values that are at the heart of reconciliation: peace, truth, justice, and forgiveness.

Culture of Peace/Nonviolence

Conflict is endemic in each and every sphere of life. Out of conflict come change and innovation, but it can also be ruinous and negative. In societies emerging from violence and division, it is crucial that the value of nonviolence is acknowledged and embodied in the different institutional spheres to avoid a collapse into the ways of the past. As Michael Ignatieff has so eloquently remarked:

> Reconciliation must reach into the shared democracy of death to teach the drastic nullity of all struggles that end in killing, the unending futility of all attempts to avenge those who are no more. For it is an elementary certainty that killing will not bring the dead back to life.[6]

Culture of Truthfulness

The different parties to a conflict each have their own history, and people do not relinquish their collective memory easily, as it invariably constitutes such a key component of their collective identity. However, to ensure that rival narratives do not fuel future conflicts, it is vital that people learn to acknowledge the validity of other people's truths. This is a reciprocal process—it is far easier to render respect to the history of others, if they in turn respect one's own. In acknowledging the reality of the other's history, even when you view the past through a different lens, the basis for a kind of organic solidarity embodying a fundamental respect for difference can be laid. But this requires people to face up to the flaws in their own past, to acknowledge the reality of the grief and remorse of the other, to begin to realize that the old Manichean division between "us" and "them," good and evil, is fundamentally flawed. This is why public memorials and commemorations can play such an important role as safe symbolic spaces where competing versions of the past can be represented. Moreover, in the competition between rival histories, commemorated in different locations and on different days, there is always the possibility that new constructive meanings can be attributed to old divisive memories, meanings that emphasize a shared victory over the bitterness of the past.

Culture of Justice

In recent years Hans Kung has written a lot about the golden rule that he claims to be present in all the major religious belief systems—"Do not do to another what you would not want to be done to you."[7] This moral imperative is of course central to notions of right behavior. It might be an unattainable ideal, but this does not weaken its significance as a guide to those seeking to establish just relationships in and throughout society. In this regard it bears repeating once again that if people are to focus more on their hopes for the future than upon their fears of the past, they must be able to experience significant movement to counter the inequalities and injustices that fueled the old divisions.

Culture of Forgiveness

Perpetrators have no right to expect forgiveness from those they have abused. Forgiveness, in the sense of relinquishing the quest for revenge, is the prerogative of the victim/survivor. But in exercising that power, such people can liberate themselves, escape the grasp of the past, and become more fully human.

At the core of such a difficult process is the capacity to distinguish between the perpetrator and their deeds, and this in turn requires some recognition of the humanity of the other, however difficult this might be. But it is in this acknowledgment of our common humanity that the seeds of a shared future lie.

Notes

1. In August 2000 the Chilean Supreme Court finally stripped Pinochet of his immunity from prosecution. In May 2000 formal charges were made against three leading figures of the Guatemalan government alleged to be responsible for some of the worst massacres of the civil war during 1981–1982. This followed the charges of genocide against six military and civilian leaders in the Spanish courts by the Nobel Peace Laureate Rigoberta Menchu. See D. Campbell, "Justice in Sight for Guatemalan Victims," *The Guardian,* 20 May 2000.

2. *The Guardian,* 11 August 2000.

3. Ignatieff, *The Warrior's Honor,* p. 188.

4. Gandhi, for example, believed that nonviolence and forgiveness were the supreme attributes of the brave, although violence was preferable to cowardice. Hence, "Nonviolence is not a cover for cowardice, but it is the supreme virtue of the brave. . . . Nonviolence, therefore, presupposes the ability to strike. It is a conscious deliberate restraint put upon one's desire for vengeance. But vengeance is any day superior to passive, effeminate and helpless submission. Forgiveness is higher still." ("Has Non-violence Limits?" *Young India,* 12 August 1926.)

5. It is interesting to note that in Australia, the Council for Aboriginal Reconciliation has called for four national strategies aimed at broadening and deepening the reconciliation process between the indigenous peoples and all other Australians, which include strategies to overcome disadvantage and to promote the economic independence of the Aboriginal and Torres Strait Island peoples. For further details about the Australian reconciliation process and "Corroboree 2000," see http://www.reconciliation.org.au.

6. Ignatieff, p. 190.

7. See, for example, Kung and Schmidt, *A Global Ethic and Global Responsibilities.*

Bibliography

Adams, K. A., "What Is Just? The Rule of Law and Natural Law in the Trials of Former East German Border Guards," *Stanford Journal of International Law*, v. 29, 1993, pp. 272–314.

Alfonsín, R., "Never Again in Argentina," *Journal of Democracy*, v. 4, n. 1, 1993, pp. 15–19.

Americas Watch, *Human Rights and the "Politics of Agreements" : Chile During President Aylwin's First Year*, Washington, D.C., 1991.

Amnesty International, *Chile: The Inescapable Obligation of the International Community to Bring to Justice Those Responsible for Crimes Against Humanity Committed During the Military Government in Chile* (AMR 22/16/98), 29 October 1998.

Amnesty International, *Guatemala: All The Truth, Justice for All* (AMR 34/02/98), April 1998.

Andenoes, Johs, "La Répression de la Collaboration Avec L'Ennemi en Norvège," *Revue de Droit Penal et de Criminologie*, v. 27, part 7, April 1947, pp. 589–606.

Arendt, Hannah, *The Human Condition*, New York: Doubleday Anchor, 1959.

Arnold, J. C., *The Lost Art of Forgiving*, Farmington, Pa.: Plough Publishing, 1998.

Ash, T. Garton, *The File: A Personal History*, London: Flamingo, 1997.

Bacic, R., "Reflections on Responsibility, Impunity and Hypocrisy," *Peace News*, 7 December 1998, p. 8.

Batrawi, Walid, "Collaboration: Was It Worth It?" *Palestine Report*, 23 April 1995, pp. 10–11.

Boraine, A., "Alternatives and Adjuncts to Criminal Prosecutions," paper delivered to symposium on *Justice in Cataclysm: Criminal Tribunals in the Wake of Mass Violence*, Brussels, 20–21 July 1996.

Boraine, A., and J. Levy, eds., *The Healing of a Nation?* Cape Town: Justice in Transition, 1995.

Boraine, A., et al., eds., *Dealing with the Past: Truth and Reconciliation in South Africa*, Cape Town: IDASA, 1994.

193

Buruma, Ian, *The Wages of Guilt: Memories of War in Germany and Japan*, London: Jonathan Cape, 1994.

Carr, Raymond, and Juan Pablo Fusi, *Spain: Dictatorship to Democracy*, London: Allen & Unwin, 1979.

Chandler, Raymond, "The Simple Art of Murder," in *Pearls Are a Nuisance*, Harmondsworth: Penguin, 1977.

Cohen, S., "State Crimes of Previous Regimes: Knowledge, Accountability and the Policing of the Past," *Law and Social Inquiry, Journal of the American Bar Foundation*, v. 20, n. 1, 1995, pp. 7–50.

Collaborators in the Occupied Territories: Human Rights Abuses and Violations, B'Tselem (Israeli Information Centre for Human Rights in the Occupied Territories): Jerusalem, 1994.

Constable, Pamela, and Arturo Valenzuela, *A Nation of Enemies: Chile Under Pinochet*, New York: W. W. Norton, 1991.

Conway, Martin, *Collaboration in Belgium: Leon Degrelle and the Rexist Movement*, New Haven: Yale University Press, 1993.

Dorfman, Ariel, *Widows and Last Waltz in Santiago*, London: Hodder & Stoughton, 1997.

Evans, M., and K. Lunn, eds., *War and Memory in the Twentieth Century*, Oxford: Berg, 1997.

Feijoó, M. del Carmen, "The Challenge of Constructing Civilian Peace: Women and Democracy in Argentina," in J. S. Jaquette, ed., *The Women's Movement in Latin America: Feminism and the Transition to Democracy*, Boulder, Colo.: Westview, 1991.

Ferencz, B., "Getting Aggressive About Preventing Aggression," *The Brown Journal of World Affairs*, Spring 1999.

Fisher, Jo, *The Mothers of the Disappeared*, London: Zed, 1989.

Frost, Brian, *Struggling to Forgive: Nelson Mandela and South Africa's Search for Reconciliation*, London: Harper Collins, 1998.

Galtung, Johan, "Violence, Peace, and Peace Research," *Journal of Peace Research*, v. 16, n. 3, 1969.

Givskov, C. C., "The Danish Purge Laws," *Journal of Criminal Law*, v. 39, 1948, pp. 447–460.

Goldstone, R., "War Crimes: Linking Peace with Justice," *Amnesty*, September/October 1997, p. 12.

Gutman R., and D. Rieff, eds., *Crimes of War: What the Public Should Know*, New York: W. W. Norton, 1999.

Hamber, B., ed., *Past Imperfect*, Derry/Londonderry: INCORE, 1998.

Havel, Vaclav, "The Power of the Powerless," in Vaclav Havel, *Living in Truth*, London: Faber & Faber, 1989.

Hayner, Priscilla, "Fifteen Truth Commissions—1974 to 1994: A Comparative Study," *Human Rights Quarterly*, n. 16, 1994, pp. 597–655.

Heller, M., "Towards a Palestinian State," *Survival*, v. 39, n. 2, Summer 1997, pp. 5–22.

Hiltermann, J. R., *Behind the Intifada: Labor and Women's Movements in the Occupied Territories*, Princeton: Princeton University Press, 1991.

Honwana, A., "The Collective Body," *Track Two,* v. 8, n. 1, July 1999, pp. 30–35.

Hooper, John, *The New Spaniards,* Harmondsworth: Penguin, 1995.

Huntington, Samuel, *The Third Wave,* Oklahoma City: University of Oklahoma Press, 1993.

Ignatieff, Michael, *The Warrior's Honor,* London: Chatto & Windus, 1998.

Jaquette, J. S., *The Women's Movement in Latin America: Feminism and the Transition to Democracy,* Boulder, Colo.: Westview, 1991.

Jeffrey, Paul, "Guatemala: Healing Through Remembering," *New Routes,* n. 3, 1997, pp. 3–6.

Jelin, Elizabeth, "The Politics of Memory: The Human Rights Movement and the Construction of Democracy in Argentina," *Latin American Perspectives,* v. 21, n. 2, Spring 1994, pp. 38–58.

Kari, Leo, *De Danske Spaniensfrivillige,* Copenhagen: Rosenkilde og Bagger, 1952, pp. 187–194.

Klass, Dennis, Phyllis Silverman, and Steven Nickman, eds., *Continuing Bonds: New Understandings of Grief,* Washington, D.C.: Taylor & Francis, 1996.

Kritz, Neil J., ed., *Transitional Justice: How Emerging Democracies Reckon with Former Regimes, vol. 2: Country Studies,* Washington, D.C.: U.S. Institute of Peace, 1995.

Krog, Antjie, *Country of My Skull,* London: Jonathan Cape, 1998.

Kung H., and H. Schmidt, eds., *A Global Ethic and Global Responsibilities,* London: SCM Press, 1998.

Lederach, John P., *Building Peace: Sustainable Reconciliation in Divided Societies,* Washington, D.C.: U.S. Institute of Peace, 1997.

Littlejohn, David, *The Patriotic Traitors: A History of Collaboration in German-Occupied Europe, 1940–45,* London: Heinemann, 1972.

Macdonald, N., *Homage to the Spanish Exiles: Voices from the Spanish Civil War,* New York: Insight Books, 1987.

Mahony, Liam, and L. E. Eguren, *Unarmed Bodyguards: International Accompaniment for the Protection of Human Rights,* West Hartford, Conn.: Kumarian Press, 1997.

Mason, H. L., *The Purge of Dutch Quislings: Emergency Justice in the Netherlands,* The Hague: Martinus Nijhoff, 1952.

Mignone, E. F., C. L. Estlund, and S. Issacharoff, "Dictatorship on Trial: Prosecution of Human Rights in Argentina," *Yale Journal of International Law,* v. 10, 1985.

Minow, Martha, *Between Vengeance and Forgiveness,* Boston: Beacon Press, 1998.

Misztal, B., "How Not to Deal with the Past: Lustration in Poland," *Archives Europeenes Sociologie,* v. 40, n. 1, pp. 31–55.

Moriarty, C., "Private Grief and Public Remembrance: British First World War Memorials," in M. Evans, and K. Lunn, eds., *War and Memory in the Twentieth Century,* Oxford: Berg, 1997.

Muller, Ampie, "Facing Our Shadow Side," *Track Two,* v. 6, nos. 3 and 4, December 1997, p. 16.

Novick, Peter, *The Resistance Versus Vichy: The Purge of Collaborators in Liberated France,* London: Chatto and Windus, 1968.

Page, Michael, "The Role of Penal Policy in the Reduction of Political Violence," unpublished doctoral dissertation, University of Bradford.

Pearce, J., "Impunity and Democracy: The Case of Chile," in Rachel Sieder, ed., *Impunity in Latin America,* London: Institute of Latin American Studies, 1995.

Pearl, L., "Punishing Balkan War Criminals: Could the End of Yugoslavia Provide an End to Victors' Justice?" *American Criminal Law Review,* v. 30, n. 4, 1993.

Pehe, Jiri, "Parliament Passes Controversial Law on Vetting Officials," *Report on Eastern Europe,* v. 2, n. 43, 25 October 1991, pp. 5–9.

Pérez-Diáz, Victor, *The Return of Civil Society: The Emergence of Democratic Spain,* Cambridge: Harvard University Press, 1993.

Popkin, Margaret, "El Salvador: A Negotiated End to Impunity?" in N. Roht-Arriaza, ed., *Impunity and Human Rights in International Law and Practice,* Oxford: Oxford University Press, 1995.

Popkin, Margaret, and Naomi Roht-Arriaza, "Truth as Justice: Investigatory Commissions in Latin America," *Law and Social Inquiry,* v. 20, n. 1, Winter 1995, pp. 79–116.

Preston, P., *The Triumph of Democracy in Spain,* London: Routledge, 1986.

Preston, P., *The Politics of Revenge: Fascism and the Military in Twentieth Century Spain,* London: Unwin Hyman, 1990.

Preston, P., and A. L. Mackenzie, eds., *The Republic Besieged: Civil War in Spain, 1936–1939,* Edinburgh: Edinburgh University Press, 1996.

Report of the Chilean National Commission on Truth and Reconciliation, vol. 1 (English translation), Notre Dame: University of Notre Dame Press, 1993.

Richards, Michael, "Civil War, Violence and the Construction of Francoism," in P. Preston and A. L. Mackenzie, eds., *The Republic Besieged: Civil War in Spain, 1936–1939,* Edinburgh: Edinburgh University Press, 1996.

Rigby, A., *The Legacy of the Past: The Problem of Collaborators and the Palestinian Case,* Jerusalem: Palestinian Academic Society for the Study of International Affairs, 1997.

Rigby, Andrew, *Living the Intifada,* London: Zed Books, 1993.

Rings, W., *Life with the Enemy: Collaboration and Resistance in Hitler's Europe, 1939–1945,* London: Weidenfeld & Nicolson, 1982.

Robinson, G. E., "The Growing Authoritarianism of the Arafat Regime," *Survival,* v. 39, n. 2, Summer 1997, pp. 42–56.

Roht-Arriaza, N., ed., *Impunity and Human Rights in International Law and Practice,* Oxford: Oxford University Press, 1995.

Rosenberg, Tina, "Overcoming the Legacies of Dictatorship," *Foreign Affairs,* v. 74, n. 3, May/June 1995, pp. 134–152.

Rosenberg, Tina, *The Haunted Land: Facing Europe's Ghosts After Communism,* London: Vintage, 1995.

Semelin, Jacques, *Unarmed Against Hitler: Civilian Resistance in Europe, 1939–1943,* London: Praeger, 1993.

Servicio Paz y Justicia, *Uruguay Nunca Más: Human Rights Violations,*

1972–1985, Elizabeth Hampsten, trans., Temple University Press, 1989.

Shriver, Donald, *An Ethic for Enemies: Forgiveness in Politics*, New York: Oxford University Press, 1995.

Sieder, Rachel, ed., *Impunity in Latin America*, London: Institute of Latin American Studies, 1995.

Smith, Kathleen E., "Decommunization After the 'Velvet Revolutions' in East Central Europe," in N. Roht-Arriaza, ed., *Impunity and Human Rights in International Law and Practice*, Oxford: Oxford University Press, 1995, pp. 82–98.

Spies, Chris, "A Safe Space: How Local Leaders Can Make Room for Reconciliation," *Track Two*, v. 6, nos. 3 and 4, December 1997, pp. 11–15.

Stinchcombe, Arthur, "Lustration as a Problem of the Social Basis of Constitutionalism," *Law and Social Inquiry*, v. 20, n. 1, Winter 1995, pp. 245–273.

Sweets, John F., *Choices in Vichy France: The French Under Nazi Occupation*, New York: Oxford University Press, 1986.

Tamari, Salim, "In League with Zion: Israel's Search for a Native Pillar," *Journal of Palestine Studies*, v. 12, n. 4, Summer 1983, pp. 41–56.

Thomson, David, *Europe Since Napoleon*, Harmondsworth: Penguin, 1977.

Truth and Reconciliation Commission, South Africa: Rondebosch: Justice in Transition/Ministry of Justice, 1995.

Tucker, Aviezer, "Paranoids May Be Persecuted: Post-totalitarian Retroactive Justice," *Archives Europeene Sociolog*ie, v. 60, n. 1, pp. 56–100.

Tutu, Desmond, *No Future Without Forgiveness*, London: Rider, 1999.

Valenzuela, Arturo, "Chile: Origins, Consolidation, and Breakdown of a Democratic Regime," in Larry Diamond, Juan Linz, and Seymour Martin Lipset, eds., *Democracy in Developing Countries; vol. 4, Latin America*, Boulder, Colo.: Lynne Rienner, 1989.

Vermeylen, P., "The Punishment of Collaborators," *Annals of the American Academy of Political and Social Science*, CCXLVII, September 1946, pp. 73–77.

Villa-Vicencio, Charles, and Wilhelm Verwooerd, eds., *Looking Back Reaching Forward: Reflections on the Truth and Reconciliation Commission of South Africa*, London: Zed Books, 2000.

Waller, David, *Rwanda: Which Way Now?* Oxford: Oxfam, 1996.

Warmbrunn, Werner, *The Dutch Under German Occupation, 1940–1945*, London: Oxford University Press, 1963.

Weissbrodt, David, and Paul Fraser, "Book Review: Report of the Chilean National Commission on Truth and Reconciliation," *Human Rights Quarterly*, v. 14, n. 4, November 1992, pp. 601–622.

Weschler, Lawrence, "A Reporter at Large," *New Yorker*, 10 December 1990, p. 127.

Weschler, Lawrence, *A Miracle, A Universe: Settling Accounts with Torturers*, Chicago: University of Chicago Press, 1998.

Weschler, Lawrence, *Calamities of Exile: Three Nonfiction Novellas*, London: University of Chicago Press, 1999.

Zondergeld, G., "Non-violent Resistance in the Netherlands During World War II," in G. Grünewald and P. van den Dungen, eds., *Twentieth Century Peace Movements: Successes and Failures*, Lampeter: Edwin Mellen, 1995.

Websites Consulted

http://www.amnesty.org/ailib/aipub/1998/AMR/23400298.html
http://www.desaprecidos.org/arg/victimas/eng.html
http://www.desaparecidos.org/arg/tort/eng.html
http://www.domovina.net/complaint
http:// www.igc.org/icc/html/ferencz199907.html
http://www.polity.org/govdocs/commissions/1998/trc/schap6.htm
http://www.publicedcenter.org/rwanda.html
http://www.reconciliation.org.au
http://www.wamani.apc.org/abuelas/ingles.html
http://www.witnessforpeace.org/nwsmay14_98g.html

Index

199

About the Book

How do societies that have been wracked by violent conflict reconcile themselves to their recent history—and lay the foundations for a peaceful, stable future? How do they deal with the impulse for revenge? What should be done with those responsible for acts of state violence under a previous regime? How can individuals and communities best be helped to cope with the aftermath of national trauma? These are the sometimes wrenching issues confronted in *Justice and Reconciliation*.

Rigby investigates differing approaches to "policing" the past, ranging from mass purges at one end of the spectrum to collective social amnesia at the other. Using case studies to analyze the advantages and disadvantages of each, he makes clear the connection between how the past is acknowledged and the prospects for a present and future culture of peace.

Andrew Rigby is director of the Centre for the Study of Forgiveness and Reconciliation, Coventry University. His numerous publications include *The Legacy of the Past: The Problem of Collaborators and the Palestinian Case*.